# Migration and
# the Labor Market
# in Developing Countries

## Also of Interest

*Food, Politics, and Agricultural Development: Case Studies in the Public Policy of Rural Modernization,* edited by Raymond F. Hopkins, Donald J. Puchala, and Ross B. Talbot

*Governments and Mining Companies in Developing Countries,* James H. Cobbe

*The New Economics of the Less Developed Countries: Changing Perceptions in the North-South Dialogue,* edited by Nake Kamrany

*Technology and Economic Development: A Realistic Perspective,* edited by Samuel M. Rosenblatt

*Protein, Calories, and Development: Nutritional Variables in the Economics of Developing Countries,* Bernard A. Schmitt

*Economic Development, Poverty, and Income Distribution,* edited by William Loehr and John P. Powelson

*A Select Bibliography on Economic Development: With Annotations,* John P. Powelson

†*From Dependency to Development,* edited by Heraldo Muñoz

*Emigration and Economic Development: The Case of the Yemen Arab Republic,* Jon C. Swanson

†*The Challenge of the New International Economic Order,* edited by Edwin P. Reubens

†*The Theory and Structures of International Political Economy,* edited by Todd Sandler

†Available in hardcover and paperback.

# Westview Special Studies in Social, Political, and Economic Development

## Migration and the Labor Market
## in Developing Countries
### edited by Richard H. Sabot

Encompassing both empirical and theoretical work, this book clarifies the linkages among income distribution, migration, surplus labor, and poverty in developing countries. The authors review models of unemployment, discuss the difficulty of testing hypotheses and accurately projecting regional population growth, and treat the issue of defining income and prices when comparing laborers in different localities. Their assessment of the consequences of out-migration for rural productivity and income distribution not only challenges the neoclassical hypothesis that the incomes of nonmigrants will increase and differences in the standard of living between the source and receiving areas of migrant labor narrow, but it also suggests that in some circumstances out-migration may perpetuate and widen existing income gaps in the source area population.

An economist with the World Bank's Development Economics Department, Dr. Sabot has previously been a research officer at the Institute of Economics and Statistics, Oxford University, and a consultant to the OECD and the ILO.

# Migration and
# the Labor Market
# in Developing Countries

## edited by Richard H. Sabot

Westview Press / Boulder, Colorado

*Westview Special Studies in Social, Political, and Economic Development*

Published in 1982 in the United States of America by
  Westview Press, Inc.
  5500 Central Avenue
  Boulder, Colorado 80301
  Frederick A. Praeger, Publisher

Library of Congress Cataloging in Publication Data
Main entry under title:
Migration and the labor market in developing countries.
    (Westview special studies in social, political, and economic development)
    Based on papers from a conference convened by the World Bank in Feb. 1976.
    Includes bibliographies and index.
    1. Underdeveloped areas—Labor supply—Congresses.  2. Underdeveloped areas—Alien labor—Congresses.  I. Sabot, Richard H.  II. International Bank for Reconstruction and Development.
HD5852.M53            331.12'09172'4            80-16050
ISBN 0-89158-763-2

Printed and bound in the United States of America

# Contents

# Figures and Tables

# Preface

The last decade has seen an unprecedented amount of economic research on migration in developing countries. The World Bank convened a conference in February 1976 to take stock of what we have learned and to identify issues of particular importance for future research. Participants included economists currently involved in empirical studies and those who have undertaken theoretical work in this area. Shorter papers commented on the papers collected here and described the research design of ongoing migration and labor market studies in India, Indonesia, Iran, Sierra Leone, and Tanzania.

The principal papers were substantially revised following the conference, indicating the fruitfulness of the discussion. Many of the discussants' criticisms were met, and suggestions for change incorporated in the course of the revision process. The discussants were not asked to prepare new comments. Rather, those of their criticisms still pertinent are noted, along with relevant comments of other conference participants, in the concluding chapter. The papers on research design were not meant simply to illustrate the state of the art but to provide a possible basis for a study rigorously comparing the findings of these country studies, among the best of the recent wave of applied economic work on migration and the labor market. This did not prove feasible. Differences in sample design, in issues on which survey questions focused, and in the details of how questions were asked precluded integrating these surveys into one large micro-data base. Differences in focus between the studies also made the statistically more casual approach of a common analytic outline undesirable. Some of the points made in these methodological papers are reflected in the concluding chapter.

The advice of John Harris of Boston University and of Mark Leiserson of the World Bank on how best to organize the conference was invaluable, and they deserve much of the credit for its success. I am also grateful to the following, who as session moderators gave order to the discussions, as commentators on principal papers offered the authors further useful thought on matters large and small, and as authors of the short papers on research design did much to define the appropriate strategy for future research: M. Ahluwalia, World Bank; B. Balassa, World Bank; A. Berry, University of Toronto; J. Bhagwati, Massachusetts Institute of Technology; D. Byerlee, Michigan State University; W. Elkan, University of Durham; K. Griffin, University of Oxford; R. Gulhati, World Bank; H. Kaneda, World Bank; A. Khan, I.L.O.; D. Lal, University College, London; I. Little, World Bank; D. Mazumdar, World Bank; G. Pyatt, World Bank; G. Scully, Harvard University; J. Tommy, Michigan State University; D. Turnham, World Bank; K. Zachariah, World Bank.

Kamal Tengra typed various drafts of this volume and cheerfully bore much of the administrative burden of the conference, and Katharine Tait edited the papers, purging many of the stylistic idiosyncrasies that are often the bane of conference volumes and making the manuscript publishable. My warm thanks to both.

My greatest debt is to the authors of the principal papers, who admirably interpreted and fulfilled their rather comprehensive terms of reference and who, with no inducement other than the scholars' satisfaction in improving their work, rewrote their papers to take account of the comments of the conference participants.

*R. H. Sabot*
Washington, D.C.

# Migration and
# the Labor Market
# in Developing Countries

# Introduction

### RICHARD H. SABOT

The importance of urban migration in the process of economic development has long been recognized. As national income rises, a decrease in agriculture's share of total output and an increase in the manufacturing and services' share are observable both in individual countries over time and in different countries at various levels of development. This relationship between growth and structural change is associated with a decrease in the proportion of the labor force in agriculture and rural areas, hence with a net urban migration.

At the beginning of this century, less than 5 percent of the populations of Asia, Africa, and Latin America lived in cities. By 1950, the portion had increased to 15 percent and by 1975 to 36 percent. It is estimated (Morawetz, 1977) that between 1950 and 1975, a period of unprecedentedly rapid economic growth in less-developed countries (LDCs), the urban populations of these countries increased by roughly 546 million (Beier et al., 1975). Although the share of urban population growth accounted for by internal migration varies considerably from country to country and from one period to the next, it is not uncommon to find migration accounting for 60 percent or more of the annual increase.

Economic theory has acknowledged the contribution of migration to economic growth. The transfer of labor from low productivity rural sectors to high productivity urban sectors is the fundamental mechanism by which increase in per capita output takes place in the dual economy genre of growth models. Nevertheless, only in the last decade has an extensive scholarly discussion of internal migration been undertaken by economists, as theoreticians and applied researchers have begun to examine in detail the causes and consequences of the migration phenomena.

Among the many stimuli that explain the rapid increase in economic research on migration in developing countries, several on the demand side stand out. The analysis of the determinants of migration provided a fresh

*1*

opportunity for assessing the long-held belief that the indigenous populations of developing countries are not "economic men," in the sense that they appear to pay no heed to normal economic incentives. Advances in data processing, made possible by the computer, allowed large scale micro-data bases to be used to estimate migration decision functions, the characteristics of which could then be compared with the predictions of the newly developed human capital theory of migration. This theory viewed people as moving in response to income premiums at destination—premiums that in the long run, considering that the value of future income is lower than that of present income, will, if labor markets are highly competitive, just compensate them for the direct and opportunity costs of moving and job search. This essentially behaviorial analysis of determinants also held out the promise of improving on mechanical extrapolations of past trends as a basis for projections of rural-urban migration flows, hence as a basis for projections of urban population growth. Moreover, there was a recognition that the testing of hypotheses regarding the determinants of migration could contribute to the specification of appropriate models of the labor market, a process that was assuming greater importance in the analysis of the consequences of migration.

Indeed, the growing awareness that the ratio of migration's social benefits to its social costs might be sensitive to the nature of the urban labor market provided a second set of stimuli to migration research. Much early theorizing about the role of migration in the development process implicitly assumed that the interactions between individual sellers and employers of labor services ensured that urban migration would proceed neither too rapidly nor too slowly. Since in theory the supply of, and demand for, labor are, respectively, positive and negative functions of the real wage, it was assumed that movements of the wage rate would automatically balance supply and demand in the urban labor market. Although Keynes had cast doubt on the ability of wage adjustment to equilibrate the labor market as a whole when faced with a decline in aggregate demand, surely such adjustments could still guarantee efficient allocation of labor between sectors and prevent rapidly growing urban economies from suffering either labor shortages or surpluses.

The emergence in the 1960s of urban unemployment as a serious and chronic problem in developing countries undermined faith in the efficacy of wage adjustments even in this relatively humble area. Given the large proportion of the annual increase in the urban supply of labor accounted for by migration, it was only natural to seek an explanation for urban surplus labor in excessive urban migration. Segmentation models of urban unemployment provided such an explanation. In these models the labor market was segmented in the sense that because of minimum wage legislation, the strength of unions, or other factors, some workers receive higher real wages than other workers with the same economic characteristics, simply by virtue of their sector of employment. Workers maximize expected income (the product of wages and the probability of obtaining a job) and move from the low wage sector in excess of demand in the high wage sector. The conventional market clearing mechanism—a decline in the (rigid) wage—is thus replaced by a quantity adjustment mechanism—an increase in unemployment.

The growth of unions, the increase in government intervention in the labor market and, most important, the apparent widening of rural-urban income differentials in many developing countries were significant factors in casual assessments of the appropriateness of the segmentation model linking urban unemployment to excessive migration. The development of this model has stimulated attempts to determine whether migrants do respond to expected rather than actual differences in incomes and whether the social costs of urban unemployment significantly detract from the social benefits of migration; it has also begged several important questions in the methodology of migration research. This has led to numerous attempts to refine the model's specification.

Increased work on rural development issues by economists provided a third set of stimuli for research on migration. No one theory purporting to undermine the conventional wisdom regarding the economic consequences of migration for source areas monopolized the attention of researchers. Moreover, in most LDCs the immediate impact of migration—the demographic impact—is generally markedly less in source areas than in receiving areas because of their relatively low level of urbanization. This is the basis for the presumption that the impact on the labor market of a given flow of migrants will similarly be less in source areas than in receiving areas. Nevertheless, several factors have prompted a reconsideration of the assumption, based on simple neoclassical models of labor migration between unconstrained labor markets, that out-migration will have a beneficial impact on the level and distribution of incomes in source areas.

Most important, perhaps, has been the revisionist trend over the last fifteen years to downgrade the importance of a divergence between rural wages and marginal product as a cause of labor misallocation. Empirical work has generally shown earlier estimates of rural "surplus labor" to be too high. At the same time, a closer examination of the theoretical conditions for such a surplus has revealed that they are more stringent than first supposed, making their fulfillment on a large scale increasingly improbable. It is no longer safe to presume that significant out-migration will have little or no impact on the aggregate level of output of the rural sector. On the contrary, it is possible that out-migration actually results in a decline in per capita output; consider the selectivity by the migrant streams of the most productive workers, the loss of "surplus" previously generated by migrants whose contribution to output exceeded marginal product while their wage equalled it, migration-induced capital flows and changes in the terms of trade, and losses of economies of scale in the provision of public services due to declines in population.

Another factor to consider regarding the impact of out-migration on source area incomes and their distributions is the influence of capital markets, and their imperfections, on human capital investment decisions, particularly when labor markets also are imperfect. In a perfect labor market, the direct costs of moving are unlikely to be a significant deterrent to migration, given their low level in relation to the discounted present values of opportunity costs and returns. In a segmented labor market, however, adding the cost of subsisting in town and searching for a job to transport costs can dramatically increase direct costs of migration. The negative relationship between direct costs and the migration rate may result as much from the difficulty of financing the increased costs as from their effects on expected returns. Inability to obtain funds for the expected direct costs, which are borne before any returns, may deter even rural residents for whom expected net returns are positive from migrating to town. If intrafamily transfers or loans are the usual way to pay for migration, then perhaps the offspring of better-off rural families will have disproportionate access to the urban protected sector's high wage jobs and migration may actually widen, rather than reduce, source area income differentials.

The chapters in this volume focus on these three sets of issues, which have provided the stimulus for much of the recent economic research on migration. They assess the implications of different key characteristics of labor markets for the response of labor supply (migration) to the hiring of additional urban workers, hence for the social opportunity cost of urban labor. They review models of unemployment and show why models in which urban migration plays an important role are currently at the center of the stage and why the attention they command may be excessive. They discuss the difficulty of estimating migration decision functions precisely enough both to test hypotheses that discriminate among alternative labor market models and to project regional population growth. They deal with the issue of defining income and prices when comparing earners in different localities—a crucial issue for the behavioral analysis of migration. They assess the consequences of out-migration for rural productivity and income distribution, showing that even where wage determination and mobility are not constrained by non-market forces there are grounds for doubting the neoclassical prediction that the incomes of nonmigrants increase and the differences in incomes between source area and receiving area narrow. They also review the relevant evidence and conclude that where the labor market is segmented and the capital market highly imperfect out-migration may perpetuate and widen existing income gaps in the source area population.

It is clear that the authors' concern with improved understanding of how labor markets function, evident throughout this volume, is motivated as much by reasons of policy as by academic considerations. In the first chapter, Joseph Stiglitz presents an overview of labor market models; he also provides rigorous theoretical support for the argument that one ignores the details of the specification of such models in social cost-benefit analyses of investment projects at the risk of serious miscalculations of the acceptability of such projects. It is well established that in "labor intensive" sectors such as tourism or housing whether one takes a shadow wage equal to the market wage or one only half as great can make a big difference to a project's rate of return. What Stiglitz demonstrates is that the social opportunity cost of urban labor is highly sensitive to differences in the characteristics of labor markets and, in particular, to differences in the response of migration to additional urban employment.

It is often assumed that in economies suffering significant urban unemployment all unskilled workers can be considered as having been drawn from the pool of those unemployed, so the social opportunity cost of employing them is always zero. Stiglitz shows that open unemployment implies zero opportunity cost only if no increase in the supply of labor is induced by the hiring of an additional worker directly from the pool of unemployed. In the simple version of the segmentation model of unemployment, hiring an additional urban worker induces just sufficient migration to leave the unemployment rate unchanged; it is easily shown that the worker's social opportunity cost is simply the urban wage. In his consideration of recent refinements and extensions of that model, however, Stiglitz shows that a variety of factors determine whether the social opportunity cost of hiring an additional worker in the high wage sector will be greater than, less than, or just equal to the wage in that sector.

John Harris and Richard Sabot also focus on the relationship between migration and urban unemployment and suggest an explanation for the great attention received by segmentation models both in the scholarly literature and among policymakers. In the first section of their chapter they present a simple taxonomy of models of unemployment and review some of the principal specification problems encountered when they are used to explain urban labor market imbalance in developing countries. In segmentation models, unemployment is specific to the high wage sector; also, in these models there are economic incentives to queue for high wage jobs rather than accept available low income employment. This class of models thus passes the Harris and Sabot "test" of consistency with two common characteristics of labor markets in developing countries: labor surplus in one sector, accompanied by labor scarcity or abundance of opportunities in urban informal and agricultural sectors; and open unemployment, at least in urban areas, as opposed to disguised or hidden unemployment or underemployment. None of the other categories of models considered, in which unemployment is either economy-wide or disguised, passes this test.

The simple segmentation model is not, however, free from specification problems. Attention has been focused on one set of these problems—the tendency of the model, in some (particularly African) countries, to predict rates of unemployment significantly higher than measured rates. Harris and Sabot review the suggested means of solving this problem, which involve tinkering with the nonprice mechanism by which high wage jobs are rationed among competing job-seekers rather than changing the "hard core" of the model—the intersectoral wage gap and the labor supply function based on expected rather than actual incomes.

However, they are more concerned with a second set of specification problems. The model assumes only one or, with the addition of an urban flexible wage sector, two urban wages; it also assumes that workers have certain knowledge of urban labor market conditions. In fact, a dispersion of wages for economically homogeneous workers and uncertain knowledge of the urban labor market are clearly more characteristic of labor market conditions in developing countries. They proceed to drop these assumptions and develop a more general search model of unemployment.

Harris and Sabot begin by considering the determinants of the optimal allocation of time between unemployment (queuing for high wage jobs) and employment when a job-seeker (with certain knowledge) is faced by a whole spectrum of wages, a high proportion of which have employment probabilities that are positive but less than unity. The decision rule, which involves setting a critical minimum wage below which all job offers are rejected, is in essence the same as in simple segmentation models: forgo employment if the expected gain from continuing to look for a job with a higher wage exceeds the opportunity costs that accrue while looking. Nevertheless, this more complex segmentation model yields insights that the simple model tends to obscure. It demonstrates that segmentation within the urban labor market may result in unemployment even if that market is closed. In other words, while the rate of migration clearly may influence the rate of unemployment and vice versa, an excessive flow of migrants from rural areas is not a necessary condition for the emergence of open urban unemployment. This change increases the relevance of the segmentation category of unemployment models to countries (particularly in Latin America and Asia) where the simple segmentation model tends to predict too low or even zero rates of urban unemployment because the gaps between rural and urban areas in average wages for homogeneous labor are negligible.

Harris and Sabot then drop the assumption that workers have certain knowledge of labor market conditions, thereby converting unemployment from a queuing phenomenon to one in which workers engage in job search as a means of improving their information, and hence their own prospects. Unemployment results because workers determine their critical wage on the basis of subjective rather than objective costs and returns. While this model bears a close resemblance to search models developed for application in the industrialized market economies, it nevertheless differs significantly from those models.

The chapters by Paul Schultz and by Paul Collier and Richard Sabot focus on issues in the methodology of research on the determinants of migration. The migration function is the principal research tool of economists analyzing the determinants of migrant behavior. It is an equation expressing the relationship between the probability or rate of migration and variables measuring aspects of the environment presumed to influence geographic mobility, such as the direct costs of moving and expected income in source and receiving areas.

The estimation of migration functions in developing countries has contributed to the acceptance, even among noneconomists, of the primacy of economic motives for the geographic mobility of workers. However, demands made of migration functions have increased. They are now being put to other tasks, some of which are considerably more difficult—for example, testing hypotheses about the influence of employment probability on the decision to migrate in order to distinguish between alternative models of unemployment. When migration functions are used for regional population projections, or used to generate the supply side elasticities in simulations of the labor market, the deficiencies of the methods used for the early estimates of migration functions become glaring. For these purposes, it is not just the signs but also the coefficients of the independent variables in which we must have confidence. In his chapter, Schultz identifies some of the pitfalls into which the unwary researcher can trip in specifying a migration decision function, determining its functional form and level of disaggregation, and measuring its variables. He then suggests some changes in standard procedure that reduce the risk of a statistical mishap.

Several of Schultz's principal suggestions concern aggregation. Markedly different rates of migration among people of different age, sex, and education are a universal feature of migration. Unless functions used to explain variance in regional rates of migration by differences in economic incentives are roughly homogeneous in age, sex, and education, the assessment of responsiveness will be biased. Apparent spatial differences in economic opportunities will in reality reflect compositional differences in the labor force. While disaggregation, too, can become excessive—increasing the unwieldiness of analysis and decreasing the generality of results—Schultz argues that, with regard to the earnings and other variables in migration functions, the trend toward disaggregation has not yet gone far enough.

The how and why of including a measure of employment probability in the migration function are only two of the specification issues with which Schultz is concerned. He also considers whether the absolute or the relative earnings differential is more appropriate and demonstrates why the choice may depend on the relative importance of direct and opportunity costs. He briefly assesses the value of a series of potential independent variables, such as education opportunities, other public sector services, and the rate of natural population increase, which may reflect aspects of the structure of economic opportunities not captured by the earnings variables. It is perhaps the difficulty of unambiguously interpreting the coefficients on these variables that explains his lack of enthusiasm for them. Indeed, with the example of a variable measuring the current population of the receiving area, he shows that the tendency towards "ad hocery" manifest in a long string of independent variables may not be as harmless as it appears.

Schultz concludes with a discussion of functional form, and recommends the application of the polytomous logistic model, which can be estimated with either individual or grouped data and which involves a choice among a finite number of mutually exclusive discrete alternatives.

The increase over the last decade in estimates of migration functions for developing countries and in the application of segmentation models of unemployment has made it imperative for development economists concerned with labor market performance to confront an issue that has long bedeviled economists concerned with international comparisons of income, distribution of income, taxation, and consumer demand: what is the best way to measure income differentials. Measurement errors may bias the coefficients of income variables in migration functions and could, conceivably, cause a reversal of their true signs. Labor market segmentation models of unemployment have intersectoral wage gaps at their core. The wider the rural-urban income gap for workers with the same economic characteristics, the higher the rate of urban unemployment predicted by this type of model. As noted above, this model tends to predict, for some countries, unemployment rates significantly higher than measured rates. This has been treated as a symptom of a specification problem. Alternatively, the inaccuracy of the model's predictions could reflect inaccuracies in measures of rural-urban differences in income.

In their chapter, Collier and Sabot demonstrate that estimates of income differentials are crude not only because of excessive aggregation, statistical inaccuracies, or the insufficiency of government-collected data, but also because the conventional definition of income is inappropriate for the task and because the index number problem is neglected. First they focus on a familiar error implicit in the conventional definition of individual income as the sum of the products of all purchased goods and services and their market prices. In computing gross product for an establishment in the enterprise sector, the costs of goods and services used in current production—intermediate goods—

are deducted from the values of sales and change in inventories of final goods, to arrive at a measure of value added. In the government sector, however, national income accounting conventions ignore this distinction, treating all public expenditure on goods and services as final, despite the recognition that some government services supplied to enterprises may be inputs which are fully reflected in the prices of their outputs and therefore should be intermediate. Similarly, the distinction between intermediate and final goods in the household sector is ignored, despite the fact that expenditure on intermediate goods may be a significant proportion of total expenditure and is likely to vary within a cross section of the population and also to vary over time. They suggest that a hedonic definition of income that takes account of this distinction is more appropriate for the behavioral analysis of migration, and they give some examples of how and why measures of rural-urban income differentials would be affected by the adoption of this definition.

An index number problem arises in the comparison of rural and urban incomes whenever the areas differ in the price at which acquisitions are valued. In LDCs such differences presumably are marked: the difference in the price of housing and food alone, generally much higher in urban than in rural areas, is probably sufficient to make the choice of prices a significant influence on the income differential. Cost-of-living indices for rural areas in developing countries are scarce; as a consequence most researchers of migration find their decision made for them. Collier and Sabot emphasize, however, that urban prices are fortunately more appropriate than either rural prices or an average of rural and urban prices, such as Fisher's Ideal Index. Of course some estimate must still be made of the substitution in consumption by the average rural dweller when faced with urban prices. Despite the availability of urban expenditure surveys for calculating elasticities of demand, this is generally not done in studies of migration, and income differentials are exaggerated as a consequence.

The consequences of migration for rural productivity and income distribution are addressed in two chapters that reflect rather different perspectives. The authors differ in the consequences on which they choose to focus. Edward Schuh's perspective is macro; he examines various direct and indirect effects of out-migration and assesses their implications for the average income of nonmigrants, limiting his discussion of distribution to the difference in income between rural and urban areas. By contrast, Michael Lipton's approach is more micro. His analysis aims to identify the rural residents most and least able to migrate in order to take advantage of spatial income differentials generated by structural change and other factors. He attempts to explain these differences in ability, and to assess their implications for the evolution of the distribution of income in the original group.

Underlying most of Schuh's analysis is the presumed absence of the cultural, government-imposed, or other "institutional" constraints on labor mobility or wage flexibility, which economists generally blame for any inefficiency of decentralized labor markets in the fulfillment of their allocative function. He treats the two most widely discussed distortions, rural wages in excess of the marginal product of labor and urban wages in excess of the equilibrium supply price of labor, as special cases rather than as characteristics common to labor markets in many LDCs, and he devotes little space to considering how his analysis of emigration might take them into account.

This is not to suggest that Schuh is content with simple neoclassical models of labor migration between unconstrained labor markets, in which source area incomes rise and converge with receiving area incomes. Though he shares the general view that migration is a necessary and desirable characteristic of economic growth and forecasts continued large-scale movements, he does not by any means assume that this is the best of all possible worlds for LDCs. His conclusion is that despite increased transport costs and the sacrifice of economies of agglomeration, decentralization of industry, which permits intersectoral labor mobility without migration, may yield higher net social returns than geographic transfers of labor, though not necessarily higher private returns. Further, he concludes that measures to encourage the dispersal of nonagricultural investment should be considered by governments of countries in the process of rapid structural change. Schuh's major contribution is a first step in the construction of a taxonomy of the various economic changes in the rural sector induced by out-migration.

In contrast to Schuh's assumption that the labor market is a well-engineered and well-maintained system that fulfills its function of allocating labor among alternative activities and geographic areas with a minimum waste of productive potential, Lipton assumes that the labor market is an extremely imperfect mechanism in which channels of communication among components are only crudely developed; even when signals are received, some components are unable to respond optimally. In Lipton's analysis, labor market imperfections are important because they enhance the role financing plays in migration decisions, thus increasing the influence of the imperfections of capital markets on labor allocation in LDCs.

Lipton, however, does not ascribe the negative effects of migration on the distribution of income in the source area solely to the financing of the direct costs of migration; his principal concern is with the financing by rural residents of investment in education. If capital market imperfections prevent poor rural residents from financing the initial investment in education, there will be fewer potential students and existing students will have a higher supply price. The consequences will be a shift to the left in the supply of educated "school-leavers." For a given demand schedule for educated workers, this implies a greater difference in earnings between educated and uneducated than if finance were not a constraint on education. If the demand for educated workers is concentrated in urban areas, this also implies an association of migration with a tendency for the source area distribution of income to be perpetuated from one generation to the next.

## BIBLIOGRAPHY

Beier, G., et al. "The Task Ahead for the Cities of the Developing Countries." International Bank for Reconstruction and Development, Working Paper no. 209, July 1975.

Morawetz, D. *Twenty-five Years of Economic Development: 1950–1975*. Washington, D.C.: The World Bank, 1977.

# 1
# The Structure of Labor Markets and Shadow Prices in LDCs

## JOSEPH E. STIGLITZ

### INTRODUCTION

The object of this chapter is to delineate several characteristics of the labor market in LDCs that are important in determining the relationship between market wages and shadow prices for labor. First, systematic distortions in the allocation of labor among alternative uses generated by a variety of market imperfections will be identified. Second the implications of any perturbation in the market equilibrium will be traced, for example, the full consequences—indirect effects as well as direct—of the government hiring an additional laborer or providing a wage subsidy to employment in the private sector. And third, the consequences of various policy changes will be evaluated.

Much of the earlier cost benefit literature did not have a fully articulated model of the labor market, and as a consequence, although some distortions were identified, other perhaps equally important distortions were not. Thus, potentially at least, the consequences of certain policy changes (e.g., wage subsidies) might be quite different from the results envisioned by those who recommended such policies. (For instance, an earlier paper [Stiglitz, 1974a] showed that under quite plausible conditions a wage subsidy could lower national income and increase unemployment.) Moreover, many earlier discussions tended to evaluate consequences of alternative actions in terms of their effects on national output, rather than the more direct effects on the welfare of individuals. For example, individuals may prefer to live in rural areas and therefore a higher wage in the urban sector will be required to induce them to migrate. In such a case, if a worker migrates, national income may go up but social welfare may be decreased. A correct welfare analysis needs to take such considerations into account.

The chapter is divided into two major sections: in the first the various distortions are identified, the conditions under which they are likely to be important are discussed, and their implications are analyzed in a general way.

*13*

In the second, detailed results of the calculation of shadow prices and optimal wages are summarized. The calculations themselves are presented in a technical appendix.

Throughout, certain simplifying assumptions are employed. In particular, it is assumed that a small, open economy is being discussed, so that relative prices of agricultural and urban goods are fixed (and these are normalized at unity). For all calculations, it is assumed the government is required to pay the same wage that firms in the private urban sector pay. Most of the analysis is carried on at a fairly high level of aggregation, and for most of the analysis, the capital stock is assumed to be fixed. Most of these assumptions may be lifted without changing the basic qualitative argument of the chapter. (Some results for a closed economy paralleling those presented here are contained in Stiglitz [1977].)

In the discussion below, the opportunity cost of, say, the government's hiring a laborer is distinguished from the shadow price. The former refers to the change in *output* in the private sector; the latter takes into account other objectives, such as growth, distribution, and employment.

## SYSTEMATIC DISTORTIONS IN THE LABOR MARKETS IN LDCs

The discussion of the various sources of distortions is organized into four areas: distortions in the rural labor market, distortions in the urban labor market, distortions in the allocation of labor between the urban and rural sectors, and distortions in other markets that have repercussions in labor markets.

Full efficiency of the economy requires that the value of the marginal product of labor be the same in all uses. In the conventional competitive equilibrium model, this is ensured by having free mobility of labor, all workers receiving exactly the same wage, and firms hiring workers up to the point where the wage is equal to the value of the marginal product. Thus an analysis of why the shadow price of labor does not equal the market price must address itself to an explanation of the significant differences in observed wages and an explanation of why wages might not equal the value of the marginal product, either within the rural sector or within the urban sector.

### Distortions in the Rural Labor Market

An analysis of distortions *within* the rural sector is addressed first. If labor is to be efficiently allocated between the rural and urban sector, the supply price of labor to the urban sector must be equal to the value of the marginal product of labor in the rural sector. If *all* workers receive their marginal product, labor would presumably be efficiently allocated between the two sectors; however, the efficient allocation of labor between the two sectors requires only that the *migrating* workers receive their marginal product.

Earlier discussions of the shadow price of labor in LDCs focused primarily on the distortions within the rural sector. It was argued that the supply price of labor exceeded the value of the marginal product of labor; that is, the opportunity cost of labor was less than the market wage in the urban sector. This was based on the premise that the marginal product of workers in the rural sector was very low—perhaps zero—and considerably lower than their effective wage. Indeed, it was commonly postulated that rural workers received their average product rather than their marginal product; it was their average product that determined the supply price of labor to the urban sector. This set of distortions is probably less important in determining the difference between shadow and market wages than its widespread employment in the development literature would imply.

There is, however, another set of distortions: although the supply price of a laborer to the urban sector may be equal to the value of his marginal product, workers in the rural sector may not receive a return for their marginal effort (time) that is equal to its value; they thus supply too little effort (time). If this internal inefficiency is less in the urban sector, a reallocation of laborers from the rural to the urban sector might increase national output.

As will be seen later, even when there are no distortions within the rural sector, a primary determinant of the relationship between the shadow price of labor and the market wage within the urban sector is the elasticity of supply of laborers to the urban sector.

## The Supply Price of Labor to the Urban Sector and the Value of the Marginal Product of a Laborer

*The determinants of the supply price.* The hypothesis that the supply price of labor equals the value of the average product in the rural sector assumes that when an individual migrates, he loses his imputed rent on the land. (He obviously would not lose his rent if he owned the land; the argument requires that land be communally owned.) But it also requires more than that: it must be (implicitly) assumed that the family does not maximize either its joint income or welfare; if it did, and if the marginal productivity of a member of the family were higher in the urban sector than in the rural sector (adjusted for differences in cost of living and amenity values), then it would always pay the family to induce that individual to migrate. Indeed, the main argument for the average product hypothesis entails a degree of communality that is consistent with the family making decisions together on the allocation of labor. The widespread evidence of remittances (flowing from the rural to the urban sector and vice versa) is also consistent with the "family welfare maximization" hypothesis.

Secondly, the relevant distortion is not between the mean marginal productivity and the mean average productivity in the rural sector, but the distortion associated with the individual with the *lowest* supply price. If there is a class of landless laborers who receive a wage equal to their marginal productivity, then the supply price of labor is equal to its opportunity cost. This would be the case even if *most* workers in the rural sector receive their average product.[1]

It is sometimes argued that the landless laborers still receive a wage in excess of their marginal product for "institutional" (social) reasons. In particular it is argued that the marginal product is approximately zero while the wage is positive (though small). If that is the case, the magnitude of the relevant distortion is not the difference between the average product of labor and zero, but between the institutionally determined rural wage and zero.

*Zero marginal productivity of labor.* The argument for the approximately zero marginal productivity of labor is based on the widespread observation of unemployment. The evidence, however, is ambiguous. If all the workers are employed at any time, e.g., at planting and harvest, there may not be unemployment in any economic sense. The pattern of seasonality in the use of labor resources may constitute an efficient allocation of resources; to employ these seasonal laborers more steadily throughout the year may require allocating complementary resources (like capital) that have more productive uses elsewhere.

The other major alternative explanation of observed unemployment in the rural sector and a positive wage is the efficiency wage hypothesis, discussed by Leibenstein (1957) and developed further in work by Stiglitz (1976). The efficiency wage hypothesis argues that the productivity of a worker increases with the wage paid to him, as illustrated in Figure 1.1. As noted below, the efficiency wage hypothesis has very strong and important implications for the calculation of opportunity cost—implications that are quite different from the traditional average product hypothesis—and therefore it merits discussion in some detail.

There are several alternative explanations of the efficiency wage hypothesis. The traditional explanation is based on nutrition: below a certain level of consumption, workers simply are not very productive. An alternative explanation has to do with morale effects: the effort an individual is willing to put forth is related to the wage he receives; an individual with a wage that is low relative to the mean wage will not put forward much effort. Still a third explanation has to do with the fact that if most individuals do own some land, then the wage at which they are willing to supply their services in the labor market (say to the plantation sector) is a function of their abilities. This point is developed in greater detail later in connection with the migration of laborers from the rural to urban sector.[2] For a further development of

Figure 1.1. Efficiency-Wage Relationship

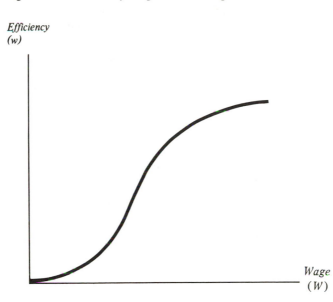

*Efficiency
(w)*

*Wage
(W)*

this kind of model, including consideration of its welfare implications, see Stiglitz (1976). The alternative versions of the efficiency wage hypothesis have quite different welfare implications. The focus of this chapter is the traditional (nutritional) version.

If the productivity of a worker is a function of his wage, as in Figure 1.1, there is a wage that minimizes costs per effective unit of labor. At this efficiency wage the supply of labor may exceed the demand, but there is no incentive to hire laborers at a lower wage.

With the efficiency wage hypothesis and a competitive labor market, there will be a positive wage and unemployment; but the supply price of labor to the urban sector will equal its opportunity cost—zero.

*Sufficient conditions for the supply price to exceed the value of the marginal product.* If there are no landless laborers and there is sharing within the family farm, but in deciding whether a particular individual should migrate or not the family does not maximize family welfare (e.g., sharing persists if the individual remains in the rural sector but ceases when he migrates), then it is possible for the opportunity cost of migration to be negative. That is, within the family farm it can be shown that the net marginal productivity of an extra individual is negative, taking into account the reduction in productivity resulting from the reduction in income, in turn resulting from the extra sharing that is required (Stiglitz, 1976).

On the other hand, in such situations it is possible that the family will not distribute income to its members uniformly since they will recognize that by increasing within-family inequality they can increase total family income. Unless they have very strong egalitarian ethics, this trade-off between total family income and within-family inequality will lead to some individuals receiving a higher income than others. In general, it can be shown that with the efficiency wage model the supply price of the marginal migrant (the lowest wage paid to family members) is less than the average product within the rural sector but greater than the opportunity cost of labor.[3]

*Surplus laborers: A red herring.* There is another situation where migration from the rural sector does not lead to a reduced rural output: if the increased productivity of laborers (due to the increased land/labor ratio) leads them to work harder, and this indirect effect offsets the direct effect of a reduced number of workers. It is important to observe that when the seasonality structure of employment is taken into account, the conditions under which this would occur are even more restrictive than those discussed by Sen (1966). (See Stiglitz [1969].) But the welfare implications of this situation—misleadingly referred to as being one of surplus laborers—is completely different from that of the conventional "zero marginal productivity" hypothesis or the efficiency wage hypothesis: welfare calculations of opportunity costs should take into account the increased effort on the part of workers.

*Concluding comments.* It seems likely that neither polar view—that the supply price equals the average product and that the opportunity cost is close to zero, or that the supply price correctly measures the opportunity cost—is correct. But where between these two views truth lies is an empirical question.

Although the focus of this chapter is on calculating the *opportunity cost* of hiring labor (in the urban sector) it is important to note that many of the same considerations that are relevant to determining the opportunity cost are also important for determining the distribution implications of hiring additional labor—and hence in determining the shadow price of labor. For instance, if the rural family acts as a unit in making migration decisions (with the individual who goes to the urban sector being supported by the remaining workers on the farm while he seeks a job, and then remitting a significant fraction back to the rural sector after he obtains a job), then the high urban wage may not have the undesirable distributional consequences usually associated with it (although it may still be undesirable on the grounds of efficiency).[4]

There appears to be some empirical evidence that bears on the issues at hand, but not enough to give one much confidence in calculating the opportunity cost of labor. It would be useful to know whether the marginal migrants are landless (or virtually landless); whether the migrants return to the rural sector, and if so, whether there is any loss of property rights; if there is not, whether the migrants receive any compensation for abandoning their implicit property rights; how significant remittances are, in both directions; and how the distribution of consumption (income) within the family farm is determined. Answers are likely to vary from country to country, so one will have to be wary of generalizing from a few case studies.

The above analysis suggests, however, that at the present state of knowledge, the hypothesis that the supply price of labor measures its opportunity cost is more reasonable than the alternative more traditional hypothesis that the supply price equals the average product and the opportunity cost of labor is zero.

### Distortions in the Allocation of Labor Within the Sector

The rules for distributing income within the rural sector induce a distortion, not only with respect to the decision of whether to migrate, but also with respect to the supply of effort in the rural sector. If labor receives its marginal product in the urban sector, and there are (uncorrectable) distortions within the rural sector, then even if each *laborer* in the rural sector receives his marginal product, there may be an efficiency gain from transferring labor from the rural to the urban sector.

That these are distinctly different distortions may be seen by observing that if labor (effort) were inelastically supplied, there would be no distortion within the sector, but as noted above, there still may be a distortion in the supply of laborers to the urban sector from the rural sector. On the other hand, it is possible that each laborer receives his marginal product—so that the supply price of labor to the urban sector correctly measures that direct opportunity cost—even when there are distortions within the rural sector. For instance, if output were proportional to effort (e.g., a constant return to scale production function with labor as the only factor), then if all individuals within the family have the same utility function and productive capacities, a rule of equal division of the output among the family members would lead each to receive his marginal productivity, but each would supply too little effort. In such situations there is likely to be an important indirect opportunity cost, since the magnitude of the distortion may depend on the migration of the individual. For instance, when there are two members in the family, each receives at the margin, in effect, half his marginal productivity; but when one of those two members leaves, the distortion is eliminated and the individual receives his full marginal product. There may be a significant gain in efficiency resulting, then, from the migration of this individual.

The importance of this is a moot question. In large families, the reduction in the distortion from the migration of a single individual is likely to be small; if migration occurs in family groups, then there will be essentially no change in the magnitude of the distortion. But there is another, more fundamental reason why this distortion is probably not important: families that share in consumption are likely to share in effort as well. Social sanctions imposed on sloth may be as effective an incentive as increased consumption of food. There seems to be an unnatural asymmetry, for small group situations at least, to assume sharing in output but not input (as Sen [1966], for instance, does).

Labor may be receiving less than its marginal product, not only because of sharing with other members of the family, but also because of sharing with the landlord; the inefficiency associated with sharecropping has been noted since at least the time of Marshall. Cheung (1968, 1969a, 1969b) and Stiglitz (1974b) have, however, argued that there may not be a distortion; if the amount of labor (effort) that an individual supplies can be costlessly observed, then the sharecropping contract will specify the amount of labor, and the contract specifications will yield an efficient allocation of resources.[5] If this labor cannot be costlessly observed, then the loss of output from the fact that individuals receive less than their marginal productivity may be less than the cost of a direct monitoring system; that is, sharecropping provides an incentive for individuals to supply effort where their effort could not be directly observed except at a great cost. It can be shown that subject to the constraint on the unobservability of labor income and the utilization of linear distribution rules the sharecropping system is Pareto optimal.[6]

*The Elasticity of Supply of Laborers to the Urban Sector*

In later discussion, it turns out that the supply elasticity of laborers to the urban sector is important in determining the relationship between the shadow price of labor and the market wage. For much of the heuristic discussion it shall be assumed that the supply is infinitely elastic; this is a simplifying assumption which has a long tradition within the development literature. Most of this grows out of the view of laborers within the rural sector as having a zero marginal product—a view on which some doubts exist. But if these laborers do have a zero marginal product and the wage within the rural sector is institutionally determined and fixed (unchanged as individuals migrate from the rural sector), then the supply function to the urban sector will indeed be horizontal, at least up to a point.

In the efficiency wage model, discussed briefly above, laborers are in surplus in the sense that additional migration from the rural sector may actually increase rural output. The opportunity cost of migration is negative. On the other hand, if families share their income amongst themselves when they live within the rural sector, but do not share once they have left, once again the supply curve will be upward sloping since as individuals migrate the lowest wage paid within the sector will normally increase. (Similar results hold if the family decides on migration communally.) Similarly in the surplus laborer model (Sen, 1966), even if output were unchanged the supply price of labor would still be upward sloping since laborers are still better off as more workers leave the rural sector.

There are two models that would seem to generate a horizontal supply schedule for laborers to the urban sector. If land is in surplus, and labor is the only scarce factor within the rural sector, it is reasonable to assume that output is proportional to the number of laborers. (Note that it is the assumption of surplus *land*, not that of surplus *labor* that is now giving us the horizontal supply schedule.) Alternatively, consider the following model that does not ignore the structure of the rural labor market as other models normally do. It is a fact that not everyone is employed full time on agricultural production— there are also manufactured goods (for example, clothing) produced within the sector. Since land and capital may not be important inputs into this activity, as individuals migrate from the rural sector, labor becomes reallocated away from rural manufacturing to agricultural production in such a way as to keep the marginal productivity of labor in agricultural production constant. In this model, it is easy to show that so long as there is some manufacturing occurring within the rural sector, and so long as the (value of the) marginal product[7] remains constant, the supply price of labor to the urban sector will be constant. Even in the two cases just presented, the supply price will be constant only if individuals have the same evaluation of the differences in amenities in the two sectors, if transportation costs are the same, and if relative skills are the same.

Although these arguments make a perfectly horizontal supply curve unlikely, it is not unreasonable to assume a fairly elastic supply curve, so long as the urban sector is small relative to the rural sector and the set of potential migrants is relatively homogeneous with respect to tastes, risk aversion, transport costs, skills, etc.

For instance, if labor were homogeneous, then the supply elasticity, $\xi$, is

$$\xi = \frac{L_r}{\bar{L} - L_r} \eta_r$$

where $L_r$ is labor in the rural sector, $\bar{L}$ is total labor supply, and $\eta_r$ is the elasticity of demand for labor in the rural sector. If the rural sector has 90 percent of the labor force and the production function is Cobb-Douglas, with laborer's share equal to $1/2$, then $\xi = 18$.

## Distortions in the Urban Labor Market

It is widely believed that wages in the urban sector exceed the supply price of labor from the rural sector; it is this discrepancy that leads to urban unemployment, as individuals queue for jobs within the urban sector. When supply exceeds demand, rather than the conventional equilibrating mechanism, in which prices fall, there is an alternative equilibrating mechanism—the number of unemployed increases.[8] As the number of unemployed increases, the expected income of job-seekers within the urban sector falls, eventually to the point where no further migration is induced.

The questions addressed in this and the next sections are: How can this failure of wages to fall be explained? What does it imply about the efficiency of the allocation of labor between the urban and rural sector?

*Alternative Explanations of High Wages*

It is important to know why the wage exceeds the supply price of labor for two reasons. First, the magnitude of unemployment (the unemployment rate) is a function of the ratio of the urban to the rural wage. If the wage is unaffected by a policy change, then if the rural wage is also constant (as, say, with constant marginal productivity in the rural sector), then the unemployment rate is fixed, and it can be shown (see Appendix A and Stiglitz [1974a]) that the opportunity cost of hiring an additional urban worker is simply the urban wage. If, on the other hand, the policy change leads to an increase in the unemployment rate, the opportunity cost of labor exceeds the urban wage. In any case, the change in the urban wage induced by any particular policy depends on the theory of wage determination within the urban sector. Second, the high wage may be performing an economic function; changes in the wage level may have consequences other than simply on the allocation of labor between the urban and rural sector and the level of urban unemployment. Again, this depends on the theory of wage determination within the urban sector.

Four alternative explanations of high wages have been discussed extensively in the literature. The first and perhaps the most widely held view is that institutional constraints—unions, political pressures on government—keep the urban wage high. If this is the case, it is still important to know how the differential between the urban and rural wage is determined. Is it likely, for instance, that a policy such as a wage subsidy will leave the urban wage unchanged? Perhaps so, if the wage is determined on political considerations relative to some standard of living; but it is unlikely if the wage is determined by union pressures. The trouble with most "institutional" explanations of the high level of wages in the urban sector is that they essentially appeal to a "black box": they fail to provide clear predictions about the consequences of various policy changes, or to provide explanations of differences in the size of wage differentials among different countries. Even if the urban wage remains absolutely rigid, the opportunity cost of hiring an additional laborer may not equal the urban wage, since as laborers migrate to the urban sector the rural wage may increase and thus the unemployment rate may decrease.

The second explanation is the "labor turnover" hypothesis that higher wages are a means by which employers reduce the not insignificant cost of labor turnover. In this view, the mere fact that wages are higher than the supply price is not necessarily evidence of inefficiency; given that indentured servitude is not allowed, high wages may be an effective instrument in reducing labor turnover. The induced unemployment is a cost that must be offset against the benefits from a reduction in turnover costs. In the model of the monopsonistically competitive labor market formulated by Stiglitz (1974a), a number of distortions were identified. Some of these led to too low a wage—the increased wage of one firm increased the unemployment rate, which reduced the quit rate faced by others at any given wage. However, the net effect is probably to lead to too high a wage. This results from the fact that each firm believes by increasing its wage it will reduce turnovers to other firms (i.e., it will enjoy a competitive advantage over its rivals), but when all firms do this none of them enjoy the competitive advantage.

In the labor turnover model (Figure 1.2), higher employment within the urban sector leads to a higher turnover rate and induces firms to pay a higher wage. The consequence is that the equilibrium unemployment *rate* increases, so the opportunity cost of hiring an additional laborer within the urban sector exceeds its urban wage. It is of some interest to note that if the urban wage is optimally set (but the government still cannot control migration directly), then the shadow price of labor is just equal to the (optimally set) urban wage.[9] (See Appendix B.)

The third explanation is the efficiency wage hypothesis—that higher wages lead to higher productivity and there is a wage that minimizes total labor costs (wages per effective unit of labor). The efficiency-wage relationship may result either from basic nutritional considerations, from morale effects, or from a correlation between the reservation wage and ability.[10] An attempt to lower the wage received by workers would lower national output and could conceivably lower employment. The urban wage will be unaffected by the government's hiring of laborers,[11] so that the opportunity cost is the same as with the "rigid wage" hypothesis. The fourth explanation, that wages are determined in such a way as to make savings equal investment in the urban sector, is discussed at greater length below.

These alternative hypotheses concerning the explanation of the high wage in the urban sector have different implications, both with respect to their predictions on the history of wages over time and on the effect of alternative policies on output and employment. For instance, the nutritional version of the efficiency wage hypothesis predicts that wages would change only in response to a change in technology in the given sector, and not in response to a change in the supply of labor (induced by, say, a change in birth rates or a change in technology in the other sectors of the economy).[12] It would predict then that different firms in the same economy might pay different wages

## Figure 1.2. The Labor Turnover Model

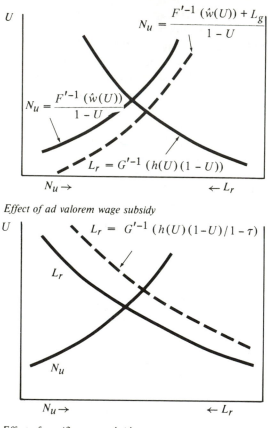

*Effect of increased government employment*

$$N_u = \frac{F'^{-1}(\hat{w}(U)) + L_g}{1 - U}$$

$$N_u = \frac{F'^{-1}(\hat{w}(U))}{1 - U}$$

$$L_r = G'^{-1}(h(U)(1 - U))$$

$N_u \rightarrow$     $\leftarrow L_r$

*Effect of ad valorem wage subsidy*

$$L_r = G'^{-1}(h(U)(1-U)/1-\tau)$$

$L_r$

$N_u$

$N_u \rightarrow$     $\leftarrow L_r$

*Effect of specific wage subsidy*

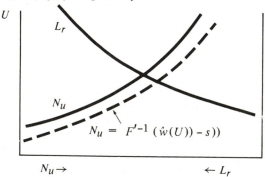

$L_r$

$N_u$

$$N_u = F'^{-1}(\hat{w}(U)) - s))$$

$N_u \rightarrow$     $\leftarrow L_r$

if they employ different technologies. The labor turnover hypothesis predicts that the urban-rural wage differential (rather than the urban wage itself) remains approximately constant if most of the labor turnover is due to labor emigrating to the rural sector, since it is that wage differential that determines labor movements. It also predicts that the magnitude of the differential depends on the magnitude of the costs of specific training.

## The Informal Urban Sector and Government Employment

The discussion so far has assumed that all of the employment in the urban sector is in modern nongovernmental enterprises and that all labor is homogeneous. In fact, neither of these assumptions is appropriate, and any adequate analysis of the relationship between shadow prices and market wages must take into account differences among the kinds of employment and the skill levels of workers within the urban sector. The discussion here deals with only the former.

It is important to distinguish between governmental and nongovernmental employment mainly because the forces that determine wages in the two sectors are likely to be different and the instruments that the government can use to control the level of wages and employment in the two are different. For instance, the main instrument for affecting employment in the private sector is a wage subsidy, while the government planners could, in principle at least, instruct government agencies to evaluate projects within the government sector according to shadow prices. The government can, again in principle, prescribe the wage to be paid in state or parastatal employment, but it appears much more difficult for the government to control wages directly within the private sector.[13] If state or parastatal firms are not profit maximizing, the explanation of high wages is likely to be different from that for private employment. Some of these distinctions will be discussed later.

A vast array of activities are included within the informal (alternatively referred to as the grey or murky) sector. The units of "production" within the sector are small—self-employed individuals or small firms. Employment is often but not always irregular. It is often thought of as temporary employment for an individual who is seeking regular employment within the urban sector, but there is some evidence that some individuals have remained in steady occupations within the informal sector for sufficiently long that their employment ought to be thought of as regular.

There is no obvious way of modeling the informal sector, but for the purpose of attempting to analyze the distortions within the urban sector, perhaps the best way to think of this sector is as one of monopolistic competition, with relatively low fixed costs of entry. The typical characterization is that of the shoeshine boy, the newspaper vendor, or the door-to-door salesman. Additional entrants essentially share the same business; the commodities produced are very close (but not perfect) substitutes, differing mainly with respect to convenience such as location or time of delivery. Thus, it is postulated that the total product of the sector (the value of output) is an increasing function of the number of workers within the sector and that there are sharply diminishing returns, but each individual receives the average product.[14] There is thus a discrepancy between his income—the average product—and his marginal productivity. If it is postulated that the marginal migrant enters employment in the informal sector, then, in deciding whether to migrate to the urban sector, an individual who expected to remain permanently within the informal sector would look at the average income within that sector and compare it with his wage in the rural sector. If the more traditional view that workers within the rural sector receive their average product were correct, then the distortion with respect to the allocation of labor between the two sectors depends simply on the relative magnitude of the ratio between marginal and average products in the two sectors. On a priori grounds, it is not possible to tell which is greater; it is possible that there is too much migration rather than too little.

In Appendix D, it is shown that taking account of the informal sector in the migration model has relatively little effect on the calculation of shadow prices, and no effect if the marginal shoeshine boy makes zero contribution to net national product.

### Skilled Versus Unskilled Labor

Laborers differ in a number of characteristics that are important for the analysis of the relationship between shadow prices and market wages. One of the most important differences is that of skills. Taking as given, for the moment, the distribution of skills within the labor market (this composition may be a reflection of an imperfection in the education market), the questions are: How are individuals of different skills assigned to different jobs? What implications does this have for shadow prices?

In some countries, it is asserted that there is a shortage of skilled workers. This must mean that wages for skilled workers are below the market clearing price, so there is an excess demand for them. Firms would like to hire more skilled workers but cannot. The question is, why don't they bid up the wages? The presumed answer is that the market for skilled labor is very thin, unlike the market for unskilled labor where there are a large number of employers of essentially the same kind of laborers. There are usually relatively few firms hiring the same kind of laborers, and each firm realizes that it faces an upward sloping supply schedule of skilled laborers. Hence, they set the marginal value product of a laborer equal to the marginal cost of hiring an additional laborer, but that exceeds the wage. But there is an alternative view, also widely held, that wages for skilled laborers—as for unskilled laborers—exceed the market clearing level, so that there is an excess supply. (Both views may be correct;

there may be excess demand for some types of skilled laborers and excess supply for others.) The explanations for this are similar to those of the high wage for unskilled workers, but the consequences may be somewhat different.

The issue revolves around rules for hiring laborers when there is an excess of applicants over jobs. A common view is that employers hire the most qualified laborers, so that if a skilled (educated) laborer applies for a job, then even if he is no more productive at the given job than an unskilled laborer he will he hired in preference to him. This has been referred to as the "bumping" model (Fields, 1972a). The consequence is that the calculations of the relation between the opportunity cost and market wage of a skilled laborer are more complicated than for the unskilled laborer. If the ratio of the productivity (say, in efficiency units) of the skilled to the unskilled laborer is $V$, then each skilled laborer hired by the government leaves $V$ vacancies for unskilled laborers. This induces migration; it can be shown that $V/(1-U)$ workers migrate, if urban and rural wages remain constant, and if the rural wage, $w_r$, equals the expected urban wage, $(1-U)w_u$, where $U$ is the unemployment rate and $w_u$ the urban wage. If $w_r$ measures the marginal product of a worker in the rural sector, the loss in rural output is thus $w_r V/(1-U)$, which is greater or less than the urban wage as $V$ is greater or less than unity.

### Distortions in Migration Patterns

*Unemployment as an Equilibrating Device*

The previous two sections discussed why the wage in the urban and rural sectors might deviate from the marginal productivity of labor in those two sectors. Even if workers in both sectors receive their marginal product, it is conceivable that labor is not efficiently allocated between the sectors. Efficient allocation of labor would require the equating of the values of marginal productivity (and hence wages) in the two sectors. But in fact wages are not equated in the two sectors. It has been postulated that the level of unemployment acts as an equilibrating mechanism. In this section, two questions are addressed. Simpler versions of the theory of equilibrium migration predicted that the *expected* wage in the urban sector would equal the rural wage, where the expected urban wage, $w_u^e$, was

$$w_u^e = w_u(1 - U) \tag{1}$$

where

$$1 - U = L_u/N_u \, ,$$

the ratio of urban employment, $L_u$, to urban labor supply, $N_u$. Hence, one minus the unemployment rate equals the ratio of the rural wage to the urban wage,

$$\frac{w_r}{w_u} = 1 - U. \tag{2}$$

Such a theory predicts a higher unemployment rate than is actually observed. The first question is: How can we explain this?

The answer to this question has important implications for the second question: What are the consequences of hiring additional laborers in the urban sector? As noted earlier, the answer to this question depends on what happens to the urban unemployment rate. If there is no induced migration as a result of hiring one additional laborer in the urban sector, then the additional labor is essentially hired out of the unemployment pool and the opportunity cost is zero. (Alternatively, the laborer may be hired from the informal sector, in which case the opportunity cost is the value of the [social] marginal productivity of a worker in that sector. Under the conditions postulated earlier, this is likely to be small.) If, on the other hand, the unemployment rate remains unchanged, then hiring one urban worker induces a migration of $1/(1-U)$ workers from the rural sector, so that, were the workers in the rural sector receiving their marginal productivity, the opportunity cost would be $w_r/(1-U)$, which, according to Equation 2, is just equal to $w_u$. Hence, if the unemployment rate were constant, the shadow price of labor could be just equal to the market wage. It is conceivable that the unemployment rate actually increases, if the government policy leads to a higher urban wage. This might be the case, as mentioned earlier, if the government uses a wage subsidy to induce employment; for the wage subsidy is likely to be shifted— that is, lead to a slightly higher urban wage—and this in turn is likely to lead to higher urban unemployment. If the unemployment rate does increase, the opportunity cost of hiring labor may exceed the urban wage.

## Modifications of the Basic Theory

There are a number of possible alternative explanations of why the unemployment rate is less than predicted. The most obvious are those associated with differences in cost of living. These simply entail an adjustment for the cost-of-living differentials or, what is harder to measure, differences in amenity values between urban and rural living. Other explanations have to do with costs of transportation, imperfections of information, and imperfections in the capital market. Individuals find it costly to migrate to the city, and therefore the expected urban wage must exceed the rural wage to induce migration. Indeed, if there are significant costs of transportation, and if there is a life-cycle pattern of returning to the rural area later in life (for example, because young individuals have a comparative advantage working within the urban sector and older individuals within the rural sector), lifetime expected incomes should be compared.

Imperfections of information mean that individuals may misperceive the expected urban wage, expecting it to be lower than it actually is. Those who remain unemployed for a very long time may make a greater impression on potential migrants than those who find jobs quickly, and thus they may overestimate the difficulty of finding a job. (There are obviously significant individual differences in this respect, some individuals being pessimists and some optimists.)

Capital market imperfections imply that individuals cannot borrow to finance a job search,[15] so that even if the expected wage in the urban sector is greater than the rural wage, individuals may not attempt to get an urban job.[16] This will be ameliorated if there is effective sharing, that is, if the part of the family remaining in the rural sector supports the individual while he is job seeking (essentially, lending him the required capital). Risk aversion is sometimes used as an explanation, but it is not obvious whether the risks of finding a job (of urban unemployment) are greater or less than those associated with agricultural income. To the extent that there is an effective sharing system, since urban unemployment is not highly correlated with agricultural income, urban employment might be desirable even if the expected wage within the urban sector is less than the rural wage.

Another possible explanation has to do with sharing: if convention dictates that those who are successful in obtaining urban jobs must remit a large fraction of their income back to the rural area, then the private incentives to migrate are lower, and the equilibrating unemployment rate will accordingly be smaller.

*Search and unemployment.* There are three more basic modifications of the unemployment urban-rural wage differential model presented above. As is recognized now, this model can be viewed as a special case of the general search models that have recently received widespread attention within macroeconomic discussions. In those models, a basic question that has been raised is whether the individual must remain unemployed to search for a better job. A similar question may be raised here: Does the individual have to migrate to the urban sector in order to search for a job? Part of the answer obviously depends on the proximity of the urban and rural sectors and the nature of the information network linking the two. If the two are closely linked, as seems the case in some countries, then word of a vacancy quickly spreads and an individual can come in from the rural sector for the day to apply for the job. In this case, there will be no urban unemployment, so long as there is a positive marginal productivity of workers (positive wage) in the rural sector.

Alternatively, if rural employment (productivity) is highly seasonal, but transportation costs are small, then one would expect there to be migration into the urban sector at slack times, and remigration into the rural sectors at planting and harvesting times. If this is true, it has important implications. It means that the appropriate rural wage for the analysis of migration is not the annual marginal productivity (or wage) of the rural worker, but his wage in slack times, and accordingly the opportunity cost of the labor engaged in job seeking is relatively small.

It is important, in this context, to observe that seasonality of employment does not necessarily imply that labor is inefficiently used—seasonal unemployment should not convey the same presumption of market failure and of inefficient use of resources that aggregate unemployment conventionally does. It is conceivable, and in many cases likely, that the efficient use of any resource requires periodic idleness; for instance, to keep labor fully employed one might develop industries within the rural sector where they could work during slack agricultural periods. But this would require the capital in those sectors to be idle at peak agricultural periods, and given the opportunity cost of capital, this might be an inefficient use of capital. This is not to say that one should not attempt to find activities—different crops, light industries, etc.—that have patterns of labor use that are complementary to that of their present usage.

*Patterns of hiring.* The second modification to the basic model takes into account the dynamics of labor markets. In the original Harris-Todaro formulation (Harris and Todaro, 1970), the labor market was modeled like a union hiring hall—all individuals came down to the hiring hall in the morning and a random selection from these received employment for that day. A more reasonable model (discussed in Stiglitz [1974a]) entails individuals coming to the labor market, waiting to get employed, and once employed, remaining on the job for an extended period (either until they quit or are fired). Thus, the period of unemployment is primarily at the beginning of their stay within the urban sector. More importantly, the expected length of time to be unemployed is related to the number of vacancies that occur, which in turn is related to the number of new jobs being created and to the number of quits (from deaths or individuals returning to the rural sector, for example) and firings that occur in old jobs. Thus, it can be shown that the expected wage in the urban sector not only decreases with the unemployment rate, but increases with the growth rate. This has one important implication: rapid expansion of the urban sector is likely to be associated with a large increase in unemployment (and, indeed, in the unemployment rate). To put it another way, the total loss of output from unemployment associated with job seeking will be a function of the rate at which jobs are created—a very rapid increase in jobs followed by a period of stable employment will induce a high unemployment rate for a short time, but a low one thereafter; a more steady increase in jobs will induce a "medium" unemployment rate throughout. At this point, it is not known what is the most efficient (i.e., loss minimizing) way of creating jobs, or indeed, whether the differences in totals would be large.[17]

*Heterogeneity of individuals.* The third and perhaps most important modification to the basic model relates to the nature of the supply function of individuals from the rural sector. In earlier work on migration models, it was essentially assumed that all individuals were identical, and accordingly, if the marginal productivity of a laborer were constant, there would be a perfectly horizontal supply schedule of labor to the urban sector. It was this assumption along with the assumption of a constant urban wage that implied that the opportunity cost of labor in the urban sector was just equal to its wage. But if individuals differ, the relationship between the opportunity cost of labor and its wage is far more complex, as the following examples illustrate.

Assume a rigid urban wage and two distinct rural areas such that transportation costs from the two differ and each has a constant marginal productivity of labor. Then as the urban sector hires more laborers, all of the laborers will come from one of the two rural areas, and the urban unemployment rate will remain constant. Eventually, however, all of the workers from that area will have migrated. Then, additional hiring of laborers will have a zero opportunity cost—it will induce no more unemployment—until eventually the expected wage in the urban sector is higher, and individuals from the second area begin to migrate, in which case the opportunity cost is again equal to the wage. The ratio of opportunity cost to market wage thus fluctuates as in Figure 1.3. Similarly, at any given level of employment, the consequences of increasing the urban wage differ markedly, depending on the level of the wage.

Similar results obtain if individuals differ, say, in their attitudes toward

Figure 1.3. Fluctuations in Ratio of Opportunity Cost to Urban Wage

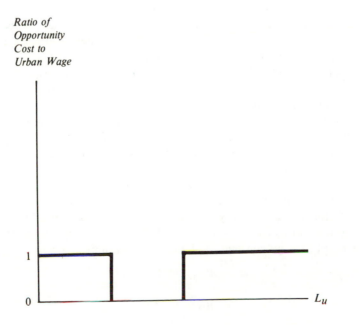

the differences in the value of amenities between the urban and rural sectors. Assume there are no transportation costs, everyone is equally productive, and the rural wage is equal to the marginal productivity of a worker, which for convenience is assumed to be constant. Again, for simplicity, assume that there are two groups, one that likes cities very much and one that dislikes cities. Then the first group of individuals to migrate would be the city-lovers; the equilibrating unemployment rate for any given urban-rural wage differential would be larger than predicted by a model that ignored amenities. One must, however, be careful in calculating the opportunity cost (a point discussed below); one ought to include these amenities values in the welfare calculation. If the amenity value is only enjoyed by those who actually receive employment, then the "corrected" opportunity cost is just equal to the urban wage, $w_u$, while the "uncorrected" opportunity cost is $w_r$; if the amenity value is enjoyed by everyone within the urban sector, then the corrected opportunity cost is still equal to the urban wage.[18]

Eventually all of the city-lovers have migrated. Additional hiring in the urban sector will come from the urban unemployed and will induce no additional unemployment; hence the opportunity cost drops to zero (or is negative, if amenity values are enjoyed only by the urban employed) until the expected wage is raised sufficiently to induce city-haters to migrate. Again, additional hiring beyond this amount will leave the unemployment rate fixed (at its now lower value), and the opportunity cost will again be the urban wage.

In general, those who migrate first will be those who have the largest comparative advantage in urban employment, those who have the largest (positive) assessment of the differences in amenity values between urban and rural living, and those who have the lowest transportation costs. (Also, consistent with the more general search models, they should be the youngest individuals.) The wage differential thus required to induce additional migration is greater than the wage differential required to induce the first group of migrants; or to put it another way, to induce additional migration the unemployment rate must fall (so the expected urban wage rises). This implies that the opportunity cost will be smaller than the urban wage by an amount that is related to the supply elasticity of labor.

For the case where there is a positively sloped supply schedule because of differences in amenity valuations, this can easily be calculated. Let $A(N)$ be the (difference in) amenity valuation placed on urban (relative to rural) living by the $N$th individual. $A'(N) < 0$. Under the assumptions given above (constant urban wage, constant rural wage), equilibrium entails

$$w_r = A(N_u) + (1 - U)w_u$$

$$= A(N_u) + \frac{L_u}{N_u} w_u$$

from which we can calculate the migration induced by hiring an additional laborer in the urban sector

$$\frac{dN_u}{dL_u} = \frac{w_u}{N_u\left(\dfrac{w_u L_u}{N_u^2} - A'\right)}$$

and the opportunity cost (including the amenity valuation of urban employment)

$$w_u \left[\frac{\dfrac{L_u w_u}{N_u}}{\dfrac{L_u w_u}{N_u} - A' N_u}\right] = \frac{\xi}{1 + \xi} w_u$$

where $\xi$ is the labor supply elasticity, given by

$$\xi = \frac{w_u^e}{N_u} \frac{dN_u}{dw_u^e} = -\frac{w_u L_u}{N_u^2} \frac{1}{A'}$$

where $w_u^e$ is the expected urban wage,

$$w_u^e = w_u(1 - U) = \frac{w_u L_u}{N_u} .$$

In the other cases (where individuals differ by such factors as transportation costs, comparative advantages, or age) the labor supply elasticity will also be important in determining the relationship between market wage and opportunity cost. For instance, if diminishing returns to labor in the rural sector were assumed, with a rigid urban wage, and no amenity values, there would still be an upward sloping supply schedule of laborers from the rural sector. Equilibrium would require

$$w_r(\bar{L} - N_u) = \frac{w_u L_u}{N_u}$$

where the rural wage depends on the number of individuals in the urban (and hence the number in the rural) sector. Straightforward calculations show that now

$$\frac{dN_u}{dL_u} = \frac{w_u/N_u}{\dfrac{w_u L_u}{N_u^2} - w_r'}$$

so the opportunity cost is

$$w_u \frac{\xi}{1 + \xi}$$

where now

$$\xi = - \frac{w_u L_u}{N_u^2} \frac{1}{w_r'}.$$

Thus, it would appear that the elasticity of supply affects the relationship between the market wage and opportunity costs in exactly the same way in both of these situations. Other cases would similarly need to be investigated in detail. It is clear, however, that an empirical parameter important in calculating a shadow wage is the elasticity of supply of labor to the urban sector. (Implicitly, in earlier calculations, an infinitely elastic supply was assumed. An elasticity as large as 2 would imply that the opportunity cost is still only two-thirds of the urban wage.)

## Distortions in Other Markets

The final set of distortions to be discussed are those in other markets, which impinge on the labor market. In any general equilibrium framework, a distortion in any sector is likely to have effects on the other sectors. Some distortions that would seem to have an important effect on the determination of the relationship between shadow wages and market wages will be presented.

### A Cambridge-Type Theory of Wage Determination

Perhaps the most important distortions are those associated with the capital market. First, if interest rates are insufficiently flexible, if there is a dichotomy between the urban and rural capital markets, and if there are differential savings rates between workers and capitalists, then when savings exceed investment, rather than the interest rate falling and equilibrium being attained at full employment by an increase in investment, the real wage rises, and savings are reduced.[19] The rise in real wages leads, in the now familiar way, to induced migration. Hiring additional workers in the urban sector (say by the government), financed by a profits tax, increases consumption, reduces savings and thus reduces the level of wages required for savings to equal investment. This lower wage reduces migration, but the higher employment increases it. For this particular policy change, the opportunity cost of hiring an additional laborer is negative (see Appendix C).

### Inefficient Capital Allocation Between Urban and Rural Sectors

Another implication of the dichotomy between urban and rural capital markets is that the return to capital may be higher in the rural sector than in the urban sector. This in turn may imply that the productivity of laborers in the rural sector is lower than it would have been had capital been efficiently allocated. But as brought out earlier this does not mean that given the distortion in the capital market labor is inefficiently distributed. If the capital allocation is unaffected by the policy changes being discussed, then what is of concern is just the productivity of labor; the fact that a particular policy change may increase the difference between the return to capital in the two sectors, and in that sense the apparent size of the distortion, is of no concern. When policy changes have an effect on the allocation of capital, this must be taken into account.

Indeed, as mentioned earlier, a distortion in one market has important implications for other markets. In particular, the unemployment induced by high wages in the urban sector implies that, if the government can control the allocation of capital among sectors, say by taxes and subsidies, it should do so: it should impose a tax on capital in the urban sector (in the rigid wage model) for this will increase the wage in the rural sector, lower it in the urban sector, and thus reduce unemployment. Similarly, the reallocation of capital induced by various government policies has important implications (see Appendix E).

For instance, hiring one more government employee (without diverting any capital from the private sector) has an immediate effect of inducing migration; the lower productivity of capital in the rural sector (as a result of the lower capital-labor ratio) induces a flow of capital to the urban sector, which increases urban employment, generating a further flow of labor. Thus, the unemployment and output loss from hiring an employee in the public sector is larger than if capital were immobile.[20]

### General Savings Shortage

The final and most widely discussed consequence is associated with the general shortage of savings. (Note that the high wage in the Cambridge model discussed earlier can be thought of as arising from a shortage of investment opportunities or an excess of savings.) There is not universal agreement on this assumption in spite of the predominant role it has played in much of the development discussion. Recent studies on capital utilization of LDCs as well as the distribution of actual returns on projects undertaken have cast doubt on the importance of capital shortages.

If there is a shortage of savings, then policies that increase employment, financed by taxes on profits, reduce savings, and this effect must be taken into account in calculating shadow prices. This effect of employment has been the central focus of much of the earlier analyses of shadow wage rates. Yet, in the context of the models discussed so far, *the effect of additional employment on savings is negligible.* For instance, with the rigid wage hypothesis, if all of the profits but none of the wages are saved, and if the marginal product of labor in the rural sector is constant, then wage income—

and hence consumption—is independent of the number of individuals hired in the urban sector (assuming no taxation of wage income); hence maximizing output also maximizes savings, and the opportunity cost calculations performed earlier are directly applicable.

On the other hand, if there are diminishing returns to the agricultural sector, hiring additional workers in the urban sector raises the rural wage and hence raises total wage income. The shadow price exceeds the direct opportunity cost. From our earlier calculations, if the urban wage, $\bar{w}_u$, is fixed,

$$\frac{dN_u}{dL_g} = \frac{w_u}{w_r}\left(\frac{\xi}{1+\xi}\right),$$

where $L_g$ is government employment and $\xi$ is labor supply elasticity to the urban sector. So, assuming workers in the rural sector receive their marginal product,

$$-\frac{dQ_r}{dL_g} = \frac{\xi}{1+\xi}\, w_u$$

where $Q_r$ is output in rural sector. Hence, the shadow price is equal to

$$w_u\,\frac{1}{1+\xi}\,(\xi + p\bar{L}/N_u)$$

where $p$ is the social value of savings relative to consumption and $\bar{L}$ is the total labor force.

It is clear that the shadow price may easily exceed the market wage. In economies with small urban sectors $\xi$ is likely to be large and $N_u/\bar{L}$ near unity so the shadow price will be near $w_u$.

## SHADOW PRICES AND OPTIMAL POLICIES

The preceding section presented a framework within which the effects of various policies can be evaluated. As noted in the introduction to this chapter, it is important to recognize that the desirability of increasing urban employment will depend not only on the presumed structure of the labor market, but also on the instruments with which such an increase in employment can be effected. For instance, the difference between the shadow price and the market wage is not necessarily equal to the optimal wage subsidy; and the optimal wage subsidy depends on the form that the subsidy takes.

An ad valorem wage subsidy has no effect on the wage in the efficiency wage model, but a specific wage subsidy does; however, in the labor turnover model an ad valorem wage subsidy has an effect but a specific wage subsidy does not.

The calculations of shadow prices and optimal wages subsidies are complicated and are presented in the appendices. Here we make a number of observations about the determination of the shadow price, based on the results presented in the appendices and the previous discussion in this chapter.

Among the factors discussed so far, several have an important effect on the value of the shadow price of labor (or on the optimal wage subsidy): (1) whether the efficiency wage model holds in the rural sector, and if so, whether the wage is below the efficiency wage; (2) the explanation of the high wage in the urban sector; and (3) the magnitude of the response of the labor supplied to the urban sector to a change in the *expected* urban wage.

A large labor supply elasticity is important for several reasons. It implies that migration from the rural sector to the urban sector will not likely have a large effect on the rural wages. If the labor supply elasticity is small, it will have a significant effect on rural wages, and this will reduce the urban unemployment rate (hence lowering the shadow price of labor). A large supply elasticity also means that there is likely to be a small difference between the marginal and average product of labor in the rural sector, so that the question of whether laborers get paid their marginal or average product becomes relatively unimportant. If the labor supply elasticity is small, it *may* be because of diminishing returns in the agricultural sector, so that the difference between the marginal and average product of labor is large. However it has been shown in this chapter that the hypothesis of a migrant's opportunity cost being the marginal product seems more reasonable than that he receives his average product; accordingly, all calculations are performed on that basis.

Some factors that might have been thought to be important (and have been extensively discussed in some earlier literature) do not appear to be particularly important: (1) the existence of an overall savings shortage (the shadow price of investment exceeding that on consumption) may have little effect on the shadow price of labor, if the urban sector is relatively small; and (2) disaggregation within the urban sector—taking into account the informal or murky sector—seems to have little effect on the calculations.

Under certain conditions, the opportunity cost of labor may be negative: (1) if there is a relation between efficiency and wages in the rural sector and the rural wage is less than the efficiency wage; or (2) if the wage in the urban sector is high in order to make investment equal savings (the Cambridge model).

In the efficiency wage model, an ad valorem wage subsidy is not shifted at all, and a specific wage subsidy actually leads to a lowering of the market wage. If there is no public employment an ad valorem wage subsidy is able to lead the economy to a constrained optimum (constrained, in the sense that the government cannot directly control migration); more generally, however, the government will need to employ both specific and ad valorem wage subsidies. With the labor turnover model, the ad valorem wage subsidy is always partially shifted, increasing the unemployment rate; a specific wage subsidy always lowers the unemployment rate.

If the government can, it should tax capital in the urban sector and sub-sidize it in the rural sector. If capital is mobile, the shadow price of labor in the urban sector is larger than if it is not.

## CONCLUDING COMMENTS

The general methodology of cost-benefit analysis now seems well estab-lished. The analysis can be divided into four steps: (1) specify objectives, for example, national output, employment, particular distribution of income; (2) formulate a model of how the economy operates; (3) consider the set of instruments available to the government, including the constraints on their implementation; and (4) derive the shadow prices to be used in cost-benefit analysis and the optimal values of the control variables on the basis of the three preceding steps.

The recent literature on cost-benefit analysis has paid too little attention to formulating a structural model of the economy and to investigating alter-native models of LDCs. The objective of this chapter has been to provide a partial remedy for that deficiency, to analyze in some detail the distortions in the efficient allocation of labor in LDCs, and to attempt to infer from that the consequences of alternative policy changes. Given the assumptions about the objectives and the structure of the economy, the derivation of optimal policies and shadow prices is a straightforward, mechanical (but often tedious) process. The shadow prices and optimal policies calculated in this chapter are those based on the simple objective of maximizing national income (al-though it has also been demonstrated how these results can be easily modified if there is a capital constraint).

It is clear that optimal wage subsidies depend on the form of the wage subsidies, that the optimal rate of wage subsidy is not necessarily equal to the difference between the shadow price of labor and the market wage, and that shadow prices and market wages may be very sensitive to the hypotheses one makes about the structure of the economy.

Much remains to be done: at the empirical level, to ascertain which of these models seems applicable to different countries, and to estimate the values of the parameters; and at the theoretical level, to derive more general (but probably less interpretable) expressions for shadow prices, particularly when there are two or more distortions operating simultaneously within the economy.

Given that the shadow price for labor seems to depend on so many variables, what is the planner to do until the empirical research called for in this chapter can be conducted? Although one must be cautious about making judgments concerning what are the important distortions to worry about, the detailed investigation of the various models and their implications has led to the following tentative conclusions: the Cambridge model is probably even less applicable here than elsewhere, but there is at least some validity to both the efficiency wage and labor turnover models; in any case, there will probably be some shifting of any wage subsidy. The elasticity of labor supply from the rural to the urban sector is likely to vary significantly from country to country, but in at least a number of important situations, it is likely to be quite large. This means that the opportunity cost of labor will probably be close to the urban wage. The correction to take account of the informal sector is likely to be small, as is the correction to take account of the difference between the shadow price of investment and consumption. The correction to take account of indirect effects on the allocation of capital between the urban and rural sectors will increase the shadow price of labor. These corrections seem likely, on a priori grounds, to be the most important, and they lead to the conclusion that on the basis of the present state of theory and empirical evidence, the best estimate for the shadow price for labor is the market wage in the urban sector.

# APPENDIX A
## CALCULATION OF SHADOW WAGE AND OPTIMAL SUBSIDIES

### 1. Efficiency Wage Hypothesis

The efficiency-wage relation is given by $\lambda(w_u)$, with $\lambda'(w_u) \geqslant 0$, $\lambda''(w_u) \gtrless 0$ as $w_u \lessgtr \hat{w}_u$ where $\lambda$ is the number of efficiency units provided by one laborer at wage $w_u$.

(a) Shadow Price Calculation: the effect on private output of hiring one more worker in public sector.

We need to calculate

$$-\frac{d[F(\lambda(w_u)L_u) + G(L_r)]}{dL_g} \equiv w_u^s$$

where

$$F(\lambda(w_u)L_u) = \text{output of urban manufacturing sector}$$
$$G(L_r) = \text{output of rural sector}$$
$$L_u = \text{urban manufacturing employment}$$
$$L_r = \text{rural employment}$$
$$L_g = \text{government (urban) employment}$$
$$w_u^s = \text{the shadow price of labor in the urban sector}$$
$$w_u = \text{urban wage}$$

and where

(A.1)  $w_u(1 - U) = w_r$  migration equilibrium condition

(A.2)  $w_r = G'(L_r)$  wage-marginal product in rural sector

(A.3)  $L_r + \dfrac{L_u + L_g}{1 - U} =$

$L_r + N_u = \bar{L}$  labor allocation condition (the labor force is either located in the rural sector, $L_r$, or in the urban)[1]

where

$$\bar{L} = \text{labor force}$$

$$U = \text{unemployment rate (in urban sector)}$$

$$N_u = \text{number of individuals in urban sector}$$

Moreover, we require

(A.4)     $w_u = w_u^*$          $\left.\vphantom{\begin{array}{c}1\\1\end{array}}\right\}$     $w_u^*$ minimizes $w_u/\lambda(w_u)$ , the cost of an effi-

(A.5)     $\lambda'(w_u^*) = \lambda/w_u^*$          ciency unit of labor. (See Figure 1.1.) Urban

(A.6)     $\lambda(w_u)F'(\lambda L_u) = w_u$          employment is set so the wage equals the
(value of) the marginal product of labor.

A change in $L_g$ will leave $w_u$ unaffected (by A.5) and hence $L_u$ (by A.6). Hence, from (A.1) and (A.2)

(A.7)                    $w_u^* d(1 - U) = G'' dL_r$

while from (A.3)

(A.8)          $$dL_r - \frac{L_u + L_g}{(1 - U)^2} d(1 - U) + \frac{dL_g}{1 - U} = 0.$$

Hence          $$-\frac{dL_r}{dL_g} = \frac{1}{(1 - U)} - \frac{L_u + L_g}{(1 - U)^2} \frac{G''}{w_u^*} \frac{dL_r}{dL_g};$$

or          $$-\frac{dL_r}{dL_g} = \frac{1}{(1 - U)\left(1 + \dfrac{N_u}{L_r \eta_r}\right)}$$

where $\eta_r = -\dfrac{G'}{G'' L_r} = -\dfrac{d \ln L_r}{d \ln w_r}$ = elasticity of demand for labor in rural sector.

If we let $w_u^e$ be the expected wage in the urban sector, so

$$w_u^e = G'(L_r) = w_r,$$

then the elasticity of supply of labor to the urban sector can be calculated as

$$\xi = \frac{d \ln N_u}{d \ln w_u^e} = \frac{L_r}{N_u} \eta_r \ .$$

Thus

(A.9)

$$\left. \frac{d(F(\lambda L) + G)}{dL_g} \right|_{L_g = 0} = -\frac{G'}{(1 - U)\left(1 + \dfrac{N_u}{L_r \eta_r}\right)} = -\frac{w_u}{1 + \dfrac{N_u}{L_r \eta_r}} = -\frac{w_u \xi}{1 + \xi} \ .$$

If the urban sector is small or the elasticity of demand for labor in the rural sector large, the shadow price of labor is approximately the urban wage. The factor $1 + N_u/L_r\eta_r$ appears repeatedly throughout the ensuing calculations. Hence, we shall define

(A.10)
$$\gamma \equiv \frac{1}{1 + \dfrac{N_u}{L_r\eta_r}} = \frac{\xi}{1 + \xi} < 1.$$

Hence, we have established that the shadow price of labor $= \gamma w_u < w_u$.

### (b) Comparison of Market Equilibrium and Government-owned Manufacturing Sector.

Assume the government determines $w_u$, $U$, and $L_u$ to

(A.11)        maximize $F + G$

$\{L_u, w_u, U\}$

subject to the constraints (A.1) to (A.3). How does the equilibrium compare with the market equilibrium?

Letting $\mu$ be the Lagrange multiplier associated with (A.1) and using (A.2)-(A.4) we obtain as our Lagrangian

(A.12)
$$\mathcal{L} \equiv F(\lambda(w_u)L_u) + G\left(\bar{L} - \frac{L_u + L_g}{1 - U}\right)$$
$$+ \mu\left[w_u(1 - U) - G'\left(\bar{L} - \frac{L_u + L_g}{1 - U}\right)\right].$$

The first-order conditions are

(A.13)
$$F'\lambda - \frac{G'}{1 - U} + \frac{\mu G''}{1 - U} = 0$$

(A.14)
$$F'\lambda'L_u + \mu(1 - U) = 0$$

(A.15)
$$\frac{G'(L_u + L_g)}{(1 - U)^2} - \frac{\mu G''(L_u + L_g)}{(1 - U)^2} + \mu w_u = 0.$$

Using (A.13) to (A.15) we obtain

(A.16)
$$\frac{\lambda'w_u}{\lambda} = 1 + \frac{L_g}{L_u}:$$

if $L_g = 0$ the government pays the efficiency wage; otherwise it pays less than the efficiency wage. Letting $L_g = 0$ we obtain from (A.13), (A.14) and (A.16),

(A.17)
$$F'\lambda = \gamma w_u$$

Since $\gamma < 1$, the market economy hires too few laborers in the urban sector and has too low an unemployment rate.

### (c) Optimal *Ad Valorem* Wage Subsidy.

Let $\tau$ be the percentage subsidy rate. Then in the market economy, $w_u$ is chosen to minimize labor costs per effective labor unit

(A.18)
$$\min \left\{ \frac{w_u(1 - \tau)}{\lambda(w_u)} \right\}$$

the solution to which,

(A.19)
$$\lambda' = \lambda/w_u,$$

is independent of the subsidy rate. Labor is hired to the point where the wage (after subsidy) equals the marginal product:

(A.20)
$$w_u(1 - \tau) = \lambda F'.$$

(A.1) to (A.3) remain unchanged. Since $w_u = w_u^*, \tau$ controls $L_u$ directly (through A.20).

Hence, if $L_g = 0$, the government can use an *ad valorem* wage subsidy to obtain a constrained optimum.

From (A.17) and (A.20)

(A.21)
$$1 - \tau = \gamma.$$

Note that if $L_g > 0$, an *ad valorem* wage subsidy is not sufficient to attain constrained optimality.

Recalling the definition of $\gamma$, we obtain

(A.22)
$$\tau = \frac{N_u/L_r\eta_r}{1 + N_u/L_r\eta_r} = \frac{1}{1 + \xi}.$$

The greater the labor supply elasticity, the smaller the optimal subsidy.
Example: (i) Assume 10% of the labor force is in urban sector.
 (ii) Assume a constant elasticity (Cobb-Douglas) production function in the rural sector

$$G = L_r^\beta.$$

Assume the share of labor in rural sector is $1/2$, so $\beta = 1/2$.
Then $\xi = 18$ and $\tau = 1/19$.

**(d)  Optimal Specific Subsidy (a wage subsidy per worker).**

The representative firm now minimizes

$$\min \frac{w_u - s}{\lambda}$$

where $s$ is the specific subsidy; i.e.,

(A.23)
$$\lambda' = \frac{\lambda}{w_u - s}$$

leading to a lower urban wage. (See Figure 1.4.)

Figure 1.4. Specific Wage Subsidy Lowers Wage in Efficiency Wage Model

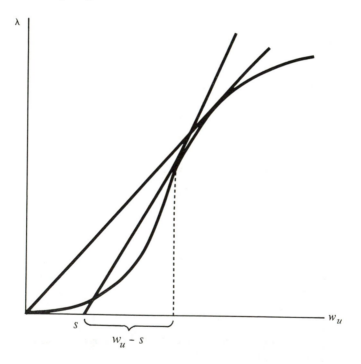

Labor is hired to the point where

(A.24)
$$\lambda F' = w_u - s.$$

Substituting into (A.23), we obtain

(A.25)
$$\lambda' F' = 1.$$

Differentiating,

(A.26)
$$[\lambda'' F' + \lambda' F'' L_u \lambda'] dw_u + \lambda \lambda' F'' dL_u = 0$$

or

$$\frac{d \ln w_u}{d \ln L_u} = \frac{\lambda \lambda' F'' L_u}{\lambda'' F' \left(1 + \dfrac{\lambda'^2}{\lambda''} \dfrac{F''}{F'} L_u\right) w_u}$$

$$= \frac{w_u - s}{w_u} \frac{m}{1 + m}$$

where

$$m = \frac{\lambda'^2}{\lambda''} \frac{F'' L_u}{F'}.$$

From (A.1)-(A.3), we have (still assuming that $L_g = 0$):

$$w_u(L_u)L_u = \frac{L_u}{1 - U} G'\left(\bar{L} - \frac{L_u}{1 - U}\right) = (\bar{L} - L_r)G'(L_r)$$

so

$$-\frac{d \ln L_r}{d \ln L_u} = \left(\frac{d \ln w_u}{d \ln L_u} + 1\right) \frac{N_u}{L_r} \gamma.$$

Hence

$$\frac{d(F + G)}{dL_u} = \lambda F' - \gamma w_u \left(1 + \frac{m}{1 + m} \frac{w_u - s}{w_u}\right) + \lambda' F'(w_u - s) \frac{m}{1 + m} = 0$$

so

(A.27)
$$\frac{w_u - s}{w_u} = \frac{\gamma}{1 + \dfrac{m}{1 + m}(1 - \gamma)}.$$

It is obvious that since the *ad valorem* wage subsidy can generate the (second best) optimum, the *ad valorem* subsidy is preferable to the specific subsidy when $L_g = 0$. Moreover, since the wage subsidy is partly shifted, the optimal subsidy is at a lower rate (comparing (A.21) and (A.27)).

Observe that when $L_g > 0$, both an *ad valorem* wage and a specific wage subsidy (tax) are required to obtain constrained optimality.

### (e) Effect of Workers in Rural Sector Receiving Average Product.

The analysis for the shadow price calculation is identical to that of section (a) except we replace (A.2) by

(A.28)
$$w_r = \frac{G(L_r)}{L_r}$$

so

$$-\frac{d \ln w_r}{d \ln L_r} = 1 - \frac{G'L_r}{G} = 1 - \beta$$

where $\beta =$ the "notional" share of labor in rural sector, i.e., $G'L_r/G$.

Hence

$$-\frac{d(F+G)}{dL_g} = \frac{w_u \beta}{1 + \frac{N_u}{L_r}(1-\beta)} = \frac{w_u \beta \xi}{1 + \xi}$$

where the supply elasticity of labor to the urban sector is now

$$\xi = \frac{L_r}{N_u(1-\beta)} \; .$$

Note that for a Cobb-Douglas production function

$$\eta_r = \frac{1}{1-\beta} \, ,$$

i.e., the supply elasticity is the same, whether workers are paid their marginal or average product. However, now the shadow price of labor

$$w_u^s = \frac{w_u \beta \xi}{1+\xi} = w_u \beta \gamma \, ,$$

i.e., it is substantially reduced.

# APPENDIX B
## LABOR TURNOVER HYPOTHESIS

Labor costs are

$$\hat{w} = w_u + Tq\left(\frac{w_u}{\bar{w}_u}, \frac{w_u}{w_r}, U\right)$$

where $T$ is the training cost and $q$ is the quit rate, a function of the wage paid by a particular firm relative to other wages paid in the urban sector, the urban-rural wage ratio, and the unemployment rate. $\bar{w}_u$ is the mean urban wage. Then $\hat{w}$ is minimized where

$$1 + T\left(\frac{q_1}{\bar{w}_u} + \frac{q_2}{w_r}\right) = 0$$

or, since in equilibrium, assuming all firms are identical, $w_u = \bar{w}_u$, and

$$(B.1) \qquad\qquad \bar{w}_u(1 - U) = w_r,$$

$$(B.2) \quad w_u = -T\left[q_1\left(1, \frac{1}{1-U}, U\right) + \frac{1}{1-U}q_2\left(1, \frac{1}{1-U}, U\right)\right] \equiv h(U).$$

Labor is hired to the point where

$$(B.3) \qquad\qquad F'(L_u) = \hat{w} = w_u + Tq = \hat{w}(U).$$

Normally, $h'(U) < 0$ and $\hat{w}'(U) < 0$ — a higher unemployment rate is associated with lower wages and labor costs.

### (a) Shadow Price.

$$(B.4) \quad \left.\frac{d(F + G - TL_u q)}{dL_g}\right|_{L_g = 0}$$

$$= -\frac{G'}{1-U} - \left\{\left[\frac{G'}{(1-U)^2} + T\frac{dq}{dU}\right]L_u\right\}\frac{dU}{dL_g}$$

$$= -w_u\left[1 + \left(\frac{U}{1-U} + \frac{qT}{w_u}\frac{d\ln q}{d\ln U}\right)L_u\frac{d\ln U}{dL_g}\right].$$

Since $dU/dL_g < 0$ and $d\ln q/d\ln U < 0$, the shadow price of labor may be greater or less than the urban wage; it is less than the urban wage if the unemployment rate is high. The exact calculation of $dU/dL_g$ is left to a footnote;[2] Figure 1.2 (see page 24) illustrates the effect of a change in $L_g$.

### (b) Optimum Wage Subsidy (*ad valorem*).

Now (B.2) becomes

(B.5)
$$w_u = \frac{h(U)}{1 - \tau}$$

but total labor costs as a function of $U$ are unchanged:

$$w_u(1 - \tau) + Tq = h(U) + Tq\left[1, \frac{1}{1 - U}, U\right] = \hat{w}(U).$$

Hence, taking $L_u$ as our control variable,

$$\left.\frac{d(F + G - TqL_u)}{dL_u}\right|_{L_g = 0} = F' - Tq$$

$$- \left[\frac{G'L_u}{(1 - U)^2} + L_u T\frac{dq}{dU}\right]\frac{dU}{dL_u} - \frac{G'}{1 - U} = 0$$

or, since $F' - Tq = w_u(1 - \tau)$,

$$\tau = -\left[\frac{U}{1 - U} + \frac{qT}{w_u}\frac{d\ln q}{d\ln U}\right]\frac{d\ln U}{d\ln L_u}.$$

Now, differentiating (B.3), we obtain

$$\frac{d\ln U}{d\ln L_u} = \frac{F''L_u}{\hat{w}'U} = -1/\eta_u\left(\frac{d\ln \hat{w}}{d\ln U}\right) > 0$$

where $\eta_u = -F'/L_u F''$, the elasticity of demand for labor in the urban sector. Notice the contrasting effects on unemployment of a change in urban employment in the private sector and public sector: one increases the unemployment rate, the other decreases it. Hence, if the unemployment rate is high relative to the effect of unemployment on training costs, while the shadow wage is less than the urban wage, the optimum policy entails a tax on employment in the urban sector, not a subsidy.

### (c) Optimum Wage Subsidy (Specific).

The wage subsidy does not affect wage decisions—the first order condition remains unchanged. Hence (B.1) and (B.2) are unchanged; (B.3) becomes

(B.6)
$$F' = \hat{w}(U) - s.$$

We can again take $L_u$ as our control variable, since

$$L_u = (\bar{L} - L_r)(1 - U) = (\bar{L} - G'^{-1}[h(U)(1 - U)])(1 - U)$$
$$= F'^{-1}(\hat{w}(U) - s).$$

We obtain an expression for $s/w_u$ which is identical to that obtained above for $\tau$, but now

$$-\frac{d \ln U}{d \ln L_u} = \frac{1}{\dfrac{U}{1 - U}(\xi + 1) - \dfrac{h'U}{h}\xi}.$$

Note that while an *ad valorem* wage subsidy increases the unemployment rate, a specific subsidy lowers it.

### (d) Government Direct Control of Urban Employment and Wages.

Then maximizing $F + G - Tq$ implies

$$F' - Tq - \frac{G'}{1 - U} - \left[\frac{G'}{(1 - U)^2} + T\frac{dq}{dU}\right]L_u\frac{\partial U}{\partial L_u} = 0$$

and

$$-\frac{G'}{(1 - U)^2} - \frac{Tdq}{dU} = 0$$

where

$$w_u(1 - U) = G'\left(\bar{L} - \frac{L_u}{1 - U}\right).$$

Hence

$$\frac{U}{1 - U} = -\frac{Tq}{w_u}\frac{d \ln q}{d \ln U}$$

and

$$F' - Tq = w_u$$

giving the optimal unemployment rate, urban employment, and urban wage. Once the optimal wage is set, labor is hired up to its net marginal productivity. To obtain the second best optimum requires a combination of *ad valorem* and specific wage subsidies (or taxes). Let $U^*$ and $w_u^*$ be the optimum unemployment rate and wage rate. Then

$$1 - \tau = h(U^*)/w_u^*$$

and

$$s = -\tau w_u^* = h(U^*) - w_u^*.$$

# APPENDIX C
## THE CAMBRIDGE HYPOTHESIS

Equilibrium is described by

(C.1)                    $w_u(1 - U) = w_r$,   the migration equilibrium condition,

(C.2)

$$\frac{I}{S_\pi} = F(L_u) - w_u L_u = F(1 - s),$$   the investment equals savings condition,

where $s$ is the share of labor, and $S_\pi$ is the saving rate out of profits.

(C.3)                    $F' = w_u$,        the wage equals marginal productivity of labor condition.

### (a) Employment in Public Sector.

Assume public employment is financed by a profits tax at rate $t$. Then

$$w_u L_g = t(F - w_u L_u)$$

and

$$I = (F - w_u L_u)(1 - t)S_\pi$$
$$= [F - w_u(L_u + L_g)]S_\pi = [F - F'(L_u + L_g)]S_\pi$$

Hence if $I/S_\pi$ is constant, urban employment increases and the urban wage falls as $L_g$ increases:

$$\frac{dL_u}{dL_g} = \frac{\eta_u L_u}{L_u + L_g}$$

$$-\frac{dw_u}{dL_g} = F'' \frac{\eta_u L_u}{L_u + L_g}$$

where, as before,   $\eta_u = - d \ln L_u / d \ln w_u$.

National output increases as $L_g$ increases:

$$-\frac{d(F + G)}{dL_g} = \frac{G'}{1 - U}\left[1 + \frac{dU}{dL_g} \frac{L_u + L_g}{(1 - U)} + \frac{N_u L_u}{L_u + L_g}\right] - \frac{F' \eta_u L_u}{L_u + L_g}$$

where

$$\left(\text{from } F'(L_u) = G'\left(\bar{L} - \frac{L_u + L_g}{1 - U}\right)\Big/ (1 - U)\right)$$

$$\frac{dU}{dL_g} = \frac{\dfrac{\eta_u F'' L_u}{L_u + L_g} + \dfrac{G''}{(1 - U)^2}\left(1 + \dfrac{\eta_u L_u}{L_u + L_g}\right)}{- G'' \dfrac{L_u + L_g}{(1 - U)^3} + \dfrac{G'}{(1 - U)^2}}$$

$$= - \frac{\dfrac{\eta_r L_r}{L_u + L_g}(1 - U) + 1 + \dfrac{\eta_u L_u}{L_u + L_g}}{\eta_r L_r + \dfrac{L_u + L_g}{1 - U}}$$

$$= -\frac{(1-U)}{L_u + L_g}\left\{1 + \frac{\eta_u L_u/(1-U)}{\eta_r L_r + \dfrac{L_u + L_g}{1-U}}\right\} < 0.$$

**Hence**

$$-\frac{d(F+G)}{dL_g} = w_u\left\{1 + \frac{dU}{dL_g}\frac{L_u + L_g}{1-U}\right\} = -\frac{w_u\,\eta_u L_u}{\eta_r L_r(1-U) + (L_u + L_g)} < 0.$$

**(b)  *Ad Valorem* Wage Subsidy, Financed by Profits Tax.**

Now, if $\tau$ is the *ad valorem* subsidy rate, $t$ the tax rate, and $L_g = 0$, then

$$F' = w_u(1 - \tau)$$

$$t = \frac{w_u L_u \tau}{F - w_u L_u(1 - \tau)}$$

$$I = (F - w_u L_u + \tau w_u L_u)S_\pi(1 - t)$$

$$= \left[F - \frac{L_u F'}{1 - \tau}\right]S_\pi = (F - w_u L_u)S_\pi.$$

Thus, the tax subsidy increases employment (for small $\tau$)

$$\frac{dL_u}{d\tau} = -\frac{L_u F'}{(1 - \tau)(\tau F' + L_u F'')}$$

and

$$\frac{dw_u}{d\tau} = \frac{F'}{(1 - \tau)^2} + \frac{F''}{1 - \tau}\frac{dL_u}{d\tau}$$

$$= \frac{F'}{(1 - \tau)^2}\left[1 - \frac{F'' L_u}{\tau F' + L_u F''}\right]$$

$$= \frac{F'\tau}{(1 - \tau)^2}\frac{\eta_u}{\tau\eta_u - 1} < 0 \ \text{ for } \tau < \frac{1}{\eta_u}.$$

We now examine the effect on unemployment and aggregate output. Recall that

$$Y \equiv F + G = F(L_u) + G\left(\bar{L} - \frac{L_u}{1 - U}\right)$$

and

$$\frac{F'(L_u)}{1 - \tau} = G'\left(\bar{L} - \frac{L_u}{1 - U}\right)\frac{1}{1 - U}.$$

Hence

$$\frac{F'}{(1 - \tau)^2}\, d\tau + \left\{ \frac{F''}{1 - \tau} + \frac{G''}{(1 - U)^2} \right\} dL_u = \left( G' - L_u \frac{G''}{1 - U} \right) d\left( \frac{1}{1 - U} \right)$$

or,

$$\frac{d \ln \left( \dfrac{1}{1 - U} \right)}{d \ln L_u} = - \frac{1 + \xi \tau}{1 + \xi} < 0.$$

Increasing employment decreases the unemployment rate, and

$$\frac{dY}{dL_u} = \left( F' - \frac{G'}{1 - U} \right) - G'L_u \frac{d \dfrac{1}{1 - U}}{dL_u}$$

$$= w_u \left( -\tau + \frac{1 + \xi \tau}{1 + \xi} \right).$$

## APPENDIX D
## SHADOW PRICE CALCULATION WITH MURKY SECTOR

Let those in urban sector not employed in the urban "employed" sector work in the murky sector, producing a total output

(D.1) $$Q_M = M(N_u - L_u - L_g).$$

The migration equilibrium condition is now

(D.2) $$w_r = \frac{(L_g + L_u)}{N_u} w_u + \frac{M(N_u - (L_u + L_g))}{N_u}.$$

If $w_r$ is constant and $w_u$ is constant

$$\frac{dN_u}{dL_g} = \frac{w_u - M'}{w_r - M'}$$

and the shadow price of labor is

$$\frac{d(F + G + M)}{dL_g} = (-G' + M') \left( \frac{w_u - M'}{w_r - M'} \right) - M' = -w_u.$$

## APPENDIX E
## CAPITAL MOBILITY AND OPPORTUNITY COSTS WITH A FIXED WAGE

A policy that induces migration from the rural sector will lower the marginal productivity of capital in that sector, leading, with the usual equilibrating mechanisms, to a movement of capital to the urban sector. This movement of capital to the urban sector will increase the productivity of labor there and hence induce more hiring. Thus, *in the long run induced migration is likely to be greater than in the short run*. More formally, assuming a fixed wage, $w_u$, and a constant returns production function in the urban sector:

$$\text{(E.1)} \qquad Q_u = Y^u(K_u, L_u) = L_u y_u(k_u)$$

where $K_u$ is capital employed in the urban sector and

$$\text{(E.2)} \qquad k_u = \frac{K_u}{L_u}.$$

Hence

$$\text{(E.3)} \qquad \bar{w}_u = y_u(k_u) - y_u'(k_u)k_u,$$

which can be solved for $k_u$, the equilibrium capital labor ratio in the urban sector. Capital is either located in the urban or rural sectors:

$$\text{(E.4)} \qquad \bar{K} = K_u + K_r = k_u^* L_u + K_r.$$

We require the return on capital to be the same in both sectors (if both produce), so if the agricultural production is of the form

$$\text{(E.5)} \qquad Q_r = Y^r(K_r, L_r)$$

with

$$\text{(E.6)} \qquad w_r = Y_L^r, \rho = Y_K^r$$

(where $\rho$ is the return on capital), we obtain

$$\text{(E.7)} \qquad Y_K^r(\bar{K} - L_u k_u^*, \bar{L} - N_u) = \rho = y_u'(k_u^*).$$

The equilibrium is described by (E.7) and the migration equilibrium condition

$$\text{(E.8)} \qquad Y_L^r(\bar{K} - L_u k_u^*, \bar{L} - N_u) = \bar{w}_u \frac{(L_u + L_g)}{N_u}.$$

Both curves of Figure 1.5 are normally upward sloping, so there may be more than one equilibrium.

The normal presumption, however, is that the capital equilibrium curve is flatter than the labor equilibrium curve and has a slope less than unity in which case the effect of increasing $L_g$ is to increase the unemployment rate. This means that the shadow wage may exceed the market wage. We first calculate the shadow wage, assuming government employment diverts (directly) no capital from the urban sector:

Differentiating (E.7) and (E.8), we obtain

$$
\begin{bmatrix}
-Y^r_{KK}k^*_u & -Y^r_{KL} \\
-N_u Y^r_{KL}k^*_u - \overline{w}_u & Y^r_L - N_u Y^r_{LL}
\end{bmatrix}
\begin{bmatrix}
dL_u \\
dN_u
\end{bmatrix}
=
\begin{bmatrix}
0 \\
\overline{w}_u
\end{bmatrix}
dL_g
$$

Hence

$$
(E.9) \quad \frac{dN_u}{dL_g} - \overline{w}_u Y^r_{KK} k^*_u / N_u k^*_u (Y^r_{KK} Y^r_{LL} - (Y^r_{KL})^2)
$$

$$
- Y^r_L (Y^r_{KK} k^*_u + Y^r_{KL} / (1 - U))
$$

where

$$
(E.10) \qquad v = - \frac{Y^r_{KL}}{Y^r_{KK} k^*_u (1 - U)} > 0 \text{ (provided } Y_{KL} > 0).
$$

$\dfrac{dL_u}{dL_g}$ may similarly be calculated. Hence

$$
- \frac{d(F+G)}{dL_g} = w_r \frac{dN_u}{dL_g} + w_u \frac{dL_u}{dL_g} ,
$$

which, after some tedious calculations, can be shown to be less than $w_u$.

Thus the opportunity cost is less than the urban wage.

Now assume that the government diverts some capital to employ labor in the government sector. Consider the case where government production has the same capital intensity as private production in the urban sector. Then equations (E.7) and (E.8) become

$$
(E.11) \qquad Y^r_K(\bar{K} - (L_u + L_g)k^*_u, \bar{L} - N_u) = \rho
$$

$$
(E.12) \qquad N_u Y^r_L(\bar{K} - (L_u + L_g)k^*_u, \bar{L} - N_u) = (L_u + L_g)\overline{w}_u ,
$$

which can be solved for $L_u + L_g$, and $N_u$. Hence an increase in $L_g$ decreases $L_u$ by the same amount: *public employment crowds out private employment on a one-for-one basis.* The reduction in output (taking into account the capital costs) equals the average productivity of labor in the urban sector.

Assume now the government controlled $K_u$ and $L_u$ but not migration, so

$$Y_L^r(\bar{K} - K_u, \bar{L} - N_u)N_u = \bar{w}_u L_u.$$

Then to maximize national income, i.e.,

(E.13) $\quad \max_{\{K_u, N_u\}} (Y^u + Y^r) = Y^u \left( K_u, \frac{Y_L^r(\bar{K} - K_u, \bar{L} - N_u)}{\bar{w}_u / N_u} \right)$

$$+ Y^r(\bar{K} - K_u, \bar{L} - N_u)$$

it sets

(E.14) $\qquad Y_K^u - Y_K^r = \dfrac{Y_L^u Y_{LK}^r N_u}{\bar{w}_u}$

or

$$Y_K^u = Y_K^r \left( 1 + \frac{Y_{LK}^r}{Y_K^r} L_u \right),$$

which, if $K$ and $L$ are complements in rural production, implies that the *marginal productivity of capital in the urban sector should exceed that in the rural.* The percentage implicit tax on urban capital for a Cobb-Douglas function with a share of labor of 50% and $L_u/L_r = .10$ is 5%.

The government sets urban employment so that

$$Y_L^u \cdot \frac{w_r}{\bar{w}_u} - Y_L^r = \frac{Y_L^u Y_{LL}^r N_u}{\bar{w}_u},$$

i.e., the implicit wage subsidy is

$$\frac{\tau}{1 - \tau} = -\frac{Y_{LL}^r}{Y_L^r} N_u = 1/\xi$$

where $\xi$ is the *short run* labor supply elasticity; if $\xi$ is large, the implicit subsidy is small. (This is identical to the expressions obtained earlier.)

Finally, assume the government imposes a wage subsidy, but cannot control the allocation of capital ( $k_u^* L_u - K_u$) directly. Then

(E.15) $\qquad \bar{w}_u(1 - \tau) = y_u - k_u y_u'(k_u).$

The wage subsidy directly affects the capital intensity in the urban sector.

Equilibrium is described by the pair of equations

(E.16) $\qquad Y_K^r(\bar{K} - K_u, \bar{L} - N_u) = y_u' \left( \frac{K_u}{N_u(1 - U)} \right)$

(E.17) $\qquad Y_L^r(\bar{K} - K_u, \bar{L} - N_u) = \bar{w}_u(1 - U).$

Thus, we can view the government as controlling the unemployment rate; for each value of $U$ there is a value of $K_u$ and $N_u$ solving (E.16) and (E.17) and an implicit wage subsidy:

(E.18)                      $$\bar{w}_u(1 - \tau) = y_u(k_u) - k_u y'_u(k_u)$$

where

$$k_u = \frac{K_u}{N_u(1 - U)}$$

For given $U$, (E.16) and (E.17) both define (under normal conditions) upward sloping loci, with the former steeper than the latter. (See Figure 1.6.)

An increase in the unemployment rate, for given $K_u$ and $N_u$, lowers the return on capital; equilibration thus requires $K_u$ to decrease. Similarly, an increase in $U$ lowers the expected urban wage, and thus $N_u$ must decrease to lower the rural wage. Thus, as $U$ increases, both $N_u$ and $K_u$ decrease.

The optimal value of $U$ is found by

$$\max_{\{U\}} Y^u(K_u, N_u(1 - U)) + Y^r(\bar{K} - K_u, \bar{L} - N_u),$$

i.e.,      $$(Y^u_K - Y^r_K)\frac{dK_u}{dU} + (Y^u_L(1 - U) - Y^r_L)\frac{dN_u}{dU} - Y^u_L N_u = 0$$

or

(E.19)                      $$\frac{1 - \tau}{\tau} = \frac{d \ln N_u}{d \ln (1 - U)}.$$

Figure 1.5.  Effect of Increase in Government Employment

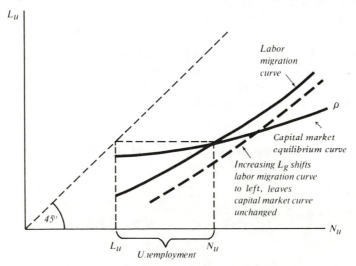

Since $dN_u/dU < 0$, optimality does entail a positive wage subsidy and a lower level of unemployment than without the wage subsidy.

The magnitude of the actual wage subsidy may be found by differentiating (E.16) and (E.17) totally, to obtain

$$
\begin{bmatrix}
-Y^r_{KK} - \dfrac{y''_u}{N_u(1-U)} & -Y^r_{LK} + y''_u \dfrac{k_u}{N_u} \\[2ex]
-Y^r_{KL} & -Y^r_{LL}
\end{bmatrix}
\begin{bmatrix}
dK_u \\[2ex]
dN_u
\end{bmatrix}
=
\begin{bmatrix}
\dfrac{y''_u k_u}{1-U} \\[2ex]
-\bar{w}_u
\end{bmatrix}
dU
$$

$$
\frac{dN_u}{dU} = \frac{\bar{w}_u Y^r_{KK} + \dfrac{y''_u}{1-U}\left(\dfrac{\bar{w}_u}{N_u} + k_u Y^r_{KL}\right)}{Y^r_{KK}Y^r_{LL} - (Y^r_{KL})^2 + Y^r_{KL}\dfrac{y''_u k_u}{N_u} + \dfrac{y''_u Y^r_{LL}}{L_u}}
$$

$$
= \frac{\dfrac{1}{(1-U)L_u}\left[\dfrac{Y^r_{KK}}{Y^r_K}L_u + \dfrac{y''_u}{y'_u}\left(1 + \dfrac{k_u Y^r_{KL}}{Y^r_L}L_u\right)\right]}{\dfrac{Y^r_{KK}Y^r_{LL} - Y^{r^2}_{KL}}{Y^r_K Y^r_L} + \dfrac{k_u y''_u}{y'_u}\left(\dfrac{Y^r_{KL}}{N_u Y^r_L} + \dfrac{Y^r_{LL}}{K_u Y^r_L}\right)}.
$$

Figure 1.6  Effect of Wage Subsidy

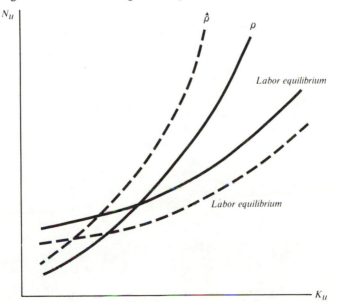

If

$$Y^u = AK_u^{\alpha}L_u^{1-\alpha}$$

$$Y^r = BK_r^{(\beta_K)}L_r^{(\beta_L)}$$

$$\beta_K + \beta_L < 1,$$

we obtain

$$\frac{1-\tau}{\tau} = \frac{L_r}{N_u} \frac{(1-\alpha)\dfrac{K_r}{K_u} - \beta_K(1-\alpha) + (1-\beta_K)}{1 - \beta_K - \beta_L + (1-\alpha)\left((1-\beta_L)\dfrac{K_r}{K_u} - \beta_K\dfrac{L_r}{N_u}\right)}.$$

If the urban sector is small,

$$\frac{1-\tau}{\tau} \approx \frac{L_r/N_u}{(1-\beta_L) - \beta_K\dfrac{L_r/K_r}{N_u/K_u}}$$

or if the capital intensity does not differ much between sectors, and defining

$$\beta_T = 1 - \beta_K - \beta_L$$

$$\tau \approx \frac{\beta_T}{\dfrac{L_r}{N_u} + \beta_T}.$$

## Notes to Appendices

1. Let $N_u$ = total job seekers in urban sector. Then

$$U = \frac{N_u - (L_u + L_g)}{N_u}$$

or

$$N_u = \frac{L_u + L_g}{1 - U} \, .$$

Since $N_u + L_r = \bar{L},$ we immediately obtain (A.3).

2. Substituting (B.2) and (B.3) into (B.1), we obtain

$$h(U)(1 - U) = G'\left(\bar{L} - \frac{F'^{-1}(\hat{w}(U)) + L_g}{1 - U}\right)$$

so

$$\frac{dU}{dL_g} = \frac{-\dfrac{G''}{1 - U}}{h'(1 - U) - h + G''\left(\dfrac{\hat{w}'}{F''(1 - U)} + \dfrac{L_u + L_g}{(1 - U)^2}\right)}$$

$$= -\frac{1}{\left(-\dfrac{d\ln \hat{w}}{d\ln U}\right)\eta_u \dfrac{L_u}{U} + \dfrac{L_u + L_g}{1 - U} + \eta_r L_r\left(1 - \dfrac{d\ln h}{d\ln U}\dfrac{(1 - U)}{U}\right)} < 0 \, .$$

3.

$$\left(\frac{dL_u}{dN_u}\right)\bigg|_{\rho} = -\frac{Y^r_{KL}}{Y^r_{KK}k^*_u} \gtrless 0 \text{ as } Y^r_{KL} \gtrless 0$$

$$\frac{dL_u}{dN_u}\bigg|_{w_u} = \frac{w_r - Y^r_{LL}N_u}{\bar{w}_u + N_u Y^r_{LK}k^*_u} = \frac{(1 - U)}{\gamma\left(1 + \dfrac{N_u}{\bar{w}_u} Y^r_{LK}k^*_u\right)}$$

where, as before (A.10),

$$\gamma = \frac{1}{1 - \dfrac{Y^r_{LL}N_u}{Y^r_L}} \, .$$

## NOTES

1. The arguments presented in this and the previous paragraph are developed in greater detail for a special model in Stiglitz (1969).

2. The alternative explanations have one important difference in their empirical implications: with the "nutritional" hypothesis, wages should be invariant over time (but differ, obviously, depending on the nature of the work performed and the climate), while with the other two explanations it is the wage relative to other wages (or income) that matters. In the third explanation, a redistribution of land might lead to a change in the (efficiency) wage, while in conventional, neoclassical analysis it would only have such a result through the indirect effect of a change in demand.

3. This is true (a) so long as there is not full employment in the rural sector at a wage exceeding the efficiency wage, that is, so long as the efficiency wage considerations are relevant; and (b) so long as there is some sharing.

4. There is some evidence in support of this situation; remittances—in both directions—appear to be significant. Note, however, that direct monetary transfers do not need to be made, for example, if there is a life cycle pattern, with young workers working in the city and returning to the rural sector when older.

5. Further difficulties arise if there is another factor (capital) that has to be provided; again, if everything is observable, then the contract would simply specify the amount of capital to be provided by each party. In effect, the sharecropping agreement is nothing more than an insurance policy in which the assumption of costless monitoring has eliminated all problems of moral hazard.

6. In an economy with more than one commodity, the price will be a random variable; the distribution of prices will be affected by the allocation of resources to that sector, but in a Nash (competitive) equilibrium, each farmer (producer) will ignore this. In general, then, the market equilibrium will not be Pareto optimal. The question of risk and efficiency is too complicated to be pursued further here. See, for instance, Newbery and Stiglitz (1981).

7. Because of the assumption of a small country facing given international prices, with all goods traded, if the marginal physical product is constant so is the value of the marginal product.

8. The notion that the unemployment rate would serve as an equilibrating device when factor prices did not adjust was presented in an appendix to Akerlof and Stiglitz (1965). The idea has received extensive application in the "search literature" attempting to explain frictional unemployment in developed economies (see, e.g., Phelps [1970]). Todaro (1968, 1969) and Harris and Todaro (1970) investigated some of its implications in the context of LDCs. The implications for the shadow price of labor were explored in Harberger (1971) and in Stiglitz (1971), subsequently revised as Stiglitz (1973, 1974a, 1976). The extension of the analysis to skilled laborers is due to Fields (1972b).

9. There is one important objection that has been raised to the labor turnover model: by charging an application fee, the firm can increase profits; the fee will shorten the queue, but will not increase the quit rate (and indeed if all firms charge a fee, the quit rate may be reduced). Presumably the fee should be increased to the point where there is no queue, or the queue is at an optimal length for the firm (i.e., for small firms, the average length of job search increases as the interarrival time of applicants decreases, so that the average time that it takes for a firm to fill a vacancy is reduced).

There are a number of reasons that firms may not raise the application fee to reduce queues to zero. If, for one of these reasons, the queue is not reduced to zero, then the kinds of considerations discussed here become relevant. Firms do seem aware of the effect of wage levels on quit rates.

10. See Stiglitz (1976).

11. This may not be true if the reason for the efficiency wage is not nutritional. If government jobs pay a high wage per unit effort (as is often alleged to be the case) then the wage required to elicit the appropriate effort in the private sector may be increased when more jobs become available in the government subsector. More generally, since in both the second and third explanations the productivity of a (randomly selected) individual will be a function of his wage at that job in relation to the whole wage distribution, any policy, such as hiring more workers in government jobs, could affect the efficiency wage.

12. This is not quite accurate, since if individuals share their income with other members of their family, the efficiency wage will be affected by the incomes received by all the individuals with whom they share their income. If the efficiency-wage relationships result from morale effects, the fact that wages in other areas are lower may result in increased productivity at any given wage. The implications of sharing in the efficiency wage hypothesis are discussed in Stiglitz (1973).

13. Minimum wage legislation is not particularly effective in the informal urban sector but is probably effective in the "organized" urban sector. Attempts to legislate maximum wage rates (or rates of change of wages) appear to have run into severe difficulties, largely arising out of the heterogeneity of jobs and individuals.

14. The reason this model is proposed is as follows: the suggestion is usually made that these individuals in this sector are *underemployed* (not that they are fully employed at a low wage)—they have excess capacity. In a conventional competitive model, they would lower their price, and competitive equilibrium would be attained at full employment.

15. It is probably inappropriate to refer to this as a capital market imperfection. Restricted lending would be a characteristic of a perfectly competitive capital market with imperfect information.

16. This has one important implication: improving rural incomes or rural credit markets may increase urban unemployment.

17. The answer would seem to be related to the convexity or concavity of the function relating unemployment or job search to hirings.

18. The equilibrating relation is that

$$w_r = A + w_u(1 - U)$$

if urban residency $U$ yields the amenity $A$, while

$$w_r = (w_u + A)(1 - U)$$

if the amenity is obtained only through employment.

The opportunity cost, taking account of amenity values is

$$\frac{w_r}{1 - U} - A = w_u,$$

in the second case, and

$$\frac{w_r - A}{1 - U} = w_u$$

in the first case.

19. The assumption of insufficient demand for investment as well as the implications of the Cambridge model are sufficiently implausible that the model should probably not be taken seriously.

20. It is important to note from this argument that capital need not be mobile in the short run; all that is required is that the capital markets in the two sectors be linked together sufficiently clearly so that, in the long run, rates of return are equalized (or bear a fixed relationship with one another).

## BIBLIOGRAPHY

Akerlof, G., and Stiglitz, J. E. "Capital, Wages and Structural Unemployment." Mimeo. Cambridge, Mass.: Massachusetts Institute of Technology, 1965.

Bardhan, P., and Srinivasan, T. N. "Crop-Sharing Tenancy in Agriculture: A Theoretical and Empirical Analysis." *American Economic Review* 61 (1971).

Cheung, S. "Private Property Rights and Share-Cropping." *Journal of Political Economy* 76, no. 6 (1968).

____. *The Theory of Share Tenancy.* Chicago: University of Chicago Press 1969a.

____. "Transactions Costs, Risk Aversion and the Choice of Contractual Arrangements." *Journal of Law and Economics* 19, no. 1 (1969b).

Dasgupta, P., Marglin, S., and Sen, A. *Guidelines for Project Evaluation in Developing Countries.* UNIDO, 1972.

Dasgupta, P., and Stiglitz, J.E. "Benefit Cost Analyses and Trade Policies." *Journal of Political Economy* 82, no. 1 (1974).

Dixit, A. K. "Optimal Development in the Labour Surplus Economy." *Review of Economic Studies* 35, no. 1 (January 1968), p. 23.

____. "Short-run Equilibrium and Shadow Prices in the Dual Economy." *Oxford Economic Papers* 23, no. 3 (November 1971), p. 384.

Fields, G. "Private and Social Returns to Education in Less Developed Countries." *Eastern Africa Economic Review* (June 1972a).

____. "Rural-Urban Migration, Urban Unemployment and Underemployment, and Job Search Activity in L.D.C.'s." Economic Growth Center, Yale University Discussion Paper no. 168, December 1972b.

Harberger, A. "On Measuring the Social Opportunity Cost of Labor." *International Labor Review* (June 1971).

Harris, J., and Todaro, M. "Migration, Unemployment, and Development." *American Economic Review* 60, no. 1 (March 1970), pp. 126–142.

Hornby, J. M. "Investment and Trade Policy in the Dual Economy." *Economic Journal* 78, no. 1 (March 1968), p. 86.

Leibenstein, H. *Economic Backwardness and Economic Growth*. New York: Wiley, 1957.

Little, I.M.D., and Mirrlees, J. A. *Manual of Industrial Project Analysis in Developing Countries*. Paris: Organization for Economic Cooperation and Development, 1968.

Newbery, D.M.G. "Public Policy in the Dual Economy." *Economic Journal* 82, no. 2 (June 1972), p. 567.

____. "Robustness of General Equilibrium Analysis in the Dual Economy." *Oxford Economic Papers* 26, No. 1 (March 1974).

Newbery, D.M.G., and Stiglitz, J. E. *The Theory of Commodity Price Stabilization*. Oxford Economic Press, 1981.

Phelps, E. S. *Micro-Economic Foundations of Employment and Inflation Theory*. New York: 1970.

Rao, C. H. "Uncertainty, Entrepreneurship and Share Cropping in India." *Journal of Political Economy* 79, no. 3 (1971).

Sen, A. K. "Peasants and Dualism With or Without Surplus Labor." *Journal of Political Economy* 74, no. 5 (October 1966), pp. 425–450.

Stiglitz, J. E. "Rural-Urban Migration, Surplus Labour, and the Relationship Between Urban and Rural Wages." *Eastern Africa Economic Review* (1969).

____. "Alternative Theories of the Determination of Unemployment and Wages in L.D.C.'s." Institute for Development Studies, University of Nairobi, 1971.

____. "The Efficiency Wage Model." Cowles Foundation paper, 1973.

____. "Alternative Theories of the Determinations of Wages and Unemployment in L.D.C.'s–I. The Labor Turnover Model." *Quarterly Journal of Economics* 88, no. 12 (1974a), pp. 194–227.

____. "Incentives and Risk Sharing." *Review of Economic Studies* 41 (1974b).

____. "The Theory of Screening, Education, and the Distribution of Income." *American Economic Review* 65 (1975).

____. "The Efficiency Wage Hypothesis, Surplus Labor, and the Distribution of Incomes in L.D.C.'s." *Oxford Economic Papers* 28, no. 2 (1976).

____. "Some Further Remarks on Cost Benefit Analysis." In H. Schwartz and R. Barney (eds.), *Social and Economic Dimensions of Project Evaluation*, 1977, pp. 253–281.

Todaro, M., "An Analysis of Industrialization, Employment and Unemployment in Less Developed Countries." *Yale Economic Essays* (Fall 1968).

____. "A Model of Labor Migration and Urban Unemployment in Less Developed Countries." *American Economic Review* 59 (March 1969), pp. 138–148.

# 2

# Urban Unemployment in LDCs:
# Towards a More General Search Model

## JOHN R. HARRIS
## RICHARD H. SABOT

### INTRODUCTION

It is often said that the social costs of urban unemployment are so high in many developing countries that planners should give the problem high priority. However, those who make these assertions often do not consider the causes of the problem or make an error in diagnosis. Accuracy in diagnosis is a matter of concern because costs vary with causes as do appropriate policy responses. Observers of unemployment also often draw inferences as to the optimal level of the shadow wage for unskilled labor and the consequences of the emigration of high-level manpower for the source country without specifying the underlying model of the labor market. And yet, the implications of unemployment for the social-opportunity cost of labor also vary with its causes.

The first section of this chapter includes a simple taxonomy of models of unemployment and a review of some of the principal specification problems encountered in using these models to explain urban labor market imbalances in developing countries. Also included is a demonstration of why the category of models termed labor market segmentation models (which includes the well-known Harris-Todaro model) is more appropriate for explaining imbalances than the other categories, though clearly not free from specification problems. The second section develops a model that resolves two of the most serious of these specification problems and shows how the Harris-Todaro model is a rather special case of this more general search model.

The authors are grateful to Jagdish Bhagwati for extensive comments and for suggesting major improvements in this chapter.

## SOME PROBLEMS WITH THE SPECIFICATION
## OF UNEMPLOYMENT MODELS

A variety of economic models, with markedly different implications for social costs of unemployment and opportunity cost of labor, have been used to explain surplus labor in developing countries. These models can be divided into two groups: those that treat unemployment as a generalized phenomenon for the economy and those that are sector specific. The first group can be divided into three subgroups based on different views of what causes labor market imbalance: aggregate demand deficiency models,[1] technical lack of substitution models[2] and models that rely directly on the fixity/stickiness of real wages[3] to explain unemployment. Similarly the sector-specific models can be subdivided into two categories: those that see the wedge driven between earnings and the marginal product of labor within a sector[4] as the root of the problem and those that view differences between sectors in earnings for economically homogeneous labor[5] as the root of the problem.

With the exception of labor market segmentation models, these five categories of models were not formulated specifically to explain urban unemployment in developing countries. The concern here is not with the "degree of corroboration" of these models, but with the appropriateness of using them for a task for which they were not designed. It is not surprising that in certain important respects their specification has been shown to be inappropriate.

In developing countries where the underutilization of urban labor coincides with the underutilization of capital, the latter is usually attributed to such factors as supply bottlenecks, maintenance problems, or other factors unrelated to the level of aggregate demand for output. Also, the level of effective demand can alone determine the volume of employment only in the short run. Although demand deficiency models may fit the cyclical pattern of production and employment in the industrialized countries, they are hard pressed to explain the chronic unemployment of LDCs.

There are two other respects in which demand deficiency models do not fit the observed characteristics (stylized facts) of urban unemployment in LDCs. First, they cannot explain excess supply occurring in one sector but not in another; yet the coincidence of unemployment in the urban sector with full employment or even labor scarcity in the rural sector is quite a common phenomenon. Keynesian models presume that the direction, if not the rate, of change in aggregate demand is the same in all sectors. Likewise models in which unemployment is traceable either to technical lack of substitution or to a rigid wage in excess of the level required for full employment are sector nonspecific. The Lewis model is an exception but one that does not contribute to the explanation of unemployment that is specific to the urban sector. It does, however, point to a more fundamental specification problem that it shares with economy-wide models, namely an inability to explain *open* unemployment.

A characteristic of the urban unemployed, widely observed if not universal in developing countries, is that they fulfill the three interrelated conventional criteria for open unemployment: the division of all of the individuals' time between leisure (noneconomic activities) and job search, no earned income, and no contribution to output. It is difficult to make sense of the notion of long-run unemployment of specific members of the labor force without taking into consideration some mechanism by which the unemployed subsist. Since the unemployed in LDCs tend to be young, savings cannot be considered as the subsistence mechanism. Given the absence of government transfer schemes, the choice is either direct transfer payments or, in the case of disguised unemployment, work sharing or employment creation. Thus, to explain open unemployment consideration must be given to the circumstances under which the employed support those without jobs by direct transfers.

Demand deficiency, technical lack of substitution, and economy-wide rigid wage models cannot explain why employed workers should offer, and workers in excess supply prefer, direct transfers to work-sharing arrangements. Certainly work sharing and the creation of unproductive jobs are not incompatible with an excess supply of labor. These models imply that there is a given stock of man-hours available for employment, and demand sufficient to absorb only part of that stock; however, they do not discuss the number of workers meeting the demand. The excess supply of labor could just as easily be manifested in underemployment—workers desiring more work than is available at the existing rate—or in disguised unemployment—workers employed at a wage in excess of their marginal product—as in open unemployment. Abstracting from the utility implications of eleemosynary behavior, from the perspective of the employed the distinction between sharing work and transferring income is that, in the latter case, there is a gain of leisure. Where employment creation is feasible there is a gain in output as well as leisure. This gives rise to the presumption that, ceteris paribus, the employed with an obligation to support workers in excess supply will prefer work sharing or employment creation to transfers.

Lewis' (1954) view, similar to that presented here, and apparently based on the same reasoning, is that where there is an economy-wide rigid wage, workers will be in disguised, rather than open, unemployment. When faced with the obligation of supporting workers, peasant farmers will employ them at the fixed wage rather than simply provide them with direct transfers. In this way the farmer reduces the cost of support by the value of his additional leisure, and, given a neoclassical production function, by the value of the worker's output. Even if the marginal productivity of labor is zero, the farmer will prefer to subsidize the worker in employment rather than in unemployment. Only if the marginal product of labor is negative or increased leisure has negative utility would the excess supply of labor be manifested in open unemployment. It would be wrong to conclude, however, that deficiencies of aggregate demand for output, lack of substitution between factors, or wage rigidities do not cause labor allocation and utilization problems in developing countries. The point here is simply that problems of this nature are unlikely by themselves to be manifested in open unemployment.

Neither the economy-wide models nor the Lewis model provides a basis for an economic incentive for direct transfers that could outweigh the benefits of work sharing or employment creation because in none of them does *open* unemployment offer the prospect of an economic return directly to the job-seeker. The Harris-Todaro segmentation model (Harris and Todaro, 1971) does provide the basis for such an incentive, hence for an explanation of *open* unemployment. It is the only one of the five categories of unemployment models that does so, which may explain why it has received so much attention in the scholarly literature and from policymakers.

Segmentation itself, however, is no more a sufficient condition for open unemployment than is an economy-wide rigid wage. Indeed, it is not even a sufficient condition for the derivation of an excess supply of labor, either in the sense of an aggregate imbalance in the supply of and demand for man-hours (as distinct from workers) or in the sense of an intrasectoral gap between the wage and marginal product of labor. As long as there is a sector in which entry is free, the consequence of raising the fixed wage to a level above the laissez-faire equilibrium is simply a decline in the flexible wage (marginal product of labor) to a level at which all the workers who could not find urban jobs can be absorbed in employment. There is excess supply to the high wage sector in the limited sense that workers employed in the flexible wage sector prefer a job in the rigid wage sector; thus the supply curve to the latter is infinitely elastic.

In the Harris-Todaro model the incentive to workers to remain in open unemployment rather than accept a job readily available at a lower wage derives from the implicit assumptions that employment and rural residence, on the one hand, and seeking an urban job, on the other, are mutually exclusive activities. That is to say, workers employed in the rural sector have no chance of obtaining a job in the rigid wage sector. The unemployed worker is not a victim of circumstances, as he is in models characterized by an aggregate imbalance between labor supply and demand. Rather, this type of unemployment is a hybrid of "voluntary" and "involuntary" elements. It would be involuntary if it were taken for granted that the worker is limited to a specific sector. Yet because employment is available elsewhere, he voluntarily limits himself.[6] With regard to subsistence, the worker expects to have more income if he does not work than if he took a low-paying job. Because of the prospect of high wage jobs, the worker can offer those who support him a return in direct transfers. They, in turn, can expect greater benefits from this arrangement than they would get through work sharing or employment creation.

The Harris-Todaro model is not, however, free from specification problems. Attention has been focused on one set of these problems by the tendency of the model to predict rates of unemployment in some (particularly African) countries that are significantly higher than the measured rates.[7] The suggested means of solving this problem involve tinkering with the nonprice mechanism by which high wage jobs are rationed among competing job-seekers, rather than changing the "hard core" of the model—the intersectoral wage gap and the labor supply function based on expected rather than actual incomes.

There are a variety of ways to alter Harris and Todaro's assumptions that $P_{uu} > P_{re} = P_{ru} = 0$ (where $P$ is the probability of obtaining a high wage job; the first subscript indicates rural [$r$] or urban [$u$], and the second subscript indicates employment [$e$] or unemployment [$u$]) so as to decrease the advantage urban open unemployment offers to the job-seeker. Thus, for a given difference between rural and urban incomes, the equilibrium rate of urban unemployment can be lowered, and hence the gap between predicted and measured rates can be lessened. With this aim, and recognizing that friends or relatives in urban areas may serve as proxy job-seekers; that application for some jobs may be made by mail or other jobs may be filled by a central labor exchange; and that a job-seeker may spend part of his time in urban areas, though maintaining his primary residence in a rural area, Fields (1975) suggests the assumption $P_{uu} > P_{re} > 0$.[8] A more interesting suggestion, $P_{uu} > P_{ue} > 0$, has come from the analysis, motivated by evidence of substantial employment opportunities in urban "informal" sectors, of the implications for labor allocation and the distribution of income by introducing a third sector into the segmentation model. This third sector is urban, but has free entry and hence flexible wages. It has been shown that if workers in the urban flexible wage sector have a better chance of obtaining a high wage job than rural workers (though not as good as the unemployed), then some of the workers comprising the excess supply to the high wage sector, who otherwise would select unemployment, enter the urban free entry sector and depress its wage to an equilibrium level below the rural wage.[9]

In the above case the excess supply of labor to the high wage sector assumes three forms: hidden rural unemployment, in the sense of workers employed in the rural sector willing and qualified to work at the rigid wage, but discouraged from seeking such work by the costs of doing so; urban underemployment, in the limited sense that the transfer of workers from the urban flexible wage to the rural sector would increase national output; and open urban unemployment. The rate of open urban unemployment predicted by the segmentation model is lower when the model includes such an urban flexible wage sector than when it does not.[10]

The Harris-Todaro model suffers from another set of specification problems that is more serious. The model assumes only one or, with the addition of an urban flexible wage sector, two urban wages and also that workers have certain knowledge of urban labor market conditions; a dispersion of wages for economically homogeneous workers and uncertain knowledge of market conditions are clearly more characteristic of conditions in developing countries. In the sections that follow these assumptions implicit in the Harris-Todaro and other simple segmentation models are dropped and a more general search model of unemployment is developed.

Consider the determinants of the optimal allocation of time between unemployment (queuing for high wage jobs) and employment when a job-seeker (with certain knowledge) is faced by a whole spectrum of wages, a high proportion of which have employment probabilities that are positive but less than unity. The decision rule, which involves setting a critical minimum wage below which all job offers are rejected, is in essence the same as in simple segmentation models: forgo employment if the expected gain from continuing to look for a job with a higher wage exceeds the opportunity costs that accrue while looking. Nevertheless, this more complex segmentation model yields insights that the simple model tends to obscure. It demonstrates that segmentation within the urban labor market may result in unemployment even if that market is closed. In other words, while the rate of migration clearly may influence the rate of unemployment and vice versa, an excessive flow of migrants from rural areas is not a necessary condition for the emergence of open urban unemployment. This change increases the relevance of the segmentation category of unemployment models to countries (particularly in Latin America and Asia) where the simple segmentation model has a tendency to predict too low or even zero rates of urban unemployment because of negligible gaps between rural and urban areas in average wages for homogeneous labor.

Dropping the assumption that workers have certain knowledge of labor market conditions converts unemployment from a queuing phenomenon to one in which workers engage in job search as a means of improving their information and hence their own prospects. Unemployment results because workers determine their critical wage on the basis of subjective rather than objective costs and returns. While this model bears a close resemblance to search models developed for application in the industrialized market economies it nevertheless differs significantly from those models in ways that will soon become apparent.

## MODELS OF UNEMPLOYMENT AS A JOB-SEARCH PROCESS

### Search Within a Geographically Specified Labor Market

*Distribution of Wage Offers Known*

Consider the optimal job-search-and-acceptance behavior by a utility-maximizing individual seeking employment within a particular geographic area. In the neoclassical theory of labor markets, as modified by Harris and Todaro (1971), it is assumed that a single wage prevails and that the only problem facing the job-seeker is to find a job—in perfect markets even this is supposed to present no problem. In most LDCs, however, individuals with similar characteristics receive widely differing wages and even the distinction of "formal" and "informal" sectors conceals the wide range of variation within each sector. It is also assumed, quite unrealistically, that accurate information is instantly available to all market participants without cost.

A job-seeker in a market with wage dispersion must first obtain an offer of employment and then decide whether to accept it or to continue looking for something better.[11] For purposes of analysis, it is useful to define a function of the probabilities of obtaining an offer at each wage in a single search period. Such a function $\rho(w)$ is shown in Figure 2.1 under the assumption that there is a mean wage ($\overline{w}$) with a normal distribution of offers around that mean. This distribution will be identical with the distribution of actual job offers only under the naive assumption that the number of seekers is the

Figure 2.1. Probability of Obtaining an Offer at Each Wage in a Single Search Period.

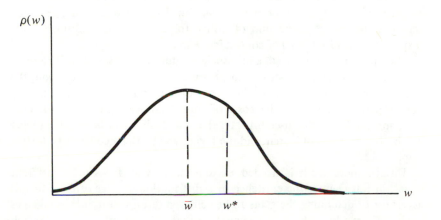

same at all wage levels. (This argument will be developed further below.) In a single period a searcher will obtain one offer from this distribution, with the probability $\rho$ $(w)$ that the offer will be at wage level $w$. The cumulative distribution of these probabilities will sum to one.[12]

An individual who receives an offer must either accept or reject it—if he rejects the offer, he searches again in the next period. In this case, the optimal strategy is for the searcher to determine a critical minimum wage $(w^*)$ such that any offer received at or above this level will be accepted and any offer at a lower wage will be rejected.[13] The logic of determination of $w^*$ is straightforward—it should be set where the expected gain from future search outweighs the value of earnings from accepting the offer plus direct costs of additional search. At $w^*$ these parameters will be equated. Since the probability of obtaining an acceptable offer in any period $i$ is

$$\pi_i = \int_{w*}^{\infty} \rho(w) \, dw,$$

the expected number of periods of search required to obtain an acceptable offer will be

$$t^* = 1 \left/ \left[ \int_{w*}^{\infty} \rho(w) \, dw \right] \right. ;$$

it follows that, for any distribution, the higher the critical minimum wage, the longer the required duration of search. The expected value of search in any period is

$$\int_{w*}^{\infty} \rho(w)u(w) \, dw$$

where $u(w)$ is defined as the present value in terms of utility of the future earnings from accepting a job paying wage $w$. The cost of refusing a job at a wage just below $w^*$ is the sum of utility forgone plus the additional costs (expressed in utility terms) of continuing search.

Therefore, the optimal $w^*$ and associated duration of search will be functions of the probability distribution of wage offers, the utility function, the rate of time preference, and the costs of undertaking further search.[14] Ceteris paribus, the lower the costs of continuing search, the less risk aversion, and the lower the discount rate, then the higher will be $w^*$, the longer will be the duration of search, and the higher will be the income earned when employed.[15]

Though more work is needed to understand why firms offer different wages, in this chapter the existence of a distribution of wage offers, which is necessary to determine the gains to be achieved through search,[16] is taken as given. In a world with perfect capital markets, the identification of search costs ($c$) would be simple. One could always borrow the resources needed for subsistence plus direct costs of search, to be repaid from earnings when employment is obtained. The real costs of search would then depend on consumption during search—such direct costs as transportation, application fees, and newspapers—and the rate of interest. In reality, however, the difficulty of financing extended search becomes a critical constraint on search behavior. One can model inability to finance continued search as high costs of search (perhaps infinitely high when the alternative to accepting any wage offer is starvation). It follows, therefore, that access to subsistence resources during search will be an important determinant of $w^*$, duration of search, and the wage received when employed.

### Distribution of Wage Offers Known Imperfectly

Since we have taken the frequency distribution of wage offers as known to the searcher, theory so far deals with behavior under conditions of risks but not uncertainty. But search is generally defined as a process of obtaining information about an objective distribution initially only imperfectly known. Perhaps it is easiest to think about an individual whose *subjective frequency distribution* and wage offers at any given time are based on a range of available information, guesses, past experience, state of mind, etc. Although he will have to devise immediate strategies based on his subjective distribution, the process of search provides information that will cause him to revise his subjective distribution. His strategies for further search will thus be revised continually during his search. Although the implications of this kind of process for observed behavior in the labor market seem clear, formal solution of the problem has so far defied repeated attempts.[17]

Figure 2.2 depicts the situation in which a job-seeker begins with a subjective distribution $\hat{\rho}(w)$. Corresponding to that distribution there is a critical minimum wage $\hat{w}^*$ that would in fact be optimal were $\hat{\rho}(w)$ the actual distribution of offers. However, the objective distribution that this seeker faces is $\rho(w)$ and the optimal critical wage associated with that distribution is $w^*$. As represented in Figure 2.2 the probability that this individual will receive a wage offer he will accept is zero. However, as lower offers are repeatedly received and rejected, the subjective distribution should shift toward the actual, with the critical wage being revised downwards. What is clear from this example is that differences between subjective and objective distributions will cause either too much or too little search. In the case represented in Figure 2.2 search will be excessive—the individual will remain unemployed longer than necessary. On the other hand, if the subjective distribution lies to the left of the objective one, the searcher is likely to accept a low wage offer and will end up with less search and lower earnings than would have been appropriate—he will have devoted too little time to search.

Figure 2.2. Frequency Distribution Considering a Critical Minimum Wage

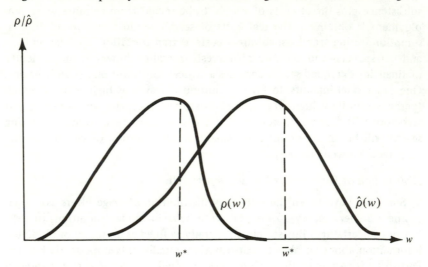

The critical questions to be asked at this juncture are: How are subjective distributions established and revised? Does this tend to produce excessive or insufficient search from the standpoint of individuals?[18] It is useful to begin by examining more closely the objective probability distribution facing an individual searcher, and distinguishing it from the wage distribution of job offers. The latter frequency distribution is depicted as $f(w)$ in Figure 2.3 where $f(w)$ is the number of vacancies that exist offering wage $w$ in the particular labor market.

This leads to a further consideration in defining the distribution of offers that a searcher will receive. The function $f(w)$ is defined across vacancies, or jobs to be filled in the period in the particular geographic labor market. Just as an individual searcher has to decide to accept or reject an offer, once an offer has been accepted, the vacancy ceases to exist. Therefore the probability of an individual receiving a wage offer for a vacancy for which he is qualified depends both on the probability that he will sample that vacancy and the probability that the vacancy will already have been filled. The latter is the joint probability that another qualified searcher will have sampled that vacancy and that the other searcher has a critical minimum wage at or below the offered wage. We can draw a frequency distribution of the number of job-seekers with a critical minimum wage equal to or less than each wage. This function is shown in Figure 2.4 as $n(w)$.[19]

The probability that any particular job vacancy will have been sampled by at least one other searcher is a function of the ratio of the total number

Figure 2.3. Frequency Distribution of Number of Vacancies Offering Wage *w*

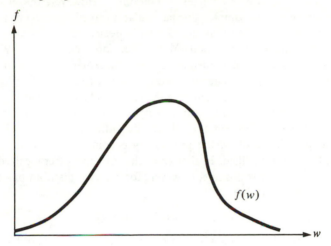

Figure 2.4. Frequency Distribution of Number of Job-Seekers with a Critical Minimum Wage Equal to or Less Than Each Wage

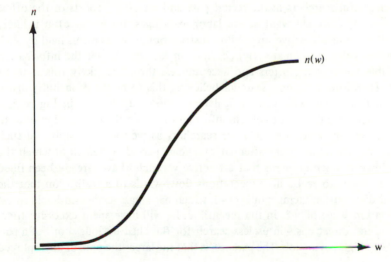

of searchers ($N$) and the total number of vacancies ($Q$), denoted as $\pi(N/Q)$ where $\pi > 0$ and will be the same for every vacancy under the assumption that the search process is completely random.[20] However, the probability that any searcher who samples the particular vacancy will accept the offer is $n(w)/N$; the probability that an offer will already have been sampled and accepted by someone else is $[\pi n(w)]/N$. Therefore, the probability of sampling a wage offer that has not already been accepted by someone else is $[f(w)/Q] [1 - \pi n(w)/N]$. The first term of this expression, $f(w)/Q$, is the probability that the offer sampled by a searcher will be at wage level $w$.[21]

The important feature to note in this figure is that $\rho(w)$ lies below $f(w)/Q$ throughout the range, except for a large discontinuity at $w = 0$. This is so because at high levels of $w$, the probability becomes high that the vacancy will already have been filled. In that case, the effective offer received by the searcher is $w = 0$. It is possible, however, for the two distributions to coincide at low levels of $w$ since if

$$n(w) = 0, \ \rho(w) = f(w)/Q.$$

That is, an offer that is so low that no one will accept it will not be filled already when sampled by any searcher—therefore, the probability of sampling an unfilled vacancy is the same as sampling a vacancy at that wage level. It should be clear that the larger the number of searchers in relation to the number of vacancies, the smaller will be $\rho(w)$ at positive $w$'s since the probability becomes greater that others will already have sampled and filled any particular vacancy.

At last we are able to explain the effects of unemployment on the duration of search. If a searcher obtains information on the wage offers accepted by successful searchers in the recent past and on other reports of the offers being made (through want ads or labor exchanges, for instance), it is likely that the initial subjective probability distribution of wage offers held by such a person will approximate $f(w)/Q$. And, in fact, the better the information available about going offers and acceptances, the more likely this is to be true. Therefore, a rational searcher believing this to be the probability distribution facing him will set a critical reservation wage of $\hat{w}^*$ in Figure 2.5. It is much more difficult to obtain information about the distribution of critical reservation wages among other searchers as well as the number of such searchers. Therefore, only after an extended period of search in which the individual frequently learns that attractive vacancies have already been filled will he begin to revise his expectations downwards to a realization that the actual distribution facing him is $\rho(w)$, which has an associated optimal critical reservation wage of $w^*$. In the meantime, he will have spent excessive time, effort, and direct costs in useless search for the elusive "long-shot" of a particularly high-paying job. The paradox is that the larger the pool of unemployed

Figure 2.5. Probability Distributions of Wage Offers

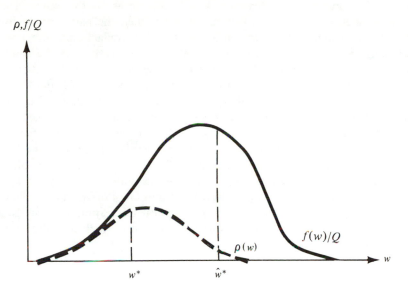

(searchers), the more likely the subjective distribution is to lie to the right of the true distribution, thereby increasing the duration of search and reducing potential output that would be created by individuals accepting lower-paying productive jobs.

This analysis departs significantly from the conventional literature on job search, such as in Phelps et al. (1970), in which it is assumed that the distribution of offers facing any searcher is independent of other searchers. In such models, unemployment varies as a result of lags in recognizing that distributions of wage offers have shifted. Transitory "Phillips curves" are generated until accurate information about the distribution of wage offers restores a "normal" unemployment rate. As such, these models have reflected only lagged adjustment to what would otherwise be perfect flex-price markets where unemployment represents a necessary cost of obtaining information. The model sketched above contains these elements of lagged adjustment, but also can take explicit account of such variables as the number of vacancies relative to number of seekers, which have otherwise been used primarily in quantity-adjustment models with less clear microfoundations. Detailed analysis of the dynamic properties of this model awaits further investigation, but it seems evident that in this context levels of unemployment *affect* as well as *reflect* underlying search behavior.

The conclusion to be drawn at this point is that unemployment in urban labor markets is a rational response of individuals who face a dispersion of wage offers and have less than perfect information about the exact set of opportunities open to them. Unemployment is then the partly productive activity of searching for information on the best available job offers and sampling the market to elicit offers. While part of this activity can be viewed as a socially desirable use of resources in generating scarce information, it is far from clear that this is the most efficient means of providing information leading to the reallocation of labor to more productive activities. It has been shown that the duration of search is likely to be longer—hence average levels of unemployment for a given labor force will be higher—the greater the dispersion of wage offers and the higher the initial level of unemployment. And it is not clear that improving the quality of information about wage offers will improve the situation—in fact, the reverse is quite possible. What is required is information not only about the distribution of offers but also about the number of other searchers and their critical reservation wage levels—a kind of information notoriously difficult to provide with any degree of accuracy.

## Non-Homogeneous Labor

So far it has been assumed that all searchers are similar and face the same set of opportunities. However, all vacancies are not open to all applicants. Employers see particular qualifications and qualities in employees, and a good part of the dispersion in wage offers can be explained by different requirements. Education is the most widely used qualification for screening potential applicants, and a plausible hypothesis with important ramifications is that people with more education will be accorded preference in hiring.[22] If this is true, the more educated (more generally those with greater human capital in the form of education, specific skills, or aptitudes) face much more dispersed distributions of potential offers—the frequency distribution is truncated on the right for those with lesser education and skills. Obviously, a number of distributions can be constructed for individuals with particular levels of qualifications, but the important point is that the less qualified job-seekers face truncated distributions. One can also add discrimination into the analysis quite easily—females, ethnic minorities, recent immigrants, or any such group that is discriminated against faces a truncated distribution of offers since many jobs will not be open to them. The analytic point is clear— one has to describe a distribution of offers that will be made if the individual in question applies before the vacancy is filled.

Thus differences observed among groups in unemployment levels and earnings may be explicable by the different job search strategies appropriate to different wage distributions. Specifically, a widespread finding in developing countries is that open unemployment levels are much higher for relatively well educated groups than for less-educated ones. Furthermore, a high proportion of such unemployment is concentrated among young persons who are initially entering the labor market. If, in fact, the more educated face a much wider dispersion of potential offers, it will pay them to invest more time in search since the potential returns to further search are much higher. The observed differences are further explained by the fact that the more educated are also more likely to have access to family resources to finance extended search. The point is that this framework provides a coherent means of analyzing different unemployment experience in terms of rational decision making by individuals.

## Migration as a Job Search Process

So far we have demonstrated that open unemployment is a manifestation of job search within a specific labor market even with an exogenously determined total supply of labor. It is likely that this manifestation will be more pronounced in urban labor markets simply because of their greater diversity of opportunities and greater dispersion of wage offers. This dispersion, which we do not here attempt to explain, is to be expected during the rapid change and transformation of specific economies in a world of imperfect information and delayed adjustments.

But the principal point of the migration literature is that urban labor force levels are not exogenously determined—that the supply of labor is an endogenous function of conditions within and between the labor markets. The Harris-Todaro model of migration is one in which the supply of labor to urban areas is a function of *expected* wages—and a particularly simple formulation of wage expectations explains why the labor force will continue to expand in the face of unemployment if significant wage differentials persist.

Migration can be viewed as a decision to move to a geographically removed labor market in order to look for a job. A rational decision maker will undertake such a move when the expected gains exceed the expected costs. But now the calculation of expected gains is more complicated than in the Harris-Todaro framework, in which wages and probabilities of obtaining employment are known. However, the principle is the same. Rather than *knowing* the urban wage, the potential migrant must now *estimate* the distribution of wage offers and the probabilities associated with each wage in order to construct an expected wage. Furthermore, rather than a straight probability of being employed, the decision maker must estimate an expected duration of unemployment during which he will be searching for work—an expected duration dependent on the strategy he chooses for establishing a minimum reservation wage, which in turn depends on the distribution of offers and the resources available for subsistence during the search. The expected income measure has to be regarded as a present value of an expected stream of earnings over a projected planning horizon. During a period of extended search, the income stream will be negative, becoming positive once a job offer is accepted. And as already mentioned, the expected duration of negative flows is a function of the search strategy selected.

Thus the determination of expected income in the Harris-Todaro model represents a very simple special case in which there is only one positive wage offer and the probability of receiving such an offer is one minus the unemployment rate (corresponding to $\pi[N/Q]$) in the previous section). All job-seekers will accept this offer if they receive it. Finally, this can easily be converted to an expected duration of search that is merely the reciprocal of the period employment probability. In a world like this, it is not unreasonable to assume that information about employment probability becomes known with a fair degree of accuracy and is taken account of by migrants. While Mazumdar (1975), Sabot (1977a) and others have generalized this model and include an informal sector with a lower flexible wage and probability of employment equal to one, the present model is completely general in that labor market opportunities are characterized by frequency distributions that, of course, can collapse into discrete distributions with only a limited number of values having positive frequencies. Since several recent studies of informal sectors suggest a wide dispersion of earnings, including considerable overlap between formal and informal sectors, it appears to be much more useful to be able to deal with wage distributions.[23]

This leads directly to the ways in which subjective estimates of the distribution of potential wages are formed. Without migrating, an individual cannot directly sample job offers in the distant labor market. The subjective distribution of $\rho(w)$ he holds is therefore dependent on secondary information that reaches him through various channels. It thus becomes important to identify the channels of information to which potential migrants have access. The literature dealing with this question suggests that personal contact through friends and relatives already in distant labor markets is by far the most important source of information. Individuals who lack access to such networks are much less likely to migrate.

The conventional theory of expectation formation is quite unsatisfactory in interpreting how uncertainty about the reliability of subjective expectations is dealt with. Conventionally, one would model the calculation of expected income as described, and the resulting expected present value would then be further discounted according to the degree of uncertainty surrounding this estimate. A more satisfactory procedure would be to model expectation formation as a joint probability problem, which takes into account that people may feel more confident about this subjective distribution in some parts of the range than in others. For instance, a potential migrant may have heard of job offers actually received by individuals he knows and trusts and therefore may expect that he too will obtain such an offer. On the other hand, he may also have heard stories or rumors about other people obtaining much better paying jobs, or going for years without finding any job. He will also consider possible outcomes and will arrive at a subjective guess of the probability of such good or bad luck occurring to him. But given the questionable reliability of the information these latter estimates were based on, the subjective probability assigned to them will be reduced further by the low probability that the information will be found to be accurate.[24]

For the purposes of the present discussion, risk avoidance is supposed powerful enough to cause individuals to assign low values to subjective expected incomes from distant labor markets without information from trusted sources. This is of considerable importance for a theory of labor migration, since migration supposedly will occur when people expect the gains from moving to a distant labor market to compensate for the forgone income accruing from searching for better employment in a labor market whose probability distribution is better known.

Within this framework, rates of migration will be affected positively by differences in mean earnings of the employed, as is true in all the theories that view migration as a form of investment in human capital. Ceteris paribus, high unemployment levels should discourage migration through lowering the $\pi(N/Q)$ term that enters into the computation of $\rho(w)$. As in the Harris-Todaro model, one would expect a positive relationship between mean income differentials and unemployment levels, since higher mean wages will encourage more new migrants to join the pool of active searchers. However, the dispersion of wages around the mean (measured by variances and higher moments) should also be positively related with average duration of search and hence unemployment. Yet, at the same time, the longer expected duration of search associated with a larger dispersion of offers will inhibit migration by lowering expected incomes.

From this analysis it becomes evident that the migration-unemployment relation is more complicated than was posited by the Harris-Todaro model. This is because unemployment is determined not only by the excess of job-seekers over vacancies, but also by the search behavior of participants in the labor market. In the present model, urban unemployment arising from search behavior is possible and likely, even in a market in which total job vacancies exceed the number of searchers since many job offers at low wages will be refused. It remains true in this more general model that the migration function serves to make the pool of searchers—the size of the labor force—endogenously determined and that increases in the labor force that exceed the rate at which individuals are finding and accepting employment will have a self-equilibrating effect in slowing further migration.

Once again, the effect of improving the quality of information has ambiguous effects. If the "true" expected incomes are higher in urban than in rural labor markets, and this condition persists because prospective migrants discount their subjective expected income functions because of uncertainty about the reliability of the information available to them, then improved information will increase the flow of migration, expand the pool of job-seekers, and, at least in the short run, increase the level of unemployment. The likely effect of improving information about the distribution of job offers in extending the period of job search and hence in raising unemployment levels has already been discussed. It is evident from this that the essential information, which must be accurate, concerns the number of seekers in relation to the number of vacancies, together with an indication of the critical reservation wage levels held by searchers. These kinds of information are difficult to provide, but it is far from evident that the market solution will generate a socially optimal level of resources devoted to unemployment in the form of job search.

### Implications of This Generalized Framework

This generalized model of migration and job search in the context of wage dispersion and imperfect information provides a more realistic description of labor market behavior in LDCs than conventional models. The widely accepted Harris-Todaro segmentation model has been shown to be a special case of the general model. However, it remains to be seen whether the increased complexity of this model enhances understanding of the processes involved and directs empirical research towards important questions.

First of all, the microfoundations of this model, rooted as they are in individual behavior in a world of imperfect and incomplete information and nonsynchronized decision making, provide a basis for a framework within which one can analyze the impacts of policy actions. Conventional neoclassical models are contained within the model as special cases when all information is freely available and all decisions synchronized. Therefore, the model provides a means for evaluating the significance of relaxing these restrictive assumptions.

Possibilities are opened for much richer treatment of labor markets and labor market institutions. Rather than being restricted to an analysis of unified or tightly compartmentalized labor markets, one can deal with continuous or discrete distribution of firms, job characteristics, wages, and worker characteristics. One need not be restricted to artificially bounded definitions of formal and informal sectors of labor markets. And, from a theoretical standpoint, the nature of unemployment and its social benefits as well as costs can be better understood to the extent that unemployment reflects search activity. It directs our attention to a number of relationships that are usually ignored or treated in superficial or ad hoc ways. Of greatest importance is the role association networks play in providing both information and financial support during periods of extended search. Although empirical studies have occasionally included variables for friends and relatives, the standard theoretical framework could not easily incorporate these institutions in other than trivial ways. Finally, within this model it is necessary to examine variances as well as means of wage distribution.

## NOTES

1. Assuming that, in disequilibrium, quantities adjust faster than prices, deviation of aggregate demand from the full employment level will be amplified rather than counteracted because the initial unemployment reduces purchasing power and creates expectations of further contractions. Aside from a strong positive effect on demand for output of the negative relationship between prices and wealth, which Keynes recognized as logically possible but socially unjust and inefficient, a decline in wages only exacerbates the situation, since its first consequence is to reduce aggregate demand, reinforcing expectations of deflation. See Leijonhufvud (1968).

2. Two basic models can be distinguished here: the static Walrasian model associated with the Eckaus (1955) paper on factor proportions and the dynamic Harrod-Domar model. In the former, with two factors (capital and labor), two commodities, and production functions characterized by Leontief-style fixed coefficients, there are flats in the production possibility curve and no market mechanism to ensure that the composition of demand will take production to the one point where both factors are fully employed. In the dynamic model, the average savings ratio and the marginal capital-output ratio are fixed. Hence, the economic system is geared to a steady rate of growth; and since, again, there is no market mechanism to equilibrate demand and supply for labor, the rate of growth of production may well be exceeded by the exogenously determined rate of growth of the (working) population. The result is an exponential rate of growth in labor unemployment. It was this "naive" growth model that Solow (1956) rescued from the inevitability of unemployment by demonstrating that the choice of technique and the savings ratio could shift in response to a growing availability of labor.

3. The simplest model in this category is the one-sector model such as that set forth by Meade (1961) to analyze the dilemma faced by the monocrop economy of Mauritius—simultaneous dramatic increases in the growth rates of both the labor force and wages. With a given supply of labor, if the real wage is fixed above labor's marginal product it is clear that capitalist employers will hire only a portion of the labor force. The deduction of unemployment is much the same in the two-sector models developed by international trade theorists. See Bhagwati (1968) and Brecher (1974). Brecher added a (real) wage floor, covering the entire labor market to the standard,

two-commodity (capital intensive, labor intensive), two-factor model and derived the feasible (constrained) production possibility curve. Capital is always fully utilized, but for a given product-price ratio there is a locus of profit-maximizing output equilibria (a Rybczynski line) along which labor is unemployed. This model shows that unemployment will vary not only with the level of minimum wage, but also with both the product-price ratio and the composition of demand for output.

4. In his seminal paper, Lewis (1954) was concerned more with the consequences of a supply of labor, perfectly elastic at a constant real wage, to the modern capitalist sector than with the cause of the unemployment in the agricultural sector that it suggested. ("Suggested" rather than "implied" is the appropriate term because what Lewis calls "unlimited supplies of labour" could be the consequence of employers in the capitalist sector, for one reason or another, paying more than the supply price of labor.) Nevertheless, a model is implicit in his discussion. It is virtually the same as the two-sector model in which unemployment is the result of an economy-wide rigid wage in excess of the market-clearing level. The wage in the agricultural sector is determined exogenously rather than by the interactions of supply and demand, which, in the economies Lewis had in mind, would produce a zero or near zero return to labor because of the abundance of labor relative to capital and natural resources. Since the modern capitalist sector must draw its workers from the agricultural sector, it too is subject to the same floor. Unemployment is sector specific in the Lewis model, though the wage floor is economy-wide, because it is in agriculture that excess workers can obtain the means to subsist.

5. There is also a rigid wage in the Harris-Todaro model (Harris and Todaro, 1971), but unlike the other models it is not economy-wide. Rather, the labor market is segmented in the sense that some workers receive higher real wages (net of psychic and direct costs of mobility) than others with the same level of human capital, simply by virtue of their sector of employment. The essential contribution of this model to the explanation of unemployment is a labor allocation mechanism under which workers migrate until the actual rural wage is equated with the expected urban wage, the latter defined as the actual (rigid) wage weighted by the probability of employment. The conventional market-clearing mechanism—a decline in the (rigid) wage—is thus replaced by a quantity adjustment mechanism—an increase in unemployment.

6. Unemployment is not, however, voluntary in the sense associated with rentiers whose reserve price exceeds the prevailing wage; it may persist even where the reserve price of the unemployed is less than the wage in the low wage sector.

7. Fields (1975) cites evidence from a number of countries where the estimated ratio of rural to urban incomes is between 1:2 and 1:8, and thus predicted rates of urban unemployment are between 12.5 percent and 50 percent and yet the highest measured rate of unemployment is 20 percent.

8. If, even for a rural resident, being without a job improves the probability of obtaining a high wage urban job, then $P_{uu} > P_{ru} > P_{re} > 0$, implying that in equilibrium there will be some rural open unemployment and that the cate-

gorization of the segmentation model as sector specific would have to be qualified. That the rural unemployed should reap such an advantage is not, however, very plausible.

9. See Sabot (1977a) and Mazumdar (1975).

10. Taking account of the heterogeneity of labor, the availability and cost of credit to finance job search, and the direct and psychic costs of migration can also lower the rates of open urban unemployment predicted by the simple segmentation model of the Harris-Todaro type. See Fields (1975).

11. A literature on optimal strategies for decision making in these circumstances has been partly developed. See in particular Alchian (1970) and Holt (1970).

12.
$$\int_0^\infty \rho(w)\, dw = 1.$$

Conceptually there is no problem including the probability that search will not yield an offer at a positive wage—in the case $\rho(0) > 0$.

13. Although in Figure 2.1 $w^*$ is greater than $\bar{w}$, it could be equal to or less than $\bar{w}$.

14. Mathematically, the expected stream of utility to be achieved from a searching strategy that takes $w^*$ as a critical acceptance wage is:

$$y = \int_0^{t^*} u(-c)e^{-rt}\, dt + \int_{t*}^\infty \left[ \int_{w*}^\infty \frac{\rho(w)}{\pi_1(w^*)} u(w)\, dw \right] e^{-rt}\, dt$$

where

$$t^* = 1/\pi_1 \text{ and } \pi_1 = \int_{w*}^\infty \rho(w)\, dw.$$

The first term is the *expected* utility cost of engaging in search for $t^*$ periods while the second term is the expected utility to be obtained from accepting a job at $t^*$ that will pay a wage $w \geqslant w^*$ in every successive period. There is in principle no problem in defining a dated stream of incomes associated with any particular initial offer but the mathematics becomes unnecessarily complicated without affecting the basic results. It should be noted that in this second term the probability term is modified to be $\rho(w)/\pi_1(w^*)$ since the expected probability of obtaining an offer greater than $w^*$ is equal to one, hence

$$\int_{w*}^\infty [\rho(w)/\pi_1(w^*)]\, dw = 1.$$

The condition for $y$ to be maximized with respect to $w^*$ is:

$$\left\{ u(-c) - \int_{w*}^\infty [\rho(w)/\pi_1(w^*)u(w)]\, dw \right\} e^{-rt}\, \frac{dt^*}{dw^*}$$

$$- \int_{t*}^\infty \left\{ [\rho(w^*)/\pi_1(w^*)]\, u(w^*) \right\} e^{-rt}\, dt$$

$$+ \int_{t*}^\infty \partial/\partial\, w^* \left[ \int_{w*}^\infty [\rho(w)/\pi_1(w^*)]\, u(w)\, dw \right] e^{-rt}\, dt = 0.$$

The first major term is of negative sign and consists of two elements: the additional direct cost of searching, plus the opportunity cost of the expected earnings forgone during the additional period of search imposed by raising $w^*$. The second term is the present value of acceptance of an offer at $w^*$. The final term is the present value of the charged expected stream of utility to be received by accepting a wage $w \geqslant w^*$. Since the first two terms are unambiguously negative, an optimum will exist only if the third term is of positive sign.

15. These propositions follow directly from the first order maximization conditions outlined in note 14. With lower direct costs of search, the first term will be smaller, hence the equality will be satisfied at a higher $w^*$ with higher gain being achieved from further search. With less risk aversion, $u(w)$ takes on higher values at high wage levels, hence the final term will be higher and the optimality conditions satisfied at higher levels of $w^*$. Finally, a lower discount rate will increase the value of the final term, which includes present values of streams of utility at high wage levels, hence the optimal $w^*$ will be increased.

It is also likely under reasonable conditions that increased variance of the distribution of offers will also increase $w^*$, hence the expected duration of search. Take two distributions of $\rho(w)$ with the same mean value but let $\rho_2^2 > \rho_1^2$. The two distributions are illustrated below. Since

$$\int_0^\infty \rho(w)\, dw = 1$$

for both distributions, and

$$\rho_1(\overline{w}) > \rho_2(\overline{w}),$$

therefore the two

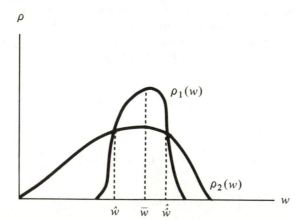

must intersect at $\hat{w}$ and $\overset{\wedge}{\hat{w}}$. Since $\rho_2(w > \overset{\wedge}{\hat{w}}) > \rho_1(w > \overset{\wedge}{\hat{w}})$ it follows that

$$\int_{w*}^{\infty} \rho_2(w)\, u(w)\, dw \;>\; \int_{w*}^{\infty} \rho_1(w)\, u(w)\, dw, \text{ if } w^* \geqslant \overset{\wedge}{\hat{w}}.$$

In such a case $w^*$ must have increased with an increase in variance of offers since the final term, the gains to further search, must increase. However, if $\hat{w} \leqslant w^* \leqslant \overset{\wedge}{\hat{w}}$, then $\rho_1(w^* \leqslant w \leqslant \overset{\wedge}{\hat{w}}) < \rho_2(w^* \leqslant w \leqslant \overset{\wedge}{\hat{w}})$ so that probabilities of higher acceptable offers increase. The effect on $w^*$ is ambiguous and will depend critically on the specific utility function. The logic is clear— a greater variance of offers around a constant mean increases probabilities of receiving very attractive offers if one engages in enough search. The extremely risk averse may reduce search in such conditions and take a quick sure thing—the less risk averse will be encouraged and search further. While research is needed to establish which groups respond in each way, it is reasonable to assume that in many cases increased variance in offers will elicit additional search.

16. One hypothesis is that high wages are offered by firms that have high returns to filling vacancies. Therefore, wage dispersion becomes a function of dynamic adjustments in the economy. Empirical testing of this hypothesis has not been done.

17. The difficulties in formulating and solving this kind of optimal search problem are referred to by Alchian (1970). However, the assumption here will be that an optimal critical wage $w^*$ exists for the subjective distribution held at any particular time by each seeker.

18. Of course, the other important question is whether or not actual levels of search are socially optimal. This question cannot be answered yet but one should not accept too easily Alchian's assumption that in markets actual levels of search will necessarily be socially optimal.

19. This function is drawn under the assumption that $w^*$ is dispersed among searchers reflecting different preferences, search costs, and subjective estimates of the true wage distribution function. If everyone had the same $w^*$, $n(w)$ would be discontinuous, having a value of 0 below and $n$ above $w^*$. However, it is extremely difficult to explain persistence of a dispersion of wage offers in such a case since any offer made by an employer at or above $w^*$ would be accepted by any searcher and any offer below that level would be refused. Therefore, the probability of filling any vacancy in a particular period is independent of the level of the wage offered.

20. What this actually is, is a probability distribution of the numbers of other searchers who will sample the particular vacancy. This distribution is binominal and the expected number of searchers will be $N/Q$. The exact expression is not needed, since it will have the same value for every vacancy.

21. This follows from the usual assumption that each searcher is able to sample one offer in each period.

22. See Fields (1975), Sabot (1977a).

23. See Sabot (1977b), Mazumdar (1976).

24. Professor Jerome Rothenberg of the Massachusetts Institute of Technology has provided many useful insights into this question.

## BIBLIOGRAPHY

Alchian, A. "Information Costs, Pricing and Resource Unemployment." In E. Phelps, et al., *Micro-Economic Foundations of Employment and Inflation Theory*. New York: W. W. Norton & Co., 1970.

Barnum, H., and Sabot, R. H. "Education, Employment Probabilities and Rural-Urban Migration in Tanzania." *Oxford Bulletin of Economics and Statistics* 39, no. 2 (May 1977).

Bhagwati, J. *The Theory and Practice of Commercial Policy*. Frank Graham Memorial Lecture, 1967. *Special Papers in International Economics*, no. 8, Princeton University, 1968.

Brecher, R. "Minimum Wage Rates and the Pure Theory of International Trade." *Quarterly Journal of Economics* 88, no. 1 (February 1974).

Domar, E. *Essay in the Theory of Economic Growth*. New York: Oxford University Press, 1957.

Eckaus, R. "The Factor-Proportions Problem in Underdeveloped Areas." *American Economic Review* 65 (1955).

Fields, G. "Rural-Urban Migration, Urban Unemployment and Underemployment, and Job Search Activity in LDC's." *Journal of Development Economics* 2, no. 2 (June 1975).

Harris, J., and Todaro, M. "Migration, Unemployment, and Development: A Two-Sector Analysis." *American Economic Review* 60, no. 1 (March 1970).

Holt, C. "Job Search, Phillips Wage Relation, and Union Influence: Theory and Evidence." In E. Phelps, et al., *Micro-Economic Foundations of Employment and Inflation Theory*. New York: W. W. Norton & Co., 1970.

Leijonhufvud, A. *On Keynesian Economics and the Economics of Keynes: A Study in Monetary Theory*. New York: Oxford University Press, 1968.

Lewis, W. A. "Economic Development with Unlimited Supplies of Labor." *Manchester School of Economics and Social Studies* 22, no. 2 (May 1954).

Mazumdar, D. "The Theory of Urban Underemployment in Less Developed Countries." IBRD Working Paper no. 198, February 1975.

____. "The Urban Informal Sector." *World Development* 4, no. 8 (August 1976).

Meade, J. "Mauritius: A Case Study of Malthusian Economics." *Economic Journal* 71 (September 1961).

Phelps, E., et al. *Micro-Economic Foundations of Employment and Inflation Theory*. New York: W. W. Norton & Co., 1970.

Sabot, R. H. "The Meaning and Measurement of Urban Surplus Labour." *Oxford Economic Papers* 29, no. 3 (1977a).

___. *The Social Costs of Urban Surplus Labour.* Paris: OECD Development Center, 1977b.

___. *Economic Development and Urban Migration.* Oxford: Clarendon Press, 1979.

Solow, R. M. "A Contribuiton to the Theory of Economic Growth." *Quarterly Journal of Economics* 70, no. 1 (February 1956).

# 3
# Notes on the Estimation of Migration Decision Functions

T. PAUL SCHULTZ

## INTRODUCTION

Differences in labor earnings among individuals may indicate differences in skills, experience, and other productive traits. These differences provide incentive to substitute lower paid skills for higher paid ones in production, and motivate individuals to acquire the higher paid skills. Differences in labor earnings among regions (and sectors) of an economy provide an analogous incentive to change the location of production to obtain lower-cost labor, and conversely the same differences motivate workers to move where their skills are more highly valued. Migration, therefore, is most often viewed primarily as a response to different earnings opportunities in spatially distinct labor markets. Needless to add, migration also occurs for political, religious, and other noneconomic motives.[1]

From an economic point of view, general equilibrium models of inter-regional factor allocation have not yet accounted for internal migration with any degree of success. Little progress has been made in distinguishing between the determinants of interregional derived demands for labor and labor supply responses of potential migrants. Therefore, a static partial equilibrium approach shall be adopted for interpreting migration that unfortunately neglects both the determinants of derived demand for labor and the interactions between regional demands and supplies of labor over time. In this regard, the current framework for the study of migration is comparable to the framework used in much of the human capital and labor supply literature, which treats individual behavior as a response to predetermined wage differentials, relative prices, and nonearned income.

The object of estimating a migration model is to learn what factors influence the response of individuals to regional differences in employment opportunities for persons with their particular skills. For example, the allocation of labor among regions may not be inefficient simply because the average

91

level of wages in one region exceeds that in another—unless, of course, the skills of the labor forces in the two regions are comparable. Even in this extreme case, the relative distribution of labor earnings by skill group may differ across regions, and one skill group could be motivated to move to one region, while another group would go to another region. Differences in aggregate wage or employment levels are difficult to interpret from the viewpoint of understanding migration or judging the efficiency of labor allocation. Disaggregation of the labor force into more homogeneous groups, according to skill classes that are relatively fixed for the individual, is an important step toward measuring labor market motivations for migration. The need for disaggregation may be even more obvious in the study of internal migration in low-income countries, for it is widely assumed that differences in wages among regions and sectors in such countries signal serious, institutionally maintained factor market distortions that may differ across skill groups.

Debate on development policy, and in particular on the choice of appropriate means for expanding production and employment in rural and urban areas, often rests on assumptions as to the nature of regional and sectoral labor markets and the relations between them. If wages are determined across both sectors by a rural subsistence wage in excess of labor's marginal product in agriculture, expansion of the urban sector is desirable at least until the "unlimited supplies" of rural labor are absorbed (Lewis, 1954; Fei and Ranis, 1961). If urban wages are institutionally maintained in excess of their market equilibrium level, migration to the urban areas may be regulated by urban unemployment that must perform the function of a market clearing "price" between sectors (Todaro, 1969; Harris and Todaro, 1970). In such a situation, it might be socially more productive to expand employment opportunities in the rural sector and thereby alleviate the urban unemployment problem. Finally, the competitive neoclassical two-sector growth model would predict only such regional differentials in employment and wage conditions as are necessary to induce the migration required by regional trends in demand and by the location of natural resources. In this case, expansion of employment in either sector is desirable according to the level of local returns on the related investments. A disaggregated description of migration, the measurement of skill-specific wage and employment differences among regions, and the estimation of migration response functions should all provide information useful for discriminating among these alternative models of intersectoral development, and hence for choosing among the prescriptions for development strategy.

Researchers of labor markets in low-income countries have only recently begun to use the human capital framework to analyze survey and census data. The structure of wages and employment by age, sex, and educational attainment is available from only a handful of countries. These labor market data are fundamental building blocks for the analysis of the determinants of migration; they are also essential for investigations into the incidence and distribution of factor market distortions, the nature of unemployment, and the personal distribution of income. This chapter has an elementary operational orientation; it consists of a collection of notes on conceptual, empirical, and statistical problems associated with the study of the responsiveness of migration to economic, social, and demographic variables.

Since this chapter is restricted to microdeterminants of migration, it does not touch on the social repercussions of migration and only briefly refers to general equilibrium models of migration and development. Consequently, the important but neglected task of measuring the elusive social externalities commonly attributed to rapid internal migration in low-income countries is not addressed here.

The chapter is ordered in the following manner. The next section explores bases for disaggregation in the study of labor markets and migration. The measurement of migration and its determinants is then discussed in the following section, with the object of specifying variables that will clarify economic issues and avoid later estimation problems. A statistical framework, developed in the fourth section, lends itself to testing a variety of economic hypotheses with better statistical techniques than are common in the field.

## DIFFERENCES IN INDIVIDUAL PRODUCTIVITY: METHODS OF STANDARDIZATION

Empirical study of migration frequently postulates an individual probability function for migration and estimates its parameters, occasionally from individual data on migrants and nonmigrants but usually from aggregate data on the occurrence of *gross* origin to destination migration. Yet at the aggregate level, migration is important as a *net* reallocator of labor that presumably enhances factor productivity and reduces the disparity in rewards to comparable factors of production (Kuznets, 1964, 1971). It is not yet clear that a satisfactory explanation of the microdeterminants of gross migration will provide the most useful information for formulating a policy to cope with net migration; it is presumed, however, that ultimately it will do so (Theil, 1954). Focusing on gross migration or the individual probability of migration at least provides a coherent rationale for applying a reasonably well developed set of concepts regarding the determinants of household demand and investment in human capital to an important economic and social phenomenon (T. W. Schultz, 1961, 1972).

The study of migration has relied heavily on aggregate statistics; little empirical evidence has yet been derived from survey information on individuals, matching origin and destination characteristics, even though these individual data sources have recently been productively exploited in estimating parameters of migration probability functions in low-income countries (Hay, 1974; Barnum and Sabot, 1975). The requirements for aggregate data, stressing criteria for stratification to obtain relatively homogeneous components of the labor force, are explored first in this section. Then an outline is presented of an approach to individual information on migration and interrelations among labor markets that relies upon indirect estimation of regional wage and employment functions imbedded in the migration function.

## Aggregate Statistics on Migration

Gross migration rates are typically obtained from a single cross-sectional survey or census that reports current residence of the respondent in conjunction with residence at a specified earlier time, such as five years ago. The number moving from each location is expressed as a fraction of all those residing in the original location in the earlier period. Often such gross flows are only available from birthplace to current residence, but it may be comforting that in India and Venezuela the one-year and lifetime gross migration rates were highly correlated, and indeed they implied similar response elasticities when used to estimate gravity migration functions (Levy and Wadycki, 1972a; Greenwood, 1971a).

A net migration rate is an aggregate concept, or, as has been noted, there is no such thing as a "net migrant." Where population registries exist, or a complete matrix of gross migration flows is at hand, net flows can be calculated. The convention is to use the initial population of the region as the denominator for the net flow to arrive at a net migration rate. Where all gross migration flows are not known, regional age and sex tabulations from two censuses may be compared, and cohort differences not explained by age and sex specific mortality rates can be residually attributed to net migration. For reasons stated previously, this chapter deals only with regularities in and interpretations of the causes of gross migration.

## Age

A strong association between age and migration is universally noted; gross migration occurs more frequently among youth at the start of their economically independent lifetime than it does at progressively later ages.[2] The economist has rationalized this age pattern of migration rates in terms of the higher reward for migration while young, when the present discounted value of income increments in the destination is maximized (Sjaastad, 1962). But a few calculations would suggest that ten fewer years to retirement might not fully account for the manyfold decrease in migration rates often observed among men between the ages of twenty and thirty.[3]

There would seem to be an important, if difficult to document, role for rising costs in this age-migration pattern, which might be called location specific capital losses. Opportunity, direct, and psychic costs are all likely to increase with age, as vocationally specific experience and goods become less readily transferred, and family obligations and social relationships less readily ruptured. Clearly all of these factors are modified by the ease of initial and return migration in a particular setting.

A cohort selectivity effect may also help to account for the pronounced concentration of migration among youth. Assuming that relevant attributes are distributed across a regional birth cohort, those for whom the expected returns from migration are highest and for whom the risks and challenges of migration are preferred will be the first to migrate as opportunity arises, typically after leaving school. Subsequently, migrants are drawn from a residual population of selectively changing character. It is hard to imagine migration across ages in a cross section, or over time in a cohort, as being generated by a constant stochastic process operating on a population of aging but otherwise unchanging composition. Yet this assumption is often implicit in empirical work on migration. Heckman and Willis (1976) have explored this problem for the study of reproduction, but it has not yet been adapted to the analysis of longitudinal information on migration, except in the mechanical short-run prediction models where current migratory behavior is explained by past duration of residence. Many gaps in our understanding of migration may be concealed by the use of convenient cross-sectional data by age where longitudinal information on individuals and cohorts is called for. A seemingly neglected objective in migration research is to develop satisfactory stochastic specifications of longitudinal migration models that can be estimated from time series. Progress along these lines could represent a major improvement over cross-sectional analyses, where differences across age groups at one point in time are assumed to measure differences that cohorts expect to experience as they age.

## Sex

Differences in migration rates between men and women are varied across regions, countries, cultures, and periods, as are the roles and relative economic opportunities of the sexes in contracting and expanding sectors of the economy. Men appear to predominate in the rural to urban migration documented thus far in Africa, India, and the Islamic countries, whereas women have on the whole led the exodus from agriculture in northwestern Europe, areas of European settlement, and Latin America. Given the variation in migration rates by age and sex, both are accepted bases for stratification in the demographic study of migration, where an objective is to discover beneath the diversity in overall migration rates greater constancy in component rates. Since life cycle differences in market wages of men and women are substantial, stratification by age and sex should also advance the economists' desire to obtain more homogeneous groups, from the point of view of the present values of future labor market earnings.

### Schooling

Within age and sex groups there remain substantial differences in lifetime earnings associated with schooling. It has been argued that these educational differences in wage rates arise from a combination of causes: statically, schooling is a useful proxy for productive skills that augment the "efficiency units" of labor a worker brings to a given task; dynamically, schooling reflects an "allocative efficiency" of the worker to deal with a changing productive environment (Welch, 1970; T. W. Schultz, 1975). It would seem to follow from Welch's reasoning that, if schooling affects allocative efficiency within a firm or a job, it should exert a parallel effect on worker ability to respond by migration to changing job opportunities.

A growing body of evidence from a variety of sources confirms the expectation that the better educated will migrate more frequently and respond to smaller income differences than the less educated.[4] For example, Table 3.1 shows the monotonic relation between schooling and lifetime migration rates for both men and women in all but one coterminous state of Venezuela. As a first step toward clarifying the response of migration to wages across spatially distinct labor markets, comparisons should be conducted within groups that are as homogeneous as possible with respect to education, sex, and age.[5] This is not to deny the existence of substitution possibilities in production among age, sex, and educational groups in most contexts, but without holding constant for these basic attributes of labor force composition and productivity, differences in wages and employment conditions may only reflect compositional differences in the labor force across regions and will not have a bearing on incentives for migration. With more understanding of the migratory response of homogeneous groups, empirical estimation of "cross-wage effects" should be feasible, that is, how wages of one group affect the migratory behavior of another. Eventually, substitution possibilities in production across homogeneous groups should also be estimable, and progress could be made in specifying regional derived demands for labor.

An obvious explanation for the lack of studies disaggregating migration by age, sex, and educational attainment is the scarcity of associated employment and wage data for these economic and demographic divisions of the population. It is to be hoped that investigations based on individual data files

Table 3.1. Percentage of Venezuelans 7 Years and Older in 1961 Not Currently Residing in Their State of Birth, By Sex and Educational Attainment: The Sum of Gross Lifetime Out-Migration

| Code | State | Men | | | | Women | | | |
|---|---|---|---|---|---|---|---|---|---|
| | | No Schooling | Some Primary | Some Secondary | Some Higher | No Schooling | Some Primary | Some Secondary | Some Higher |
| 01 | Federal District | 17.26 | 20.44 | 28.85 | 42.25 | 16.96 | 19.81 | 27.45 | 30.80 |
| 02 | Anzoátegui | 15.21 | 24.97 | 59.50 | 83.91 | 16.00 | 25.49 | 47.48 | 81.58 |
| 03 | Apure | 17.86 | 32.31 | 77.85 | 95.17 | 20.43 | 35.18 | 73.23 | 97.80 |
| 04 | Aragua | 22.18 | 28.80 | 52.67 | 83.22 | 25.75 | 29.45 | 45.88 | 72.00 |
| 05 | Barinas | 13.21 | 23.03 | 67.81 | 86.27 | 16.14 | 26.15 | 62.27 | 92.54 |
| 06 | Bolívar | 13.34 | 22.81 | 58.95 | 81.78 | 16.52 | 27.55 | 56.28 | 80.97 |
| 07 | Carabobo | 18.50 | 24.49 | 43.42 | 64.27 | 21.52 | 26.19 | 37.09 | 67.24 |
| 08 | Cojedes | 24.50 | 39.28 | 62.23 | 87.59 | 30.20 | 40.54 | 56.56 | 100.00 |
| 09 | Falcón | 29.34 | 37.20 | 56.69 | 79.35 | 27.80 | 30.46 | 44.11 | 59.59 |
| 10 | Guárico | 17.06 | 30.00 | 60.21 | 82.70 | 20.96 | 32.39 | 47.76 | 93.55 |
| 11 | Lara | 26.70 | 30.51 | 46.26 | 70.76 | 24.76 | 26.19 | 34.25 | 71.10 |
| 12 | Mérida | 19.57 | 36.04 | 65.57 | 74.51 | 23.20 | 37.73 | 51.14 | 66.80 |
| 13 | Miranda | 28.60 | 41.81 | 56.28 | 49.21 | 34.21 | 42.90 | 47.91 | 58.30 |
| 14 | Monagas | 18.72 | 34.63 | 63.67 | 85.90 | 22.03 | 34.97 | 50.21 | 90.70 |
| 15 | Nueva Esparta [1] | | | | | | | | |
| 16 | Portuguesa | 10.92 | 22.75 | 57.26 | 83.33 | 13.86 | 25.64 | 50.00 | 84.06 |
| 17 | Sucre | 23.50 | 41.15 | 69.47 | 86.57 | 25.00 | 39.36 | 56.03 | 89.46 |
| 18 | Táchira | 16.82 | 29.95 | 62.35 | 84.46 | 22.71 | 32.19 | 48.68 | 89.95 |
| 19 | Trujillo | 28.77 | 40.73 | 67.62 | 85.50 | 29.77 | 39.31 | 54.47 | 91.63 |
| 20 | Yaracuy | 29.41 | 43.14 | 72.11 | 91.09 | 34.46 | 44.06 | 50.07 | 87.23 |
| 21 | Zulia | 5.25 | 9.78 | 29.92 | 42.13 | 4.86 | 9.32 | 27.29 | 48.07 |

[1] Nueva Esparta, a small island of 89,492 persons, is excluded from this study for a variety of reasons, as are the Amazon, Amacuro Delta and Federal Dependent Territories.

Source: T. P. Schultz, 1975(a).

containing this minimum necessary information will provide more valuable detail to fill this gap in empirical research. A major, and as yet unresolved, problem in using individual records for the analysis of migration, however, is "selectivity bias," or the inability to infer without bias from cross sections what opportunities the migrant has forgone at origin and what opportunities the nonmigrant might have expected at destination. On the other hand, some information on labor markets that might be useful in the study of migration, such as quit, hire, fire, and turnover rates, is more likely to come from employers. Other data, such as the duration and frequency of unemployment and the intensity of job search are infrequently available from surveys.

### Individual Statistics on Migration

Individual information on residence, employment, and earnings status permits one to dispense with the crude assumption underlying most aggregate analyses of migration—that the potential migrant occupies a representative position in the aggregate distribution of characteristics thought to determine the probability of migrating. Even the seemingly weaker assumption that the migrant retains his relative position in the size distribution of wages as he shifts from origin to destination need not be realistic.

This assumption is likely to *overstate* the realizable gains for a typical rural-urban migrant in most low-income countries. Migrants are *positively* selected, under most circumstances, and they therefore exhibit above average education and earnings when compared with populations at origin. At the same time, however, they are likely to suffer at least a temporary disadvantage in the more urban destination job market, compared with other workers of the same age, sex, and educational qualifications.

In developing areas, where the agricultural sector has exhibited relatively little change in inputs or techniques, rewards for educated skills and innovative and entrepreneurial talents are probably greater in urban than in rural activities. Positive selectivity among rural-urban migrants is consequently common, though negative selectivity in migration may also arise. Lipton (1976) shows evidence of a bimodal distribution of migrants from rural Indian villages, with the lower-class landless being displaced short distances by agricultural changes, and higher-class youth being sent long distances to acquire education and better jobs. Both negative and positive selectivity are seen in these disparate groups of Indian migrants. Fragmentary evidence on interregional migration in low-income areas suggests that, as in Venezuela (Table 3.1), the positive selectivity of migration will outweigh the negative, given the evolving distribution of opportunities and returns to education in the urban and rural sectors of most developing areas. Of course, a shift in development priorities reducing the bias toward urban interests and introducing new inputs and techniques into agriculture could change this pattern of migration in the future.

Individual data can be used to reduce some of these sources of aggregation bias, but forms of selectivity bias will persist. It is assumed that these sources of bias are of a second order of magnitude,[6] and the goal here is to estimate the real wage and employment opportunities a migrant could expect in each region, explicitly allowing for job opportunities to improve with duration of residence. Opportunities probably also differ according to the migrant's region of origin, since quality of schooling and relevance of vocational skills differ among regions. Estimated real wage and employment rates could be multiplied to obtain average real earnings at origin and destination, and the discounted sum of these earnings streams could then become an argument in a migration decision function (Sjaastad, 1962). But attitudes toward unemployment and risk could perhaps be better understood if both the wage and the employment probability entered separately in the migration function.[7] If both the wage and employment functions are estimated in semilogarithmic form, their sum is the logarithm of "expected income." Consequently, it is straightforward to test whether the "expected income" hypothesis is strictly consistent with observed migration behavior. It seems desirable, therefore, to explore empirically how migrants trade off the wage level against the probability of obtaining a job at destination and, where data are sufficiently abundant, how this trade-off changes over various time horizons.

## PARALLEL SPECIFICATION OF REGIONAL EMPLOYMENT AND WAGE FUNCTIONS

In the study of migration and labor markets in general, there is reason to estimate both a real wage rate function and an hours (or weeks) worked function for each regional labor market, rather than a single semilogarithmic earnings function as elaborated by Mincer (1974). Both these wage and employment functions are treated as reduced forms, where both dependent variables are expressed in logarithms and the same right-hand-side variables appear in each equation. In certain circumstances, the employment function might be viewed as a labor supply function, but a more complex interpretation is probably justified, in which time not spent working may be devoted to job search or odd jobs in the informal sector.

Though the specification of these functions might depend on the institutional setting in a particular country as well as the available data, a hypothetical example illustrates how labor market data might initially be explored. The two labor market functions would be estimated over $k$ individuals separately within each sex and education group $j$ in each region $i$ of a country, as follows:

$$\ln W_{ijk} = \alpha_{ij0} + \alpha_{ij1}A_{ijk} + \alpha_{ij2}A^2_{ijk} + \alpha_{ij3}X_{ijk} + \alpha_{ij4}X^2_{ijk} + \sum_{m=5}^{n} \alpha_{ijm}R_{ikm} \qquad (1)$$

$$\ln L_{ijk} = \delta_{ij0} + \delta_{ij1}A_{ijk} + \delta_{ij2}A^2_{ijk} + \delta_{ij3}X_{ijk} + \delta_{ij4}X^2_{ijk} + \sum_{m=5}^{n} \delta_{ijm}R_{ijk} \qquad (2)$$

where $W$ and $L$ are the real wage rate and the units of time worked, respectively; $A$ is calendar age (or some transform such as years since end of schooling or, preferably, actual years of work experience); $X$ is proposed to capture the nonlinear effect of years of experience in the destination region $i$, in its quadratic form; and the $R$s are $n - 4$ origin region dummy variables representing the quality of schooling, perhaps. Parsimony in specifying and parameterizing such wage and employment functions would, of course, depend on the extent and form of data at hand. Hierarchical $F$ ratio tests could be applied to test for coefficient equality across origin regions, or even across education and sex groups, in an effort to reduce the number of parameters estimated. Having adopted this parallel semilogarithmic specification, the relative effects of any right-hand-side variable on total expected earnings is directly obtained by summing the respective parameter estimates, i.e., $\alpha_{ij} + \delta_{ij}$.

The purpose of estimating these wage and employment functions by migratory status is to obtain predicted values for the labor market conditions in all regions. These predicted values, conditional on the individual's age, sex, and education, should be relevant to his decision to migrate to the specified destination. If individual migration decisions are independent of each other, the mean proportion migrating, or gross migration rate, is a maximum likelihood estimator of the migration probability. Such rates could be obtained from aggregate data sources as before, or by tabulation of a survey or census. But if these rates are based on small enough subpopulations, their instability may necessitate the use of a more efficient estimation procedure that weighs observations accordingly. If individual data are used directly, the dependent variable in the migration function becomes dichotomous. The form of a statistical model that might be useful for estimating the migration function itself is then discussed and conclusions are made in the last section of this chapter.

The empirical exercise proposed above requires a considerable amount of work, and it has not been performed in a low-income country.[8] The intermediate products pertaining to the regional distribution of wage and employment opportunities would be informative, adding substantially to our understanding of the sources of personal income inequality that are rooted in regional factor market differences. Also, the second stage of analysis directed at explaining migration would probably yield quite different migration response parameters than those usual in aggregate studies.

## Empirical Specification and Economic Hypotheses

Since migration requires resources and time to realize a new set of employment and consumption opportunities, it is often treated as an investment opportunity. For ranking and choosing among investments, it is appealing to summarize the associated costs and returns over time as an internal rate of return or present (discounted) value. But the traditional problems of thus ranking physical capital investments are at least as severe when these summary approaches are applied to human capital investments, particularly migration.

The gestation period of a human capital investment can be a crucial feature in its attractiveness, and yet plays no distinct role in the above summary measures. The importance of timing inputs and outputs can be attributed both to imperfections in the human capital market that largely necessitate self-financing and to the inability of investors to diversify commitments to reduce risk, since only one migration destination can be pursued at a time. These features of migration help to explain the usefulness of "stepwise" patterns of migration noted since the Industrial Revolution (Ravenstein, 1885), the widespread networks of relatives who facilitate and mobilize capital for migration in some societies, and the relative infrequency of return migration where substantial costs of relocation and job search have been incurred by migrants.

Risk, for which measures are imperfect and possibly misleading, is a dominant element in the migration decision. There is not only the risk of pecuniary failure, which would weaken the incentive to any investor, but also the uncertainty of how fundamental changes in the migrant's mode of life and opportunities will change his values and family attachments. Both risks might restrict a youthful migrant's access to family savings, though the normal altruism of families should assure that the extended family will be the primary source of funds used in migration. Changes in life-style might reasonably be disquieting to the migrant's elders, but the ability to bequeath these locational "benefits" to heirs makes migration unusual as a clear source of intergenerational externalities. Whatever summary measure of gain or return is associated with migration, it will be a very partial measure of the expected psychic, pecuniary, and opportunity costs and benefits, appropriately adjusted for risk.

## Relative or Absolute Differences in Earnings

There is no known unambiguous logic that implies that migration responds to either the difference or the ratio of earnings. It is simple to show, however, that this specification choice could depend on whether direct costs or opportunity costs of time are the primary deterrent to migration (DaVanzo, 1972). Neglecting consumption benefits from migration, the present value of migrating from region $i$ to $j$ can be expressed:

$$V_{ij} = \sum_{t=1}^{n} (W_{jt} - W_{it})/(1 + r)^t - C_{ij} - P_{ij} - T_{ij}W_{i1} \qquad (3)$$

where $W_{jt}$ and $W_{it}$ are the earnings opportunities available to the potential migrant in period $t$ in regions $j$ and $i$, respectively; $n$ is the retirement age minus the migrant's current age; $r$ is a constant discount rate; and $C_{ij}$, $P_{ij}$, and $T_{ij}$ are the direct, psychic, and time costs, respectively, of migrating from $i$ to $j$, all of which are assumed to be incurred in the initial period. Time costs are valued, in this example, at the initial period origin wage.

For simplicity it is assumed that regional wages do not vary over time and age, $t = 1, \ldots, n$; the internal rate of return, $r^*$, is then defined as that discount rate that equalizes the present value of current costs and annuity benefits.

$$C_{ij} + P_{ij} + T_{ij}W_i = (W_j - W_i)/(r^*(1 - r^*)^{-n}) \qquad (4)$$

Abstracting from the finiteness of the working life by letting $n$ approach infinity,

$$r^* = (W_j - W_i)/(C_{ij} + P_{ij} + T_{ij}W_i). \qquad (5)$$

If migration costs were only opportunity costs of forgone earnings during the period of relocation and job search, $C_{ij} = P_{ij} = 0$, the migration function might have as its arguments the ratio of wages minus one, and the reciprocal of the time units forgone by migration,

$$r^* = (1/T_{ij})\left(\frac{W_j}{W_i} - 1\right). \qquad (6)$$

However, if direct and psychic costs were the only costs of migration, and they were unrelated to origin or destination wages, i.e., $T_{ij} = 0$, then the absolute difference in earnings might be an argument in the migration decision function with the reciprocal of the direct costs:

$$r^* = (1/(C_{ij} + P_{ij}))(W_j - W_i). \qquad (7)$$

In both cases, the internal rate of return is expressed as a product of the arguments representing the cost and benefit components; actual specifications of these terms would, of course, depend on the nature of available data, but the rationale for a logarithmic specification of the migration decision function is clear in both Equations 6 and 7.

The proxy usually available for costs is that of distance from $i$ to $j$, which leaves much to be desired. And though direct costs, $C_{ij}$ and $P_{ij}$, are probably well-behaved monotonic functions of distance, the link to opportunity costs, $T_{ij}W_i$, is unclear. To approximate regional differences in $T_{ij}$ one needs added information on job turnover and an explicit model of how jobs are allocated.

## Private Internal Rates of Return to Migration

In contrast to the literature estimating earnings functions (Mincer, 1974), estimating parameter values associated with a migration function does not obviously tell one, even approximately, the internal rate of return to migration. But at a more descriptive level, the relative standard deviation (of the logarithms) of earnings across regions indicates the average magnitude of gains available to migrants in terms of time costs. The time costs in Equation 6 that determine the internal rate of return reflect the years of forgone earnings, valued at origin real wages, expended to progress to the destination real wage level. $T_{ij}$ is then not a period of total unemployment, but more accurately a discounted integral of time unemployed (actual $W_t = 0$) and "underemployed" ($W_t < W_j$), during which the migrant gradually closes the gap between his earnings and the "equilibrium" level received by long-term ($\lambda$ year) resident at the destination,

$$T_{ij} = \int_{t=0}^{\lambda} (W_j - W_t)(1 + \gamma)^{-t} \, dt, \tag{8}$$

where $\gamma$ is a rate of time preference.

In these simplified terms, interregional relative variation in wages within education, sex, and age groups is one measure of disequilibrium returns available to migrants.[9] For example, Tables 3.2, 3.3, and 3.4 present comparative statistics on wages and migration across regions for the United States and Venezuela. As observed earlier, migration notably increases with educational attainment. Despite the tendency for personal variation in earnings to increase with education,[10] the regional variation in earnings diminishes. For example, males with some primary schooling in Venezuela report a regional variation in wages of 0.22 in 1961 (Table 3.3). With a lognormal distribution of regional wages, a representative potential migrant residing in a state with an average level of wages would find about 16 percent of the alternative regions offering him a wage at least 22 percent greater than he currently receives. For males with some secondary schooling, a similar fraction of alternative regions would yield at least a 12 percent gain, and for those with some higher education, a comparably common gain would be less than 10 percent. If the time costs needed to obtain these destination average earnings were equivalent to one year, these percentage gains would also be approximately internal rates of return.[11]

The regularity of declining relative returns to migration with educational

Table 3.2. Level and Variation in Incomes and 5-Year Interdivisional
Migration Rates for Males Age 25–29 in the United States, 1960
(Arithmetic Weighted)

| | White | | Nonwhite | |
|---|---|---|---|---|
| | Mean | Standard Deviation | Mean | Standard Deviation |
| Expected Family Income ($/yr) by Years of Education | | | | |
| 0–4 years | 1859 | 520 | 1553 | 630 |
| 5–7 years | 3138 | 598 | 2122 | 637 |
| 8 years | 3871 | 576 | 2440 | 575 |
| 9–11 years | 4440 | 460 | 2733 | 536 |
| 12 years | 5175 | 393 | 3413 | 663 |
| 13–15 years | 4980 | 325 | 3479 | 766 |
| 16+ years | 5880 | 337 | 4341 | 497 |
| Gross Migration Rate 1955–1960 by Years of Education | | | | |
| 0–4 years | 8.64 | 11.2 | 6.02 | 8.83 |
| 5–7 years | 11.6 | 13.4 | 8.37 | 10.9 |
| 8 years | 14.0 | 14.0 | 11.1 | 15.4 |
| 9–11 years | 15.3 | 13.3 | 12.6 | 15.6 |
| 12 years | 17.8 | 13.9 | 16.9 | 18.5 |
| 13–15 years | 24.5 | 17.4 | 21.7 | 23.8 |
| 16+ years | 37.1 | 26.9 | 30.6 | 30.2 |

Source: DaVanzo, 1972, Table 9.

attainment in both countries confirms the notion that there are important
earnings differences among individuals in the market for human capital. Yet
it is still consistent with the working hypothesis that individuals, within their
capital constraints, equalize the returns they require from alternative human
capital investments. In a normal long-run equilibrium, the marginal rate of
return to human capital is thought to diminish for an individual as the quantity
invested is increased. Though this relationship is not necessarily observed in
a reduced form earnings function estimated across individuals (Becker, 1975),
it is noted in many countries that estimated "returns" to schooling are lower
for higher levels of education.[12]

The magnitude of returns to migration diminishes by 72 percent for both

Table 3.3. Levels and Variation in Male Wage and Lifetime Interstate
Migration Rates in Venezuela in 1961 Among Coterminous States

| | Arithmetic | | Logarithmic | |
|---|---|---|---|---|
| | Mean | Standard Deviation | Mean | Standard Deviation |
| *Monthly Average Wage Rates* | | | | |
| No schooling | 368 | 145 | 5.84 | 0.345 |
| Some Primary | 558 | 118 | 6.30 | 0.220 |
| Some Secondary | 1629 | 201 | 7.39 | 0.120 |
| Some Higher | 6119 | 530 | 8.71 | 0.096 |
| *Lifetime Average Migration Rates* | | | | |
| No Schooling | 1.03 | 2.26 | −1.43 | 1.74 |
| Some Primary | 1.61 | 3.39 | − .808 | 1.56 |
| Some Secondary | 3.03 | 6.57 | − .083 | 1.48 |
| Some Higher | 4.04 | 8.62 | .140 | 1.57 |
| *Nonmigration Rates* | | | | |
| No Schooling | 80.4 | 6.63 | 4.38 | 0.082 |
| Some Primary | 69.7 | 8.51 | 4.24 | 0.121 |
| Some Secondary | 42.4 | 12.3 | 3.71 | 0.276 |
| Some Higher | 23.7 | 15.4 | 2.97 | 0.590 |

*Source:* T. P. Schultz, 1975a, Table 4.

men and women in Venezuela from those with no schooling to those with
some higher schooling; the approximate decline in returns to migration between the extreme education classes of males age 25–29 in the United States
is about 80 percent for whites and 71 percent for nonwhites.[13] The puzzle
remains why the educated migrate more frequently although they derive
smaller rates of returns from their time investments. At least two hypotheses
warrant study: one, that greater ability of the better educated to process information reduces the risks of migration, or the time required to change jobs,
or both; the other, that the increased access to investable funds among the
better educated, perhaps because of family background, encourages them to
invest more in human capital formation, lowering the marginal return they
find acceptable.

Table 3.4.  Levels and Variation in Female Wage and Lifetime Interstate
Migration Rates in Venezuela in 1961 Among Coterminous States

|  | Arithmetic | | Logarithmic | |
|  | Mean | Standard Deviation | Mean | Standard Deviation |
|---|---|---|---|---|
| *Monthly Average Wage Rates* | | | | |
| No Schooling | 251 | 79.7 | 5.48 | .297 |
| Some Primary | 347 | 47.2 | 5.84 | .143 |
| Some Secondary | 912 | 79.2 | 6.81 | .085 |
| Some Higher | 1574 | 138 | 7.36 | .084 |
| *Lifetime Average Migration Rates* | | | | |
| No Schooling | 1.17 | 2.69 | −1.52 | 1.93 |
| Some Primary | 1.63 | 3.70 | −1.03 | 1.74 |
| Some Secondary | 2.63 | 5.62 | − .434 | 1.65 |
| Some Higher | 6.30 | 12.7 | .496 | 1.61 |
| *Nonmigration Rates* | | | | |
| No Schooling | 77.8 | 7.08 | 4.35 | .091 |
| Some Primary | 69.0 | 8.23 | 4.23 | .117 |
| Some Secondary | 51.9 | 10.8 | 3.93 | .221 |
| Some Higher | 22.6 | 17.7 | 2.90 | .807 |

*Source:*  Derived from Venezuelan Census of 1961 according to methods
reported in T. P. Schultz, 1975a.

## Expected Income Hypothesis

In the Harris-Todaro model of migration (Harris and Todaro, 1970), it is
assumed that potential migrants behave as though they maximized their expected earnings, defined as the product of their expected wage rate, and their
perceived probability of finding employment, expressed over time and discounted to present values. In determining who gets the available urban jobs,
it is assumed that all job-seekers have an equal chance, and consequently expected employment in each period is one minus the average unemployment
probability. Stiglitz (1972) showed that the same expression holds for the
expected urban wage in the absence of urban growth for either the queuing
model, in which individuals are hired in the order of urban arrival, or the
random selection Poisson model, in which individuals are hired irrespective
of their arrival times.

In a migration function in which the explanatory variables are expressed in logarithmic form, the expected income hypothesis implies that the coefficients of the logarithm of the wage rate and of the logarithm of the employment rate should be identical.[14] This is, of course, a severe empirical test of the expected income hypothesis. Nonetheless, the adequacy of the data or the model may be questioned if the destination employment rate coefficient is not positively and significantly associated with migration.

On the other hand, a number of factors might explain a tendency for the coefficient of the employment rate to exceed the coefficient of the wage rate. Fields (1975) has identified several such factors in explaining why the large gap between urban and rural wages has not contributed to even greater urban unemployment. First, a rural resident may have some positive probability of obtaining an urban job without first migrating to the city and incurring opportunity and real costs in job search. Second, "unemployed" urban workers may find low-paying jobs in the traditional urban sector, which do not bar them from searching for a better job but do reduce the opportunity costs of effective job search and lower the rate of urban *open* unemployment. Third, turnover of urban jobs can affect the equilibrium level of unemployment, as can modified forms of queuing or preferential treatment in hiring. Risk aversion, which is neglected in the expected income model, may also play a role if migrants emphasize the probability of employment more heavily than the expected wage rate. All of these modifications to the expected income hypothesis imply that the empirically estimated migration trade-off between the employment probability and the expected urban wage rate at destination will exceed unity.

## Uncertainty, Job Turnover, and Allocation

The strict Harris-Todaro expected income formulation (Harris and Todaro, 1970) neglects information on the period of job turnover, the duration of unemployment, and the manner in which the job-seeker responds to uncertainty in the labor market. Where more information is available on the functioning of regional labor markets, more satisfactory and rigorous testing of models of migration should be possible. Fields and Hosek (1975) have proposed a framework for interpreting turnover that characterizes the job allocation mechanism as a first-order Markov process, where the probability of being hired if unemployed and fired if employed is expected to be constant over time. Applying this model to migration, the expected earnings gained from migration is a function of $W[P_{ue}/(r + P_{ue} + P_{eu})] (1 + r)/r$, rather than $W(1 - U)/r$, as in the Harris-Todaro model, where $r$ is the discount rate, $W$ the real wage gain in urban compared with rural employment, $U$ the urban unemployment rate, and $P_{eu}$ and $P_{ue}$ are the probabilities of being fired if employed and of being hired if unemployed during the reference period, respectively. Clearly, the two formulations are the same when the current employment state does not influence the probability of next period employment, i.e., $P_{ue} = 1 - P_{eu} = P_{ee}$. Proxies for these probabilities have been drawn by Fields (1976) from monthly "layoffs" and "new hires" for Standard Metropolitan Statistical Areas (SMSAs) in an application of the framework to intermetropolitan U.S. migration. Empirical approximations for these concepts in low-income countries are not likely to be found in standard data sources, but the formulation could be a guide for future data generating efforts aimed at understanding the determinants of migration.

### Asymmetry of Origin and Destination Conditions

Additional considerations suggest that the treatment of employment conditions in origin and destination regions may be asymmetric. The potential migrant may anticipate that as a new arrival in the city he would encounter more than the average difficulty in finding work; and he may equally well discount origin unemployment, given his existing job, established contacts, and family ties. Consequently, origin employment coefficients would tend to be distinctly smaller than destination employment coefficients. This appears to be implicit in the Harris-Todaro formulation where rural employment probabilities are ignored or assumed equal to one (Harris and Todaro, 1970).

As an illiquid investment in the productivity of the human agent, migration is undoubtedly limited by imperfections in capital markets. The income or wealth of the potential migrant or his family is likely to augment his supply of investable funds and contribute to lowering the return he requires to migrate. This investable-funds effect of origin wage variables would offset, to some degree, the origin wage's restricting effect on out-migration. Origin wage variables therefore may be expected to have somewhat smaller (negative) coefficients in absolute value than the destination wage (positive) variables.[15]

Another common characterization of migration involves the selectivity with which migrants are drawn from their origin populations. Lee (1966) concluded that when the opportunities of the destination region prompt migration, migrants are positively selected, which could imply that better educated migrants would be more responsive to destination variables. Conversely, when deterioration in origin conditions stimulates out-migration, a negative selectivity arises, according to Lee, suggesting that greater weight should be given to origin conditions in the migration of less-educated groups. This selectivity hypothesis has not often been directly documented; testing for the asymmetry of origin and destination effects by education level is a start, although it does not do justice to the subtle dynamic considerations that may be important in Lee's interpretation of historical evidence. Yet, if Lee's reasoning is applicable, one would expect the positively selected highly educated migrant stream to respond more sensitively to destination effects.

## Urban-Rural Sectors

The comparability of real wage rates and employment opportunities in urban and rural sectors is hard to achieve with existing data from low-income countries. Employment levels are reportedly high in rural-agricultural regions, and lower in urban-industrial regions. Yet it is commonly assumed that the majority of self-employed workers in agriculture are less fully employed throughout the year than unrefined census data indicate (Turnham, 1971). Moreover, the greater frequency of payments in kind and lower prices of food and shelter in the rural sector understate *real* wage rates in comparison with urban. On the other hand, the prices of manufactured goods are somewhat lower in urban than in rural areas. Without relative price indices and confidence in the comparability of employment data in urban and rural sectors, wage and employment equations might be usefully estimated for both urban and rural sectors of each region. Migration should also be distinguished by rural and urban subareas within a region if feasible.

## School Enrollment Rates and Other Factors

Stratification of the migrant population by sex and educational attainment is essential to quantify the diverse effects of schooling on migratory behavior and to recognize explicitly the heterogeneity of labor. In addition, the educational opportunities of a location are often reported by migrants as an important reason for moving, for either their own or their children's access to improved schools (J. Nelson, 1970). Consequently, school enrollment rates may be considered as a measure of the region's provision of public sector services. Public housing, health, and other services may also influence the choice of migrants, though evidence of such effects is as yet impressionistic.

In many countries, military service shifts youth about the country, with lasting effects on their subsequent mobility. Migration of youth to obtain higher education has similar effects—once the educational goal is achieved, return migration requires a decisive break with established routines. All of these factors have not yet been explicitly incorporated into econometric studies of migration, though disaggregation by educational attainment provides a starting point for this analysis.

### The Rate of Natural Population Increase

One potentially important determinant of migration that may be amenable to social policy is the difference between regional birth and death rates. Regional differences in the rate of natural increase of the population stimulate migration to the extent that these differences do not correspond with regional employment growth. Population growth has often been greater in rural areas than in urban areas, and these rural areas have also frequently experienced slower growth in derived demands for labor. Consequently, both supply and demand shifts have contributed to the disequilibrium among regional labor markets. The partial equilibrium framework adopted here interprets employment conditions as motivating individuals to migrate, but does not attempt to determine how these conditions were produced by shifts in regional derived *demands* for labor and regional differences in natural increase in *supplies* of labor. Kuznets (1964), in his introductory essay to *Population Redistribution and Economic Growth, United States, 1870-1950,* concludes that "the effects of population increase are far less important than those of structural changes in the economy's productive system." But in understanding contemporary migration in developing countries, regional differences in population increase may no longer by secondary to changes in the structure of production (T. P. Schultz, 1969, 1975a). Exploration of population growth effects on migration would seem to require a broader general equilibrium approach to internal migration and development.

### Can Migration and Destination Be Independent?

Before turning in the next section to a statistical framework for the study of migration determinants, the limitations of the dependent variable and the ambiguous meaning of regional population size require discussion. The dependent variable is the probability of migration from region $i$ to region $j$, $P_{ij}$, or given independence of individual movement, a consistent estimator of this probability is the gross migration rate.[16]

The longer the period over which migration is observed, the more serious are various measurement problems. Differential mortality among migrants and nonmigrants can probably be neglected except perhaps for lifetime migration rates. The importance of repeat and return migration varies greatly from setting to setting. The migrant's birthplace, which is the starting point for lifetime migration data, may not be the place of permanent residence, particularly where regional units are small and municipal hospitals provide maternity services for dispersed populations. More serious, however, is the measurement error introduced by the passage of time over which concurrent employment and wage conditions may be inadequately measured.

Differences in the population size of regions make it difficult to infer with confidence what factors cause regional rates of migration to vary. This will be evident later when a rationale for the gravity formulation for the study of migration is sought. The normalization of migration to a probability or a gross rate seems unavoidable. Once an individual migration probability function has been specified, no more difficulty attaches to aggregating over individuals to obtain a gross regional migration rate than is encountered in deriving aggregate relations in other areas of discrete consumer choice.[17]

Although origin and destination population size have long been interpreted as determinants of migration flows in the literature using the gravity model, this presumption is not without its pitfalls. For example, many "gravity" studies account for past migration in terms of *current* population size variables.[18] Since migrants are counted in current destination populations and excluded from current origin populations, a positive and negative definitional correlation (bias) is introduced that distorts any time-ordered association between migration and population size variables. This bias can be particularly serious when migration is measured over substantial periods, and in settings where migration is "efficient" or flows are predominantly in one direction.[19] By redefining population size variables ex ante as the number of persons born in the region this definitional bias can be removed (T. P. Schultz, 1975a), but there remains another, more subtle, bias that arises from the persistence of interregional patterns of development and population growth.

Populous regions are frequently so because they contain early centers of commerce, industrialization, and urbanization and have consequently attracted a net inflow of migrants. When migrants continue to gravitate toward more populous regions, this may not be due to the larger numbers of persons in the destination regions, as implied by the gravity model, but only to a persistence of unobserved economic variables that influence migration.[20] The regions with large populations once had the prerequisites to amass a large population, and these advantages, if eroded at all, appear to be eroded slowly by the development process. Caution must be exercised, therefore, in interpreting the coefficient of the destination population size variable, for it may reflect a "size effect" or the effect of many omitted regionally persistent variables. An improved dynamic approach to migration flows over time and across regions will be required to resolve this ambiguity.[21]

## A STATISTICAL MODEL

The objective here is to specify a set of relationships that describe how the mutually exclusive and exhaustive probabilities of migration, including the outcome of not migrating, depend on a set of conditioning variables. One model for such a phenomenon is the polytomous logistic or log linear model, as applied in bioassay for a number of years (Mantel, 1966; Cox, 1970) and more recently in economics (McFadden, 1968; Theil, 1969). In particular, Domencich and McFadden's (1976) study of consumer choice among urban transportation modes is analogous to the problem analyzed here. They provided a theoretical basis for studying individual choice among discrete alternatives within the traditional framework of economic rationality and utility maximization. Differences among individuals in tastes or utility functions are posited in a stochastic form, providing an economic link between observed discrete choices individuals make and attributes of the alternatives and observable traits of individual decision makers.

An individual is confronted with $n$ alternative locations in which to reside including his origin location (e.g., birthplace), denoted by subscript $i$. The probability that he resides in location $j$ in a specific time period is assumed to depend on a vector of weighted personal and regional characteristics, $Z_{ij}$, as follows:

$$P_{ij} = \frac{e^{Z_{ij}}}{\sum_{j=1}^{n} e^{Z_{ij}}}, \quad \begin{matrix} i = 1, \ldots, n \\ j = 1, \ldots, n \end{matrix} \tag{9}$$

where for each region of origin, probabilities sum to one:

$$1 = \sum_{j=1}^{n} P_{ij} \qquad i = 1, \ldots, n. \tag{10}$$

The odds ratio of any two probabilities implied by this specification is independent of the characteristics of other (hence, irrelevant) locations. Though this lack of differential substitutability or complementarity between alternatives may appear to be a shortcoming of the polytomous logistic model, this functional specification provides a flexible and symmetric way to treat multiple choice situations and implies a plausible, if not ideal, characterization of the determination of interregional migration.[22]

A possible specification of $Z_{ij}$ would be a linear function in natural logarithms[23] of the pertinent characteristics of the origin and destination regions, $X_i$ and $X_j$; the average distance between persons in the two regions, $D_{ij}$; and individual traits associated with susceptibility to migration, $Y_i$. Where theoretical guidance on scaling of $Y$s is limited and the effect of a trait, such as education, is thought to operate in conjunction with the $X$s and $D_{ij}$, stratification of the population according to these traits is a reasonable research strategy. Homogeneity restrictions on parameter estimates across groups defined by such variables as age, sex, and educational attainment may then be tested.

$$Z_{ij} = \alpha + \sum_{k=1}^{K} \beta_k \ln X_{ki} + \sum_{k=1}^{K} \gamma_k \ln X_{kj} + \delta \ln D_{ij} \quad \begin{matrix} i = 1, \ldots, n \\ j = 1, \ldots, n \end{matrix} \tag{11}$$

where $\alpha$, $\delta$ and $\beta_k$, $\gamma_k$ for $k = 1, \ldots, K$ are the $2K + 2$ parameters of the migration probability function for each stratum of the population. Restrictions may be considered to reduce the number of independent parameters for estimation. First, however, this framework may be elaborated to allow for structural differences between the process that determines whether a potential migrant leaves his origin location and where he relocates, if he does migrate.

The above "uniform" specification of migration as a single integrated decision process provides one way for considering migration probabilities, $P_{ij}$, where $i \neq j$, but neglects complications that might arise with nonmigration, namely the occurrence of $P_{ii}$.[24]

A general "two stage" view of migration might assume all response parameters in the process determining *non*migration are distinct, indicated by asterisks:

$$Z_{ii} = \alpha^* + \sum_{k=1}^{K} (\beta_k^* + \gamma_k^*) \ln X_{ki} \qquad i = 1, \ldots, n \qquad (12)$$

whereas the $Z_{ij}$ for $i \neq j$ are still determined according to Equation 11.

Another modification to the migration model may be denoted the "symmetry" hypothesis, in which origin and destination conditions are thought to exert equal but opposite effects (elasticities) on the probability of migration, namely $\beta_k = -\gamma_k$, $k = 1, \ldots, K$. It follows that only the ratio of origin to destination conditions then matter:

$$Z_{ij} = \alpha + \sum_{k=1}^{K} \beta_k \ln (X_{ki}/X_{kj}) + \delta \ln D_{ij} \qquad \begin{matrix} i = 1, \ldots, n \\ j = 1, \ldots, n \\ i \neq j \end{matrix} \qquad (13)$$

$$Z_{ii} = \alpha^* \qquad i = 1, \ldots, n. \qquad (14)$$

Clearly, certain factors may be symmetric and others not; these may be tested as restrictions on the estimated parameters.

## Estimation

The uniform polytomous logistic model of migration, summarized in Equations 9, 10, and 11, can be estimated by maximum likelihood techniques based on individual or grouped data. It has been shown that when the likelihood function for this model converges to a maximum it will be a unique maximum (McFadden 1968). Information on migration frequencies can also be obtained from tabulations of large surveys or censuses. For those cells in which the expected migration probability is greater than zero and less than one, the polytomous logistic model can be estimated by ordinary least squares.

In order to impose the $n$ adding-up constraints in Equation 10, it is convenient to express the migration probabilities as ratios. The nonmigrant probability, $P_{ii}$, can be used as the normalizing factor. Taking logarithms of these probability or odds ratios, one obtains the linear estimation equation:

$$\ln (P_{ij}/P_{ii}) = Z_{ij} - Z_{ii} \qquad \begin{aligned} i &= 1, \ldots, n \\ j &= 1, \ldots, n \\ i &\neq j \end{aligned} \tag{15}$$

which becomes for the "uniform model":

$$\ln (P_{ij}/P_{ii}) = \sum_{k=1}^{K} \gamma_k \ln (X_{kj}/X_{ki}) + \delta \ln D_{ij}. \tag{16}$$

Thus, aggregate estimates of the uniform model provide no direct information on $\alpha$ (no intercept) or $\beta_k$ (origin effects), and rationalize a "symmetric" treatment of origin and destination conditions as ratios.

When nonmigration is not restricted to be a response to the parameter vector allocating migrants among destination, the "two-step" model can be estimated,

$$\ln (P_{ij}/P_{ii}) = (\alpha - \alpha^*) + \sum_{k=1}^{K} (\beta_k - \beta_k^* - \gamma_k^*) \ln X_{ki}$$

$$+ \sum_{k=1}^{K} \gamma_k \ln X_{kj} + \delta \ln D_{ij}. \tag{17}$$

Estimates of Equation 17 permit a test of the hypothesis earlier advanced that migration should be approached as two separate decisions—whether and where to migrate. Where one finds that the regression coefficients of $\ln X_{ki}$ are of approximately equal absolute value but opposite sign to the coefficients of $\ln X_{kj}$, one could impose the restriction of symmetry, replacing the origin and destination variables with their ratio as in Equation 13. However, $F$ tests of coefficient equality (Fisher, 1970), or likelihood ratio tests for maximum likelihood estimators, would not actually test whether both $\beta_k = \beta_k^*$ and $\gamma_k = \gamma_k^*$, but only test whether $(\beta_k - \beta_k^* - \gamma_k^*) = \gamma_k$. Incremental tests could be calculated for the hypothesis that $\alpha = \alpha^*$.

The symmetry hypothesis is implied, as observed above, by the uniform polytomous logistic model. Moreover, the only change in the aggregate estimation Equation 16 when a distinct nonmigration parameterization is assumed with symmetry is the addition of an intercept term, $\alpha - \alpha^*$. Should this intercept be negative, nonmigration tends to occur more frequently than predicted by the uniform model of migration. The existence of an "inertia" (negative) or "wanderlust" (positive) effect would seem to be a suggestive distinction between the uniform and two-stage migration formulations.

Nested tree decision models may also be constructed that are consistent with the logit formulation but seem particularly well suited to the study of migration as a segmented process. McFadden (1974) showed that in such cases it is possible to apply a moderate cost stepwise estimation procedure, estimating by stages the conditional probabilities proceeding from the final stage to the initial stage. In the case of migration polytomous logit estimates are first estimated for the decision of destination conditional on migrating, and then second stage estimates are obtained by fitting a binary logit model for whether migration or nonmigration occurs. The performance of the uniform and the nested tree decision models can then be compared in terms of likelihood ratios to determine goodness of statistical fit.

### The Gravity Model of Migration

Most empirical research on migration has applied some modification of the "social interactions" or "gravity-type" model of interregional migration. Similarities and differences between the polytomous logistic and the gravity model should therefore be noted. The gravity framework presumes that aggregate gross flows of migration from one location to another are directly proportional to the population in the origin *and* destination, inversely proportional to the distance between regions, and perhaps conditional on other attributes of origin and destination, measured as differences or ratios.

$$M_{ij} = N_i P_{ij} = \frac{N_i^{g_1} N_j^{g_2}}{D_{ij}^{g_3}} Z(\cdot) \qquad \begin{array}{l} i = 1, \ldots, n \\ j = 1, \ldots, n \\ i \neq j \end{array} \qquad (18)$$

where $M_{ij}$ is the gross aggregate number of migrants going from $i$ to $j$, and $N_i$ and $N_j$ are the number of persons initially residing in regions $i$ and $j$, respectively; $Z(\cdot)$ is a migration function of other attributes of regions $i$ and $j$ including an intercept; and $g_1$, $g_2$, and $g_3$ are parameters.

Frequently $g_1$ is restricted to one, and the gravity model is rearranged to obtain an estimation equation where the dependent variable is the gross migration rate.[25]

$$\ln P_{ij} = a + \sum_{k=1}^{K} b_k \ln X_{ki} + \sum_{k=1}^{K} c_k \ln X_{kj} + d \ln D_{ij} \qquad \begin{array}{l} i = 1, \ldots, n \\ j = 1, \ldots, n \\ i \neq j \end{array} \qquad (19)$$

where $a$, $b_k$, $c_k$, and $d$ are analogous to the logistic parameters obtained by least squares, and $N_i$ and $N_j$ may be contained in the vector of regional attributes $X_{ki}$ and $X_{kj}$. In this formulation the parameters obtained from Equation 19 can be interpreted in terms of an individual migration probability model, although predicted "probabilities" may exceed one.

In addition, the gravity model assumes that migration varies in proportion to the size of the destination population, in other words, that the elasticity of migration with respect to destination population size is constant; some studies also restrict this elasticity to one.[26] It is difficult to derive this responsiveness to destination population from behavioral assumptions although this is attempted by Niedercorn and Bechdolt (1969). It is also difficult to devise an appropriate test for this normalization procedure as implied by the gravity model, because serial correlation over time in the unexplained component of migration (i.e., the disturbance) is likely to yield high and misleading correlations between initial population size and current migration in a single cross section.

Finally, the gravity model does not make use of the information contained in the relative frequency of nonmigration, $P_{ii}$; the $n$ adding-up constraints that are incorporated into the logistic model by means of Equation 10 imply residual estimates of $P_{ii}$ for the gravity model, but these have not been reported before.[27]

It may be noted that the gravity formulation, as estimated by Equation 19, could yield similar estimates to the logistic model (as in Equation 16), if the $P_{ii}$ were the same magnitude for all $i$ ($i = 1, \ldots, n$), and the same characteristics were specified in the vector of determinants, $X_k$. In the limit, as the unit of time diminished over which migration is measured, the $P_{ii}$s would approach one, and differences between these two model specifications would tend to diminish. The observed "good fit" of migration data to the gravity model would tentatively suggest that the logistic model will also provide a better fit to data when determinant characteristics are expressed in logarithms, as they are here, rather than in conventional units.

## CONCLUSION

Several conceptual, empirical, and statistical problems of the framework commonly applied in the empirical study of internal migration in low-income countries have been reviewed in this chapter. Some of the specification problems discussed are sufficiently serious that available parameter estimates are not particularly helpful, either in considering policies or in understanding underlying individual behavior. A priority in this field would therefore seem to be to move toward a somewhat more satisfactory statistical and empirical specification of the migration function that would then be applied more uniformly across countries. Much richer characterizations of the institutional operation of labor markets will be required, and demands will grow for new and better data. A promising route for obtaining these multidimensional data is the household survey representing all national labor markets. The optimal degree of aggregation for final estimation, however, may not be the individual or family. But it is strongly felt that the closer one gets to the individual decision unit, the less serious will be many of the problems discussed here.

## NOTES

1. Migration has not only been analyzed as a long-term human capital investment (Sjaastad, 1962); it has also been interpreted as a select response of more energetic and adaptable individuals to the changing distribution of economic activity (Kuznets, 1964) and as the summation of presumably asymmetric "push and pull" factors associated with individuals and their environment (Lee, 1966). All of these approaches reduce more formally to maximization by the individual of the present (discounted) value of future streams of benefits minus costs (opportunity, direct, and psychic), subject to his limited knowledge of the world and his preferences. Consumption benefits would also matter, in terms not only of the amenities of the environment but also of the actual consumption effects of migration itself. Clearly upon retirement from the labor force, locational choice is likely to emphasize such environmental amenities and relative prices and deemphasize labor market opportunities. Migration for retirement purposes must be relatively unimportant in developing countries, given their age composition and income level.

2. After retirement, labor-market production attributes of a location are largely displaced by consumption attributes, contributing to a second post-retirement wave of migration in some, generally affluent, societies. Here the primary concern is with the regional reallocation of labor up to the retirement age.

3. Assume, for example, that a person enjoyed a constant certain-dollar premium on his annual wage by migrating. With a 5 percent discount rate, these potential income streams would have a present value of about $16.40 if retirement were thirty-five years off, and $17.80 if forty-five years off. If a 9 percent differential explained a 50 percent reduction in migration rates between ages twenty and thirty, then a similar degree of responsiveness would be expected for migration between alternative destinations that exhibited 9 percent differences in wage-employment opportunities. Such interregional responsiveness of migration is uncommon.

4. See, for example, Caldwell (1968, 1969), Lee (1970), Schwartz (1971), and DaVanzo (1972). In Venezuela around 1961 lifetime migration rates increased in all twenty-one states without exception for men and for women as educational attainment increased across four classes (T. P. Schultz, 1975a).

5. Since it is assumed that comparable labor is paid different wages in different sectors of the economy in many models of the development process, it is surprising how little firm evidence appears to exist on the quantitative importance of such "dual labor markets" and their institutionally maintained factor price distortions between rural and urban, craft and modern, informal and formal sectors of a low-income economy.

6. There are at least two sources of selectivity bias that are not readily eliminated from such an empirical exercise. First, persons who migrate are different from those who do not, for no other reason than that they nonrandomly chose to migrate. Stratifying by age, sex, and educational attainment

reduces the differences between migrants and nonmigrants, but is not likely to eliminate it completely. Probably there remains some positive selectivity, and therefore, the fortunes of migrants are better than what nonmigrants might reasonably expect to have were they to migrate. Second, those persons observed in the labor force are not a random sample of all persons of that age, sex, and educational attainment group. They might be recipients of higher wage offers than those not in the labor force, and therefore this exercise would attribute to all potential migrants (potential participants and nonparticipants) an upward biased wage offer.

7. Urban unemployment may play a role governing the rate of rural-urban migration, where urban wages are inflexible downward and urban jobs must be rationed (Todaro, 1969). The Todaro assumption warrants more explicit empirical testing than it has received. The expected income (utility) hypothesis invoked to allow the evaluation and calculation of expected present values implies restrictive behavioral assumptions that need not be imposed in modeling migration.

8. There is also a study by DaVanzo (1976) that performs a similar exercise with U.S. data, but she proceeds much further in refining issues relating to the husband's and wife's joint interest in family migration.

9. Many additional productive attributes of a labor force might differ across regions and explain interregional earnings differentials. As noted in the discussion of estimating wage and employment functions, other variables such as ability or quality of schooling belong in these reduced-form equations. The hazard of controlling for other characteristics is that they will be, to a greater degree, endogenous and hence bias other estimates, or that they become so collinear with each other that individual parameters and their statistical significance may lose reliability.

10. For the United States see Mincer (1974). Evidence from other countries is widely scattered, with some exceptions being found within narrow advanced specialties, for example, in the Netherlands. But across general educational classes with no less than five years of working experience, the tendency for relative variance to increase with education seems common.

11. One might expect that regions with very different wages would also tend to be separated by greater distances, or have other countervailing factors responsible for some portion of the wage gap. Another approach to estimating internal rates of return from wage relatives might be to seek to explain this relative variation and regard the standard deviation of the residual in such a model as a measure of unexplained regional variation that might warrant interregional migration. The residual in this wage model might then be entered as an argument in a migration decision function.

12. It has been suggested, however, that where institutionally inflexible supply bottlenecks have created a scarcity of the highly trained, and demand conditions have expanded rapidly, such as in contemporary Brazil, earnings disparities have widened and large rents raise the returns to higher education.

13. In the study by DaVanzo (1972) the standard deviation of the logarithms of earnings is not reported; the approximation used here is simply the ratio of the arithmetic standard deviation to the arithmetic mean.

14. Replacing the wage and employment variable with its product, an $F$ or likelihood ratio test can be performed to test the restriction of coefficient equality on the two variables. Regression studies of migration, though often in double log specification, consider the unemployment rate and not the employment rate.

15. This argument is elaborated by DaVanzo (1972) and tested against U.S. interdivisional gross migration flows. Greenwood (1971b) found rural origin income effects were even positive on Indian migration to cities. In Venezuela one would expect that the capital market constraint would be most frequently binding in the case of the migration of the least educated. Therefore, the ratio of destination to origin wage coefficients should be greatest for this group; this result was confirmed (T. P. Schultz, 1975a).

16. Some studies of gross migration rates appear to use in the denominator the population currently resident in the $j$th state. See, for example, Levy and Wadycki (1972a).

17. A case can be made for weighting aggregate observations according to the size of the population of origin to increase efficiency in estimation. The differences in origin size are viewed as affecting the variance of the observed regional migration rate, which is itself sampled from a particular time period. Larger regions should exhibit less sampling variation in gross migration rates over time, other things being equal, and therefore are weighted more heavily in a generalized least squares estimation procedure. In practice, in the linear case all variables are multiplied by the square root of the origin population size (or the denominator in the dependent variable rate). Since the appropriate weighting scheme differs between the gravity and logistic models, unweighted estimates also are attractive (Cox, 1970). This entails only a modest loss of efficiency, given the large sample sizes, and should not introduce bias (Theil, 1969).

18. This would appear to be the procedure followed by Beals et al. (1967), Greenwood (1969b, 1971a), Levy and Wadycki (1972a, 1974a), and Sahota (1968), among others.

19. Migration is called "efficient" if the net migration flow from one point to another is large relative to the sum of the gross migration flows occurring in both directions. In low-income countries, migration tends to be more efficient (undirectional), particularly among the less educated. See related discussions by Lee (1970), Sjaastad (1962), and Schwartz (1971).

20. In several studies the prior stock of migrants has been considered as a determinant of current migration, using single equation estimation techniques. The effect of this variable is rationalized in terms of information flows or the effects of friends and family on migrant destination choice. But in this case, even more clearly than with population size variables, the prior migrant stock is an endogenous variable, and by not treating it with simultaneous equation techniques, the migration equation is seriously biased. Not surprisingly, the prior migrant stock explains current migration flows in both the United States and Venezuela very well. See P. Nelson (1959), Greenwood (1969a), and Levy and Wadycki (1973).

21. One way to test this hypothesis concerning the appropriate interpre-

tation of destination population size effects is to pool a time series of cross sections on interregional migration. The disturbance in the estimated migration equation could then be partitioned into region-specific and random components using the procedure first proposed by Balestra and Nerlove (1966). This more appropriate dynamic estimation approach would probably "wash out" the effect of both destination and origin population size variables. It would also, in all likelihood, reduce the magnitude of the coefficients of other variables that are highly serially correlated over time in the cross section. See T. P. Schultz (1973).

22. For example, one suspects that changes in the employment opportunities in Baltimore influence the number of persons from Philadelphia migrating to Washington, D.C. vis-à-vis to New York City. The cross substitution effect of Baltimore is probably greater on the Washington flow of migrants than on the New York City flow. On the other hand, changes in employment opportunities in Seattle might leave these specific flows unchanged. How the spatial organization of locations or the geographic spread of information about locations affects patterns of migration is frequently discussed in the literature, but this complication has not yet been resolved in a convincing and empirically tractable way. Levy and Wadycki (1974a) have attempted, in the context of a gravity model of migration, to operationalize Stouffer's (1940) concept of "intervening opportunities" as a determinant of interregional migration. In most low-income countries there are relatively few urban centers of growth and most have clear rural migration watersheds. Completely heterogeneous interregional migration flows with substantial cross substitution effects may be less of a problem, therefore, for the type of analysis proposed here.

23. The logarithmic form of $Z_{ij}$ is preferred for several reasons. First, the expected wage hypothesis posits multiplicative interaction between wage rates and employment rates, which is readily translated into parameter restrictions on the logarithmic variables. Second, if opportunity costs are the major costs of migration, the ratio of expected incomes in two regions approximates the return to migration between these regions (DaVanzo, 1972). Third, the empirical literature on migration has generally fit double log-linear equations permitting more nearly direct comparisons. Finally, the logarithmic form of $Z_{ij}$ explains more of the variance than other forms, such as a linear form.

24. There is first a problem of measurement. If all regions contain the same area and populations, the nonmigrant probabilities might be treated simply as an adding up constraint, implied by Equation 10. But if regions differ in size, larger ones would encompass a larger share of all changes in residence within their own boundaries, augmenting the frequency of *measured* nonmigration. One anticipates, therefore, that $N_i$ origin initial population (or perhaps jobs or area) would be positively correlated with nonmigration as a consequence of measurement conventions, other things being equal. It should be noted, however, that since unobserved socioeconomic determinants of migration may also be correlated with such a "size" variable, the measurement

effect alluded to here may be swamped by other correlated past and concurrent variables. In analysis of Venezuelan migration data it was found that the parameter estimate for the region's "size" was not negative, as anticipated, but positive and sometimes statistically significant at conventional levels.

25. An exception is Sahota's (1968) study of Brazilian migration that relies largely on double log regressions using as his dependent variable gross lifetime migration flows among the Brazilian states as recorded in the 1950 census. Although he interprets his findings in terms of individual responsiveness of migration to a host of variables, it is not clear how he can relate his estimates to the microeconomic behavioral model posited at the outset of his investigation. Sahota's specification also contradicts the classical assumption of homoscedastic disturbances in the regression equation, and since the origin of population size tends to be correlated with other determinants of migration, bias as well as loss of efficiency occurs (T. P. Schultz, 1969). For these reasons no parallels are sought between his study of Brazilian migration circa 1950 and the investigation of Venezuelan migration (T. P. Schultz, 1975a) as of 1961. Greenwood (1969b) also analyzes gross migration flows in Egypt.

26. See Greenwood (1971b) or, in arithmetic form, Vanderkamp (1971). Most applications, however, estimate $g_2$ independently, and generally obtain positive values of less than one (Beals et al., 1967; Levy and Wadycki, 1972a, 1972b, 1974b). But, as noted earlier, there are problems in interpreting these estimates.

27. The coefficient of determination $(R^2)$ is not immediately useful for comparing the fit of the logistic and gravity models of migration, since their dependent variables differ. The logistic estimates of Equation 11 or 16 can be readily converted into predicted values for all $P_{ij}$ and these compared with the $n^2$ observed values. Similarly, estimates of the gravity model obtained from Equation 19 and the implied estimates for $P_{ii}$ $(i = 1, \ldots, n)$, though not necessarily values on the 0–1 interval, can be compared with observed gross migration rates. Since both models are derived from logarithmic estimation equations, a plausible criterion for fit might be the mean squared relative error.

## BIBLIOGRAPHY

Anderson, B.A. "The Effects of Characteristics of the Province of Birth on the Decision to Migrate and the Choice of Migration Destination: The Case of Late 19th Century European Russia." Mimeo. Yale and Princeton, October 1974.

Balestra, P., and Nerlove, M. "Pooling Cross-Section and Time Series in the Estimation of a Dynamic Model: The Demand for Natural Gas." *Econometrica* 34, no. 3 (July 1966).

Barnum, H., and Sabot, R. H. "Education, Employment Probabilities and Rural-Urban Migration In Tanzania." International Bank for Reconstruction and Development, 1975.

____."Education Employment Probabilities and Rural-Urban Migration in Tanzania." *Oxford Bulletin of Economics and Statistics* 39, no. 2 (May 1977).

Beals, R. E., Levy, M. B., and Moses, L. N. "Rationality and Migration in China." *Review of Econ. and Statistics* 49, no. 4 (November 1967), pp. 480–486.

Becker, G. S. *Human Capital.* New York: Columbia University Press, 2nd edition, 1975.

Ben-Porath, Y. "The Production of Human Capital and the Life Cycle of Earnings." *Journal of Political Economy* 75, no. 4 (August 1967).

Browning, H. L., and Feindt, W. "Selectivity of Migrants to a Metropolis in a Developing Country: A Mexican Case Study." *Demography* 6, no. 4 (November 1969), pp. 347–357.

Caldwell, J. C. "Determinants of Rural-Urban Migration in Ghana." *Population Studies* 22, no. 3 (November 1968), pp. 361–377.

____. *African Rural-Urban Migration.* New York: Columbia University Press, 1969.

Cerrutti, R. G., and Kar, S. B. *Venezuela: Country Profile.* New York: The Population Council, June 1975.

Chen, C. Y. *Movimientos Migratorios en Venezuela.* Caracas: Instituto de Investigaciones Economicas de la Universidad Catolica Andres Bello, 1968.

Childers, V. E. *Human Resources Development: Venezuela.* Bloomington: International Development Research Center, Indiana University, 1974.

Corden, W. M., and Findlay, R. "Urban Unemployment, Intersectoral Capital Mobility and Development Policy." *Economica* 42, no. 165 (February 1975), pp. 59–78.

Cox, D. R. *The Analysis of Binary Data.* London: Methuen & Co., Ltd., 1970.

DaVanzo, J. *Family Migration Decision: An Econometric Model.* Santa Monica, Calif.: The Rand Corp., R-1972, 1976.

____. "A Family Choice Model of U.S. Interregional Migration Based on the Human Capital Approach." Santa Monica, Calif.: The Rand Corp., P-4815, April 1972.

Domencich, T., and McFadden, D. *Urban Travel Demand: A Behavioral Analysis.* Amsterdam: Charles River Associates Inc. Research Monograph, North Holland Press, 1976.

Elizaga, J. C. "Migracion Diferencial en Algunas Regiones y Ciudades de la Americana Latina, 1940–1950." In *Centro Latinoamericano de Demografia.* Santiago, Chile: 1963.

____. "Assessment of Migration Data in Latin America." *Milbank Memorial Fund Quarterly* 43, no. 1 (January 1965), pp. 76–106.

Fei, J., and Ranis, G. "A Theory of Economic Development." *American Economic Review* 51, no. 4 (September 1961), pp. 533–565.

Fields, G. S. "Rural-Urban Migration, Urban Unemployment and Underemployment, and Job Search Activity in LDC's." *Journal of Development Economics* 2, no. 2 (1975), pp. 165–187.

___. "Labor Force Migration: Tests of a Markovian Approach." *Review of Economics and Statistics* 58, no. 4 (1976).

Fields, G. S., and Hosek, J. R. "A Markovian Approach to Long Run Labor Market Decisions." Mimeo. Yale University, October 1975.

Fisher, F. M. "Tests of Equality between Sets of Coefficients in Two Linear Regressions: An Expository Note." *Econometrica* 38, no. 2 (March 1970), pp. 361–366.

Greenwood, M. J. "An Analysis of the Determinants of Geographic Mobility in the United States." *Review of Economics and Statistics* 51 (May 1969a), pp. 189–194.

___. "The Determinants of Labor Migration in Egypt." *Journal of Regional Science* 9 (August 1969b), pp. 283–290.

___. "An Analysis of the Determinants of Internal Labor Mobility in India." *Annals of Regional Science* 5, no. 1 (June 1971a), pp. 137–151.

___. "A Regression Analysis of Migration to Urban Areas of a Less Developed Country: The Case of India." *Journal of Regional Science* 11, no. 2 (August 1971b), pp. 253–262.

Harris, J. R., and Todaro, M. P. "Migration, Unemployment and Development: A Two-Sector Analysis." *American Economic Review* 60, no. 1 (March 1970), pp. 126–142.

Hay, M. J. "An Economic Analysis of Rural-Urban Migration in Tunisia." Unpublished Ph.D. dissertation, University of Minnesota, June 1974.

Heckman, J. J., and Willis, R. J. "Estimation of a Stochastic Model of Reproduction." In *Household Production and Consumption,* edited by Nestor E. Terleckyj (New York: National Bureau of Economic Research, 1975), volume 40 of *Studies in Income and Wealth.*

Kuznets, S. "Introduction: Population Redistribution, Migration and Economic Growth." In H. T. Eldridge and D. S. Thomas, *Population Redistribution and Economic Growth, United States, 1870–1950,* Vol. III. Philadelphia: American Philosophical Society, 1964.

___. *Economic Growth of Nations.* Cambridge, Mass.: Harvard University Press, 1971.

Lee, E. S. "A Theory of Migration." *Demography* 3, no. 1 (1966), pp. 47–57.

___. "Migration in Relation to Education, Intellect and Social Structure." *Population Index* 36, no. 4 (October–December 1970), pp. 437–444.

Levy, M. E., and Wadycki, W. J. "Lifetime Versus One-Year Migration in Venezuela." *Journal of Regional Science* 12 (December 1972a), pp. 407–415.

___. "A Comparison of Young and Middle-Aged Migration in Venezuela." *The Annals of Regional Science* 6, no. 2 (December 1972b), pp. 73–85.

___. "The Influence of Family and Friends on Geographic Labor Mobility: An International Comparison." *Review of Economics and Statistics* 55, no. 2 (May 1973), pp. 198–203.

___. "What is the Opportunity Cost of Moving: Reconsideration of the Effect of Distance on Migration." *Economic Development and Cultural Change* 22, no. 2 (January 1974a), pp. 198–214.

____. "Education and the Decision to Migrate: An Econometric Analysis of Migration in Venezuela." *Econometrica* 42 (March 1974b), pp. 377–388.

Lewis, A. "Development with Unlimited Supplies of Labor." *The Manchester School* 22 (May 1954).

Lipton, M. "Migration from Rural Areas of Poor Countries: The Impact on Rural Productivity and Income Distribution." Prepared for workshop on Rural-Urban Labor Market Interactions, International Bank for Reconstruction and Development, Washington, D.C., February 5–7, 1976.

Lowry, I. S. *Migration and Metropolitan Growth: Two Analytical Models.* San Francisco: Chandler Publishing Company, 1966.

McFadden, D. "The Revealed Preferences of a Government Bureaucracy." Department of Economics, University of California, Berkeley, Tech. Dept. 17, November 1968.

____. "Conditional Logit Analysis of Qualitative Choice Behavior." In P. Zarembka (ed.), *Frontiers in Econometrics.* New York: Academic Press, 1974.

Mantel, N. "Models for Complex Contingency Tables and Polychotomous Dosage Response Curves." *Biometrics* 22, no. 1 (March 1966), pp. 83–94.

Mincer, J. *Schooling, Experience and Earnings.* New York: Columbia University Press, 1974.

Morrison, P. A. "Chronic Movers and the Future Redistribution of Population: A Longitudinal Analysis." Santa Monica, Calif.: The Rand Corporation, October 1970, p. 440.

Morse, R. M. "Trends and Issues in Latin American Urban Research, 1965–1970, Part II." *Latin American Research Review* (Summer 1971), pp. 19–75.

Mortensen, D. T. "Job Search, the Duration of Unemployment, and the Phillips Curve." *American Economic Review* 60, no. 5 (December 1970), pp. 847–862.

Nelson, J. "Peasants in the City: Migration, Urban Poverty and Politics in New Nations." *World Politics* (April 1970).

Nelson, P. "Migration, Real Income and Information." *Journal of Regional Science* 1 (Spring 1959), pp. 43–74.

Niedercorn, J. H., and Bechdolt, B. V., Jr. "An Economic Derivation of the 'Gravity Law' of Spatial Interaction." *Journal of Regional Science* 9, no. 2 (August 1969), pp. 273–282.

O'Neill, June A. "The Effect of Income and Education on Inter-Regional Migration." Unpublished Ph.D. dissertation, Columbia University, 1970.

Ravenstein, E. G. "The Laws of Migration." *Journal of the Royal Statistical Society* 48 (June 1885), pp. 167–227.

Sabot, R. H. "The Meaning and Measurement of Urban Surplus Labor." International Bank for Reconstruction and Development, Development Economics Department, June 1975.

Sahota, G. S. "An Economic Analysis of Internal Migration in Brazil." *Journal of Political Economy* 76, no. 2 (March/April 1968), pp. 218–245.

Schultz, T. P. *Population Growth and Internal Migration in Colombia,* Santa

Monica, Calif.: The Rand Corporation, RM-5765, July 1969.

___. "Explanations of Birth Rate Changes over Space and Time: A Study of Taiwan." *Journal of Political Economy,* Supp. 81, no. 2 (March/April 1973), part II, pp. S238–274.

___. "Determinants of Internal Migration in Venezuela." Paper presented at Econometric Society, Third World Congress, Toronto, August 1975a.

___. "Long Term Changes in Personal Income Distribution." In Levine, D. M., and Bane, M. J. (editors), *The Inequality Controversy,* New York: Basic Books, 1975b.

Schultz, T. W. "Investment in Human Capital." *American Economic Review* 51, no. 1 (March 1961), pp. 1–17.

___. "Human Capital: Policy Issues and Research Opportunities." *Economic Research: Retrospect and Prospect.* Fiftieth Anniversary Colloquium VI, National Bureau of Economic Research. New York: Columbia University Press, 1972.

___. "The Value of the Ability to Deal with Disequilibria." *Journal of Economic Literature* 13, no. 3 (September 1975), pp. 827–846.

Schwartz, A. "On Efficiency of Migration." *Journal of Human Resources* 6, no. 2 (Spring 1971), pp. 193–205.

___. "Interpreting the Effect of Distance on Migration." *Journal of Political Economy* 81, no. 5 (September/October 1973), pp. 1153–1169.

Sen, A. *Employment, Technology and Development.* Oxford: Clarendon Press, 1975.

Sjaastad, L. A. "The Costs and Returns to Human Migration." *Journal of Political Economy,* Supp. 70, no. 5 (October 1962), part 2, pp. 80–93.

Stiglitz, J. E. "Alternative Theories of Wage Determination and Unemployment in L.D.C.'s: I. The Labor Turnover Model." Yale University, Cowles Foundation Dis. Paper No. 335, April 5, 1972.

Stouffer, A. "Intervening Opportunities: A Theory Relating Mobility and Distance." *American Sociological Review* 5, no. 6 (December 1940), pp. 845–867.

Theil, H. *Linear Aggregation of Economic Relations.* Amsterdam: North Holland Publishing Company, 1954.

___. "A Multinomial Extension of the Linear Logit Model." *International Economic Review* 10, no. 3 (October 1969), pp. 251–259.

Todaro, M. P. "A Model of Labor Migration and Urban Unemployment in Less Developed Countries." *American Economic Review* 59, no. 2 (March 1969), pp. 139–148.

___. "Migration and Economic Development: A Review of Theory, Evidence, Methodology and Research Priorities," World Employment Program, Population and Employment Project ILO, June 1975.

Tolley, G. S. "Management Entry into U.S. Agriculture." *American Journal of Agricultural Economics* 52, no. 4 (November 1970), pp. 485–493.

Turnham, D. *The Employment Problem in Less Developed Countries.* Paris: Organization for Economic Co-operation and Development, 1971.

Vanderkamp, J. "Migration Flows, Their Determinants and the Effects of Return Migration." *Journal of Political Economy* 79, no. 5 (September/October 1971), pp. 1012–1931.

Venezuela, Direccion General de Estadistica y Censos Nationales. *Octavo Censo general de poblacion 26 de Noviembre de 1950, Resumen general de la Republica, Parte A. Poblacion.* Oficina Central del Censo Nacional, Caracas, 1957.

_____. *Noveno Censo general de poblacion (26 de febrero de 1961), Resumen General de la Republica, Parte A.* Caracas, 1966 and state volumes 1–25, Caracas, 1964–69.

Welch, F. "Education in Production." *Journal of Political Economy* 78, no. 1 (January/February 1970), pp. 35–59.

# 4

# Measuring the Difference Between Rural and Urban Incomes: Some Conceptual Issues

PAUL COLLIER
RICHARD H. SABOT

## INTRODUCTION

The concern in this chapter is with two conceptual issues in the measurement of differences between rural and urban incomes in developing countries. The first section attempts to clarify the definition of income that is appropriate when estimates will be used for behavioral analysis of urban migration; the second section focuses on the index number problem that arises when a set of prices and quantities is selected for comparative purposes.[1]

Recognizing employment problems in urban labor markets and the links between rural-urban migration and income distribution, economists are turning increasingly to the analysis of migrant behavior. An exercise such as that presented in this chapter is therefore timely. Advanced microeconomic empirical research on the supply of labor must rest on large, integrated data bases, with income as a principal dimension, generated by sample surveys specially designed for the purpose. Indeed, several such surveys have already been run, and many more should follow. Most current measures of rural-urban income differences, however, are crude, and statistical inaccuracies and the insufficiency of government-collected data are only a partial cause. Conceptual errors are also involved, and these should be resolved before costly investments are made in empirical research.

Since some types of errors, as a proportion of a variable's absolute magnitude, tend to be constant over time and thus not reflected in the variable's rate of change, the importance of imprecision in measurement for economic analysis is sometimes discounted. This practice is not an effective defense of conventional procedures for the measurement of differences in income.[2] There is a definitional error that is likely to be large in magnitude and to change significantly as a proportion of income. Moreover, segmentation models need the absolute magnitude of income differences as input if they are to yield accurate estimates of the magnitude of urban labor market imbalance without

direct observations, or if comparisons between predicted levels of urban surplus labor and observations are to be used to test the theory. In this regard,
the first section of this chapter can be viewed as an extension of work begun
by Todaro, in the sense that his essential contribution to the theory of unemployment lies in his redefinition of income to take into account probabilistic
outcomes.[3]

## THE DEFINITION OF INCOME

We begin with a general definition of an individual's income, $Y$, as the sum
of the products of all acquisition, $q$, and their prices, $p$:

$$Y = \sum_i^n p_i q_i .$$  (1)

Abstracting from the imputation problem and assigning monetary equivalents
to nonmarket acquisitions, income is conventionally defined so that the quantities are purchased commodities (goods and services) and prices are those
observed in market transactions.[4] Divergence between market prices and the
opportunity cost to the economy of commodities raises a problem with this
definition of income for which, at least conceptually, there is a readily available solution. An individual's income is equal to each of the other baskets of
commodities that could be produced by the resources employed in producing
the one he acquires. Using any commodity as the numeraire, any other commodity can be valued by a shadow price equal to the opportunity cost of the
commodity in terms of the numeraire. But there is a more fundamental
problem. Though the above definition may be appropriate for national income accounting, production opportunity cost is not a suitable basis for the
valuation of acquisitions for the purpose of behavioral analysis. Assuming
individual utility maximization, what one needs is a valuation based on the
private, rather than the social, costs of acquisitions.

The ideal measure of an acquisition's cost to an individual is its subjective
benefit, which is best known as consumer surplus, the integral of the individual's demand curve for the commodity. This measure answers the question, "What would the consumer give up in order to make a particular acquisition?" Unfortunately, the consumer surplus concept is open to Little's (1957)
objection that "areas under demand curves cannot be measured." Observed
demand curves show market rather than individual demand for a good. Also,
in order to avoid double counting due to complementary goods and omissions
due to substitutes, a rather special type of individual demand curve would be
required. Suppose, for example, that income is comprised of three acquisitions
$X$, $Y$, and $Z$. Then, in order to arrive at the value of total income, measurements must be made for the demand curve for $X$ imposing the constraint that

neither $Y$ nor $Z$ are available, the demand curve for $Y$ imposing the constraint that $X$ but not $Z$ is available, and the demand curve for $Z$ allowing both $X$ and $Y$ to be available. The sum of the integrals of these three demand curves would then yield the value of total income.

Consumer opportunity cost provides another way to evaluate acquisitions. It reflects what the consumer must sacrifice to make an acquisition rather than what he is prepared to sacrifice or what the economy must sacrifice. It has the advantage of coinciding with the valuation by the consumer surplus approach of marginal acquisitions. Thus, consumer opportunity cost is the one practicable means of valuing acquisitions for a measure of income to be used in behavioral analysis. Moreover, the market price is a better measure than the shadow price of the consumer opportunity cost of a commodity. This does not imply, however, that income should be defined as the aggregate of commodities acquired, valued at market prices.

Two changes in the concepts of acquisitions and prices are proposed here, with potentially important implications for the level of income in any given area, and for income comparisons. Since income is realized consumer demand, changes in the theory of demand have corollaries for the definition or concept of income. Beginning from the proposition that the existing theory of consumer demand, whatever its merits, has nothing to say about the demand for new commodities, Lancaster (1966) has developed a new approach, the hedonic approach. It assumes that utility does not depend on the consumption of commodities per se, but rather depends on the satisfaction of wants by "qualities" or "characteristics" inherent in physical goods and services. Nerlove (1974), who traced the historical roots of this idea to Bentham, Banfield, and Marshall, quoted Leontief to support the contention that the new approach is closer than the conventional to commonsense notions of demand:

> The assumption of the existence of general categories of needs, different from demands for particular individual commodities, but still specific enough to be clearly distinguishable from each other, is basic to the man-in-the-street idea of consumer's demand. One speaks of the demand for food as existing behind and separately from the particular demand for bread (or) apples . . . (and) at the same time . . . distinguishable from the similarly general needs for clothing or, say, for shelter.

Income should then be redefined as

$$Y^* = \sum_{i=1}^{n} p_i^* \cdot q_i^* \tag{2}$$

so that acquisitions and prices refer to "qualities" related to specific consumer objectives rather than to commodities. The direct implications of this change for the measurement and comparison of income are illustrated by the examples in the next section of this chapter.

A definition of income in terms of the acquisition of "qualities" rather than commodities is not a logically necessary antecedent, but it makes the need for the second proposal more apparent, and makes its application more feasible. When one conceives of commodities as inputs into objectives, one naturally distinguishes between commodities that are direct inputs (as an orange is an input into nutrition) and those that are indirect inputs (as a bus trip to the store is an input into nutrition). Commodities of the first kind confer utility directly, those of the second kind do not. The latter may be a necessary means of making acquisitions of direct inputs or, more generally, they may reduce the price that must be paid for a direct input. This distinction does not imply that indirect inputs should be excluded from the definition of income, for then the opportunity cost to the consumer of a direct input would be understated. It does mean that they should enter the definition as components of the prices of utility conferring acquisitions, rather than as quantities of such acquisitions, as is conventional.[5] The proposal here, then, is to redefine income as

$$Y^* = \sum_{j=1}^{m} (p_j^* + \sum_{i=1}^{n} p_i q_{ij}) \, q_j^* \tag{3}$$

where $q_{ij}$ is the input of item $i$ used to acquire one unit of $j$.

The distinction between direct and indirect inputs is by no means novel. In a somewhat different guise, it is basic to the concept of gross national product (GNP) originating in enterprises. In computing gross product for an establishment in the enterprise sector, the costs of goods and services used in current production, or intermediate goods, are deducted from the values of sales and change in inventories of final goods to arrive at a measure of value added. Whether this distinction should be comprehensive or remain limited to certain sectors is a controversial matter. The convention is to treat all public expenditures on goods and services as final output, despite the argument that government services supplied to enterprises may be inputs that are fully reflected in the final output of the enterprises. Housing expenditures provide another example. The convention in this case is that they should be treated as final output even though a large proportion of them can be considered intermediate.

Errors resulting from logical inconsistency in procedures among sectors in income estimated for national accounting purposes may indeed be significant,[6] and Ruggles and Ruggles (1970) have emphasized that they imply an underestimate of "the increasing costs of maintaining the society."[7] The failure to distinguish intermediate and final inputs in the household sector, however, is likely to lead to still greater errors when income is estimated for the purpose of behavioral analysis for two simple reasons. Given that intermediate and final goods are distinguished and treated appropriately in the measurement of income generated by the enterprise sector, the change in estimates resulting from the extension of this procedure will be less for national income than for income generated by the government and household sectors. The second, and perhaps quantitatively more important, reason is that labor supply decisions are based on comparisons of income. For example, the composition of consumption may differ between rural and urban areas. If the gap between the actual and estimated level of income is consequently minimal in the relatively large rural sector and highly significant in the small urban sector, the ratio of the actual to the measured difference of income between the urban and rural sectors will be in excess of the ratio of the actual to the measured aggregate income.

## Illustrations of the Input-Output and Hedonic Approaches to the Measurement of Income

### Leisure as a Quantity

Leisure can be treated as an acquisition like goods and services, being valued at its opportunity cost, which is the marginal wage rate. Hence, as seen in Table 4.1, the boundaries of the ratio of A's income to B's income would be 28:36 at A's prices and 18:20 at B's prices. The choice of a measure within that range depends upon the treatment of the index number problem, which will be considered later in this chapter. This approach rests upon the assumption that a quantity of leisure contributes to welfare in the same way as the consumption of a quantity of rice.

### Leisure as a Price

The opposite view was advocated by Becker (1975), who suggested that leisure should be regarded, not as a welfare-giving quantity, but as a component of the cost of making particular acquisitions of goods and services. Hence, if a visit to the cinema takes two hours and the marginal wage rate is one dollar per hour, the opportunity cost of a visit to the cinema is the price of the ticket plus two dollars. If the figures from Table 4.1 are retained but leisure is allocated between rice and cinema acquisitions, then A is shown in Table 4.2 as unambiguously better off than B (28:26 at A's prices, 22:20 at B's prices), whereas when leisure was treated as a quantity, A was unambiguously worse off than B.

In Becker's approach a wider concept of price and a narrower concept of goods than in the preceding approach is adopted. As such it constitutes an early example of the general principle that should be taken into consideration when measuring income: not only leisure but many other items can be classified

Table 4.1. Measurement of Income with Leisure Treated as a Quantity

| | Acquisitions | | | | | | Income | |
| | Rice | | Cinema | | Leisure | | $(a \cdot b) + (c \cdot d) + (e \cdot f)$ | |
| Consumers | a Price | b Quantity | c Price | d Quantity | e Price | f Quantity | A's prices | B's prices |
|---|---|---|---|---|---|---|---|---|
| A | 2 | 4 | 2 | 2 | 2 | 8 | 28 | 18 |
| B | 2 | 2 | 1 | 4 | 1 | 12 | 36 | 20 |

Table 4.2. Measurement of Income with Leisure Treated as a Price

| | Acquisitions | | | | | | | | | | Income | | |
| | Rice | | | | | | Cinema | | | | $(d \times e) + (i \times j)$ | | |
| Consumers | *a* Price | *b* Hours per Unit | *c* Wage | *d* Oppor- tunity cost/unit | *e* Quan- tity | *f* Price | *g* Hours per Unit | *h* Wage | *i* Oppor- tunity cost | *j* Quan- tity | A's prices | B's prices |
|---|---|---|---|---|---|---|---|---|---|---|---|---|
| A | 2 | 1½ | 2 | 5 | 4 | 2 | 1 | 2 | 4 | 2 | 28 | 22 |
| B | 2 | 2 | 1 | 4 | 2 | 1 | 2 | 1 | 3 | 4 | 26 | 20 |

as components of opportunity cost rather than as acquisitions in themselves.

The hedonic approach, to which the specification of the reasons for acquisitions is basic, can be used to resolve these conflicting treatments of leisure in income. A critical distinction is that between time spent on activities that reduce the cost of making acquisitions and thus increase the bundle of consumable goods, and time spent on activities that do not do this and that must therefore confer utility directly.

The more time spent on acquiring rice, the less the consumer will pay. He may spend the time walking to a more distant market or comparing prices within a market. There does exist a dispersion of prices, a manifestation of ignorance in the market, and it takes time to find cheaper rice. Stigler (1961) offers a simple illustration:

> At any time there will be a frequency distribution of the prices quoted by sellers. Any buyer seeking the commodity would pay whatever price is asked by the seller whom he happened to canvass, if he were content to buy from the first seller. But, if the dispersion of price quotations of sellers is at all large (relative to the cost of search), it will pay on average to canvass several sellers. Consider the following primitive example: let sellers be equally divided between prices of $2 and $3, then the distribution of minimum prices, as search is lengthened, is shown in the table [Table 4.3]. The buyer who canvasses two sellers instead of one has an expected savings of 25 cents per unit, etc.

Because of this relationship between time and the total cost reduction on rice purchases, the price actually paid for the rice does not reflect the true opportunity cost. The consumer has spent time, which has an opportunity cost, in

Table 4.3. Distribution of Hypothetical Minimum Prices by Number of Bids Canvassed

| Number of prices canvassed | Probability of minimum prices of | | Expected minimum price |
|---|---|---|---|
| | $2 | $3 | |
| 1 | 0.5 | 0.5 | $2.50 |
| 2 | 0.75 | 0.25 | 2.25 |
| 3 | 0.875 | 0.125 | 2.125 |
| 4 | 0.9375 | 0.0625 | 2.0625 |
| 5 | 1.0 | 0 | 2.00 |

order to achieve a particular price level. If one values rice at this price, one understates its value.

However, time spent at the cinema does not achieve any cost reduction. It is intrinsically a direct input into the objective of entertainment. Consequently the price of the cinema ticket accurately reflects its value. Becker is surely wrong to contend that since the man could have been working one must treat time spent at the cinema in the same way as time spent shopping. A man shopping for rice *is* working, for he is increasing the total bundle of goods that he can acquire. The man at the cinema has chosen not to work. He has decided to consume leisure. The time thus spent should be viewed as an acquisition to be valued at its opportunity cost, like any other acquisition. This approach applied to the previous data secures a set of prices and quantities as shown in Table 4.4, with the ratio of A's income to B's income being 28:34 at A's prices and 20:20 at B's prices. The result is a resolution of the conflicting approaches of treating all time not spent earning income as a quantity of the acquisition "leisure," or allocating all time as part of the opportunity cost of acquisitions.

Finally, since it is hard to determine how much leisure is needed to maintain human capital, any figure being highly arbitrary, it is proposed that in income comparisons one should value only the difference in the amount of leisure acquired by A and B. This method prevents domination of the estimates by a large and hypothetical leisure component. Thus, the treatment of the data would be as shown in Table 4.5.

*Transport*

Transport offers an important practical example of a good most plausibly regarded as an intermediate input that is conventionally treated as a final good. Transport expenditure is a necessary input into both the sale of labor and the purchase of final goods. In most instances it should therefore be regarded as raising the cost of achieving objectives, rather than as being itself a final objective. The comparison of rural and urban incomes will be sensitive to the treatment of transport because urban transport (by bus) typically requires spending cash, while rural transport (by foot) requires spending time. Time spent walking to the field has an opportunity cost predominantly in the form of labor time and agricultural output. Conventional measures of income, which only take account of output, exclude this rural transport from income. As noted in the introduction to this chapter, this is not a legitimate procedure; intermediate inputs should be assigned as part of the cost of some final acquisitions. Nevertheless, because conventional measures do not regard rural transport as a final acquisition, they must implicitly view it as intermediate, while they treat urban transport as a final acquisition, with the expendi-

Table 4.4. Hedonic Approach to Measurement of Income

| Consumers | Rice | | Cinema | | Leisure | | Income | |
| | a | b | c | d | e | f | $(a \cdot b) + (c \cdot d) + (e \cdot f)$ | |
| | | q | p | q | Wage | Hours | A's Prices | B's Prices |
|---|---|---|---|---|---|---|---|---|
| A | 5 | 4 | 2 | 2 | 2 | 2 | 28 | 20 |
| B | 4 | 2 | 1 | 4 | 1 | 8 | 34 | 20 |

Table 4.5. Measurement of Income, Taking into Account Leisure Excess

| Consumers | Acquisitions | | | | | | Income | |
| | Rice | | Cinema | | Leisure excess | | $(a \cdot b) + (c \cdot d) + (e \cdot f)$ | |
| | $a$ | $b$ | $c$ | $d$ | $e$ | $f$ | A's Prices | B's Prices |
| | | $q$ | $p$ | $q$ | Wage | Hours | | |
| A | 5 | 4 | 2 | 2 | 2 | 0 | 24 | 18 |
| B | 4 | 2 | 1 | 4 | 1 | 6 | 30 | 18 |

ture upon urban transport conferring utility in the same way as expenditure upon rice does.

This inconsistent treatment of transport by conventional measures distorts the comparison of income in two ways. First, because the acquisition of transport is counted as a quantity of final consumption in urban areas but not in rural areas, urban incomes are overstated. Second, the correct treatment of expenditure of cash and time on transport is to assign it as part of the cost of certain acquisitions. The conventional approach, by ignoring this component of the cost of transport-intensive items, misstates the price structure in both rural and urban areas and also, almost inevitably, the relative price structure between rural and urban areas. Since incomes are compared using the wrong set of relative prices, one gets an erroneous comparison of income in addition to the direct misstatement of quantities of goods consumed.

### Housing

While the preceding examples have been cases in which many different goods contain a few characteristics that serve as inputs into a single objective, the pattern of consumption will contain more complex cases. Sometimes a single good will have many characteristics that, in turn, enter into more than one objective. It is in these cases that some of the most substantial corrections to income estimates are likely to occur.

Housing provides an example of a good that serves more than one objective. In urban areas especially part of the expense of some houses is the cost of a convenient location. Expenditure on a convenient location is an alternative to the acquisition of transport and should therefore be regarded as an intermediate input. In addition to this difference in the objectives that housing serves, rural and urban houses differ in quality; but because they frequently do not exist in the same spatial market, market prices cannot be used directly to value these differences. The conventional approach interprets urban expenditure on a convenient location as raising the urban cost of housing relative to the rural cost and fails to take into account quality differences.

The hedonic approach specifies housing as a set of quantifiable characteristics such as floor area, roofing material, and location, which relate to the objectives of shelter and spatial access. Each of these characteristics can be assigned by comparing housing with differing characteristics in the same spatial market, though this may require econometric techniques. Having priced each of the characteristics, one can then assign the characteristics to more than a single objective. That part of urban housing expenditure that has the objective of a convenient location is better assigned to transport than to shelter expenditure. By means of the hedonic approach one can disaggregate differences in expenditure upon housing into components due to quality differences, quantity differences, price differences, and the attainment of objectives other than shelter. In each of these components, there is likely to be a substantial difference between rural and urban housing. Urban housing is commonly of higher quality, some characteristics are generally cheaper per unit (for example tin roofs will be cheaper in urban areas), and the implicit component of transport expenditure is greater.

## DIFFERENCES IN THE TRANSFORMATION FUNCTION BETWEEN INPUTS AND OBJECTIVES

A direct advantage of the hedonic approach is that the attainment of an objective can be measured in units of the relevant characteristics that are inputs into the objective, rather than by the input of commodities.

Taking food, for example, the income elasticity of demand for calories has empirically been found to be low. This might be explained by an income elasticity of demand for calories lower than that for food. Perhaps food acquisitions serve the dual objectives of nutrition and taste, the latter being more income elastic than the former. Or maybe attainment of the objective of nutrition is subject to varying levels of efficiency because the transformation function between food and nutrients is imperfectly known. The previous example of housing has already demonstrated the case of a single good serving two objectives. Concentrating upon this latter possibility, the simplifying assumption can be made that food consumption has the sole objective of nutrition. The attainment of the objective of nutrition can thus be measured, not in units of food, but in units of calories and protein. The average cost per unit is the total number of units consumed divided into total expenditure on food. This change in the basis of measurement from goods to characteristics as the units of quantity can significantly affect the valuation of rural and urban incomes.

If consumers have perfect knowledge of the characteristic content of goods, so that purchases of goods represent an efficient attainment of an objective; and if rural and urban consumers face a common transformation function between goods and objectives, then the valuation of incomes is unchanged. But, as seen below, if either of these assumptions is not made, the result will not hold.

### Inperfect Knowledge

Consider first the case in which both rural and urban consumers have a common, though imperfect, level of knowledge about the nutritional value of foods. The extent of the inefficiency in consumption that this lack of knowledge induces will generally vary with the structure of relative prices. The consumer may err both by overestimating the value of one food relative to another and by oversubstituting one food for another in response to a price change. Such a case is illustrated in Figure 4.1. The vertical axis measures the relative consumption of two foods, $x_1$ and $x_2$, and the horizontal axis their relative prices, $P_{x_1}$ and $P_{x_2}$. The schedule $E$-$E$ denotes efficient consumption and $C$-$C$ denotes chosen consumption. With a common state of knowledge, $C$-$C$ describes choices in both urban and rural areas. However, if relative prices of the two foods differ between urban and rural areas in the manner indicated in Figure 4.1, then rural consumption patterns will be more efficient than urban. A common level of knowledge has yielded systematic differences in the level of welfare.

Now consider the case in which the level of knowledge itself differs systematically between rural and urban areas. A particularly striking feature of rural-urban dualism is that frequently the same consumer objectives are satisfied by traditionally designed goods in rural areas and by modern goods in urban areas. The dichotomous consumption patterns of rural and urban areas are frequently due not to any physical lack of modern goods in rural areas, but to limited information about the combination of characteristics that might make modern goods more efficient than traditional goods in achieving a particular objective. It has been suggested that information about the characteristics of new goods is disseminated among the population by a process

Figure 4.1. Imperfect Knowledge and the Efficiency
of Consumption

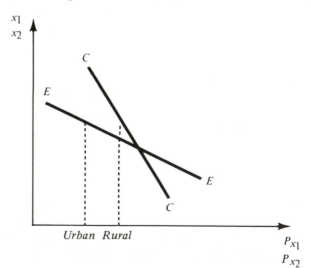

similar to contagion. If innovation, or the adoption of more efficient patterns of consumption, occurs first among a small group of urban consumers, then dualism in consumption may reflect the lag of rural dwellers behind urban dwellers in learning of the innovation.[8]

This correction for the difference in efficiency between rural and urban consumption would change not only the level of rural-urban income disparities, but also the trend; it is expected that, over time, information would increase in rural areas so that disparities would narrow. An example of the greater efficiency of modern goods might be the use of metal versus earthenware cooking pots. Metal pots might be less liable to break and be better heat conductors, yet their use is diffused only gradually from the urban to the rural population.

However, precisely because consumers often do not have perfect knowledge about the transformation between goods and objectives, the greater knowledge available to urban consumers may lead to less efficient consumption patterns than those in rural areas. An example of this is the use of powdered milk instead of mother's milk in urban areas. While this may be partly explained by differences in the opportunity cost of women's time in rural and urban areas, a major reason is the greater urban awareness of powdered milk. Information on powdered milk is disseminated primarily through advertising, which has a predominantly urban impact. But advertising does not convey enough information for efficient consumer choices. As a substitute for mother's milk, powdered milk is nutritionally inferior. Here the urban consumption pattern is a less efficient means of achieving a common objective.

**Differences in Environments**

Even if all consumers have perfect knowledge, the measurement of objectives in units of characteristics instead of goods can lead to a change in the valuation of relative incomes, if rural and urban consumers have different possibilities of transforming goods into objectives. An example of this, a familiar paradox in the literature, is that of different weather conditions: to attain the same temperature, consumers in cold areas use more fuel than those in warm areas. The conventional approach expressed by Kravis (1975) is to describe the former group of consumers, ceteris paribus, as having the higher income:

> The production of heat is an economic activity that adds to welfare and must be counted as a part of the contribution the economy is making to welfare where the heat is produced. Thus, the income of a country that requires and produces heat is higher than the income of a country in a warm climate that does not require or produce heat, the production of all other products being equal in the two countries. It is equally

clear, on the other hand, that added inputs or costs to attain a given level of welfare that are necessitated by a harsher environment do not represent more production. A potato remains a potato whether it takes one hour to produce in a rich soil in a hospitable climate or three hours in a barren soil in an unfavorable climate.

This approach is justifiable if the measurement is of productive potential, but not if it is of household welfare. In the latter case warmth can be regarded as a final objective regardless of its means of production. The extra fuel needed to attain a given level of heat has the same status as the extra time needed to grow a potato in barren soil. This procedure concludes that the price of the objective is higher in the cold area.

### Probable Future Income

So far the comparison has been of actual current incomes in rural and urban areas. The approach suggested to define income corrects some of the deficiencies of the conventional approach, but it must still be adjusted for the purpose of behavioral analysis, to take account of expected future incomes in alternative opportunities. Involved are not only estimates of differences in the path of income for employed workers but also, following Todaro (1968), estimates of employment probabilities as well. First this approach considers the appropriate income concept for a riskless future income stream. Then the problems posed by probabilistic outcomes are encountered. Even if the direct costs of moving and psychic costs and returns are not considered and the decision to move is made solely on the grounds of whether permanent income (the discounted stream of future income) is greater in urban than in rural areas, the original assumption of maximizing behavior may be contradicted, depending on the determinants of the rise in income over time.

In Figure 4.2 the rural wage is assumed to be constant while the urban wage rises. If the rise in urban wages is institutionally determined and is related to the age of the worker, then urban permanent income is higher than rural permanent income at all times; but the household maximizes permanent income if it remains in the rural area until $t_1$ and then migrates. In this case, maximizing current income in each period maximizes permanent income, and measures of the former are sufficient for use in a migration function.

If, however, the urban wage rises, not with age but with experience on the job (seniority), the maximizing individual migrates prior to $t_1$. Each year he stays in the countryside, the migrant reduces the urban wage he will earn subsequently, the discounted present value of this reduction representing a fall in permanent income. Only if this fall in permanent income exceeds the reduction in current income brought about by migrating to the city does migration maximize permanent income. This is illustrated in Figure 4.2 by a

Figure 4.2. Effect of Age of Worker on Wage in Urban and Rural Sectors

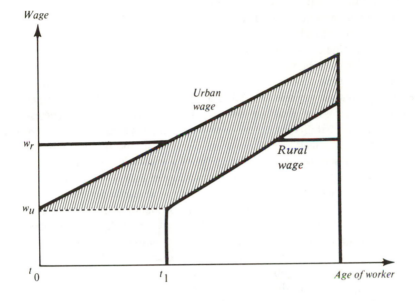

comparison of the shaded area, the (undiscounted) loss in future income from postponing migration from $t_0$ to $t_1$, with rectangle $w_r$, $w_u$, $t_0$, $t_1$, the total value of the higher current income achieved by postponing migration. Thus, when urban wage scales are a function of seniority (as is generally the case), neither current nor permanent income provides an appropriate income concept. The maximization of current income does not maximize permanent income because it ignores the change in permanent income caused by deferring the acquisition of job experience. Hence, the appropriate income concept is the sum of current income plus the value of this change in permanent income. Only if this sum is maximized is permanent income maximized.[9]

This issue has been raised to illustrate the importance of knowing how the urban labor market functions in order to specify the income measure appropriate for the behavioral analysis of migration. It is necessary to know not only the wage structure in various urban activities and the rationale for the wage structure, but also the expected movements of migrants among activities. A typical migrant may move from the unorganized to the organized sector, or he may rise within the hierarchy of activities in the unorganized sector. In each case, the promotion may be due to the man's having grown older, or to his having acquired, by his urban employment history, characteristics that secure him access to higher jobs. As was shown in the first example, current income does not need to be amended for the promotions due to aging, but does for those due to acquiring characteristics for access to higher jobs.

The resulting estimate of the change in permanent income must be discounted to a present value. This requires an estimate of the own discount rate; the best guide to this rate is perhaps the interest rate charged on consumer credit—the consumer opportunity cost.

The analysis can be extended to cover these future income streams that are probabilistic. Objectively, access to an income stream is probabilistic only to the extent that the selection criteria determining eligibility yield an excess demand for access, so that the final selection process is random. The estimation of the probability of access is therefore highly sensitive to the correct specification of selection criteria. For example, if one left out educational attainment as a criterion, one would usually overestimate considerably the job prospects of the uneducated. The probability of access cannot be estimated with confidence until it is shown that it is not sensitive to the inclusion of further selection criteria. In estimating the probability of access a comprehensive array of selection criteria must be constructed that define the set of job-seekers and this must be compared with the number of vacancies.

However, just as the labor force must be disaggregated by characteristics such as education and job experience, so should employment opportunities be disaggregated. While the original Harris-Todaro (1971) model used a single aggregate of high income employment, in practice there is a continuum of activities and wages, each activity having its selection criteria and hence its distribution of probabilities. The Harris-Sabot model (see Chapter 2) offers an explanation of unemployment as a function of this heterogeneity of employment opportunities.

One needs detailed knowledge of the labor market to estimate objective expected income correctly. But objective expected income is important in behavioral analysis only to the extent that it influences subjective perceptions of expectations, the estimation of which is rather more problematic. Two questions must be answered: what selection criteria are considered important by the particular group and how the objective facts, such as the ratio of vacancies to jobseekers with a particular selection characteristic, affect individual perceptions of probabilities. Unfortunately, since the objective probability requires a lot of data for accurate estimation, its influence upon subjective perceptions would be rather weak. This is a major difference between the probabilistic element of income and the component of income that is certain. The information requirements for accurate knowledge of wages in particular sectors is minimal by comparison with the requirements for the probability of access, except where access is certain or impossible.

Even if the researcher correctly estimates perceived probabilities of access, he must still face the problem of translating them into a certainty-equivalent level of income. The first obstacle is that the calculations are apparently too

difficult for most people to be able to aggregate probabilistic outcomes correctly. Experimental psychologists have found a systematic tendency for low probabilities to be undervalued. Further, the less successful a person has been, the more likely he is to avoid middle-range probabilities, preferring near certain probabilities (that is, very high or very low). The second obstacle is conceptually distinct from the first. When a utility function is introduced, risk aversion must be accounted for as a function of the rate or decline of marginal utility. Although the extent of the discount for risk varies greatly over the population and is extremely difficult to estimate, risk aversion is probably too powerful an influence on behavior to ignore.

The migration function requires the subjective estimate of migrants' probabilities and the discount for risk aversion; both items are important and intractable. Through surveys one can both discover the sources of migrants' information about probabilities and get some indication of their views, though this is not easy. In some cases, the researcher will then feel confident enough to apply some risk discount and include the item in income, but there are two other options. If the weak link is the risk discount, then subjective probabilistic income can be included as a separate item in the migration function (the discount being derived from the econometrically estimated coefficients). Or, if both the risk discount and the link between objective and subjective probabilities are highly uncertain, then objective probabilistic income can be included as a separate item instead.

## THE INDEX NUMBER PROBLEM

If relative prices differ between urban and rural areas, then alternate procedures will yield different measures of the disparity of incomes. No single procedure can claim to be correct a priori. However, due to the particular functions of a rural-urban income measurement, one procedure, which is usually dismissed as inferior, turns out to be the most appropriate. The standard problem will be presented first.

In Figure 4.3 tangent point $R$ depicts the rural consumption bundle and tangent point $U$ the urban bundle of goods. First, $R$ and $U$ can be compared using either urban or rural relative prices. As long as the urban community consumes relatively more of the good that is relatively cheap, the difference in income will be greater at rural than at urban prices. A sufficient, though not necessary, condition for this is that the good that is relatively cheap in the richer community should be the luxury (that is, income elastic) good. However, both of these measures misstate the true difference in welfare, since they fail to allow for substitution in consumption resulting from the change in relative prices. For example, a man facing rural prices would only need an income sufficient to purchase $U_R$ to achieve the same level of welfare

Figure 4.3. Comparison of Rural and Urban Consumption

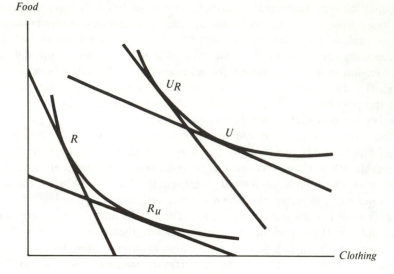

as an urban dweller. Clearly, at rural prices $U_R$ is less valuable than $U$. Similarly, at urban prices $R$ is more valuable than $R_u$. Hence, each measure which fails to allow for substitution acts as a bound to the true measure, as seen in Equations 4 and 5.

$$\frac{P_R \cdot U}{P_R \cdot R} > \frac{P_R \cdot U_R}{P_R \cdot R} \tag{4}$$

and

$$\frac{P_u \cdot U}{P_u \cdot R} < \frac{P_u \cdot U}{P_u \cdot R_u}. \tag{5}$$

Since it is known that usually

$$\frac{P_R \cdot U_R}{P_R \cdot R} > \frac{P_u \cdot U}{P_u \cdot R} \tag{6}$$

then a sufficient condition for the two nonsubstitution measures to provide outer bounds for the true measures is that

$$\frac{P_R \cdot U_R}{P_R \cdot R} > \frac{P_u \cdot U}{P_u \cdot R_u}. \tag{7}$$

The necessary and sufficient condition for Equation 7 is that the luxury good should be cheaper in the city.

In this case, if nothing is known about the pure substitution elasticities, some average of the two nonsubstitution measures is likely to be a better guide than either on its own. A commonly used average, which satisfies various statistical consistency tests, is the geometric mean. The resulting index is known as Fisher's Ideal Index number, $I$,

$$I = \sqrt{\left(\frac{P_R \cdot U}{P_R \cdot R} \cdot \frac{P_u \cdot U}{P_u \cdot R}\right)}. \tag{8}$$

This sort of averaging, however, assumes that the rural and urban weighted indexes are equally appropriate. Each index would be suitable for a particular problem. To determine the sort of rural life-style that is equivalent to the average urban life-style, $U_R$ needs to be evaluated. In comparing $U_R$ with $R$ it would be appropriate to use rural prices. Similarly, to find an urban life-style, $R_u$, that is equivalent to rural living standards, the comparison of $R_u$ and $U$ should be made using urban prices. The latter approach is probably the more appropriate.

Consider the likely distribution of income in rural and urban areas. Almost certainly the range of variation of incomes in rural areas will be narrower than in urban areas. Within each range, the distribution is likely to be tighter in rural areas; in urban areas, the distribution might well be bi-modal. Finally, the range of rural incomes will probably be within the range of urban incomes. The sort of distribution that might be expected is illustrated in Figure 4.4.

If this pattern is broadly correct, then mean income in rural areas is more descriptive of typical living standards in rural areas than mean income in urban areas is of urban living standards. Second, very few people in rural areas have a standard of living equivalent to the average urban living standard, but a substantial group of urban households probably live at a level comparable to the mean rural living standard.

In using an index to describe the distribution of income, this assymetry is important. If mean rural income is assigned a position in the urban income hierarchy, then the comparison of living standards with other urban groups is concrete and readily visualized. Particular income levels translate easily into particular life-styles; the alternative approach does not have this advantage: the notion of a rural life-style at an income level high enough to equal average urban incomes might be largely hypothetical.

Further, if the measure here is intended for use in the migration function, then the identification of $R_u$ and its comparison with other urban income groups is of particular importance, while $U_R$ is of no special significance. Hence, if the index of income differentials is to be used to describe income distribution, the Fisher index gives undue weight to rural relative prices.

The previous arguments suggest that $(U \cdot P_u)/(R_u \cdot P_u)$ will be a more

Figure 4.4. Income Distribution in Rural and Urban Areas

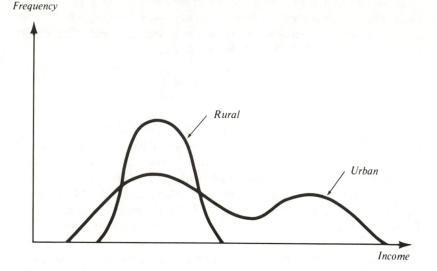

useful way in which to state rural-urban income differentials than $(U_R \cdot P_R)/(R \cdot P_R)$. However, from the inequalities in Equations 4 and 7 it cannot be concluded that $(U \cdot P_u)/(R \cdot P_u)$ is more appropriate than $(U \cdot P_R)/(R \cdot P_R)$. If the bundle $R_u$ cannot be deduced, then the Fisher index might still be the best measure possible. Fortunately, $R_u$ can be approximated without alarming demands on data collection. Since the range of income distribution in the cities is wide, the calculation of income elasticities of demand for commodities can be reliably inferred from urban expenditure surveys. The resulting urban Engel curve provides additional information, which enables bounds to be placed on $R_u$. Note that because of the narrower range of rural incomes, and their lower level, the same procedure cannot always be applied to estimate $U_R$.

The curve $E$-$E$ in Figure 4.5 denotes the observed urban Engel curve. The lower bound to $R_u$ is provided by the bundle on the Engel curve that has the same value as $R$ when both are valued at rural prices. If there is anything less than infinite substitutability between the two goods, then $R_u$ must be a more valuable bundle than $U_L$. The upper bound is provided by that bundle on the Engel curve that has the same value as $R$ at urban prices. Again, convexity ensures that $U_H$ must be more valuable than $R_u$. Thus, for all sets of prices,

$$p \cdot U_L < p \cdot R_u < p \cdot U_H. \tag{9}$$

Though these bounds are better than none, they may still leave a considerable range of uncertainty. There is, however, a distinct approach using consumer

Figure 4.5. Effect of Urban Engel Curve on $R_u$

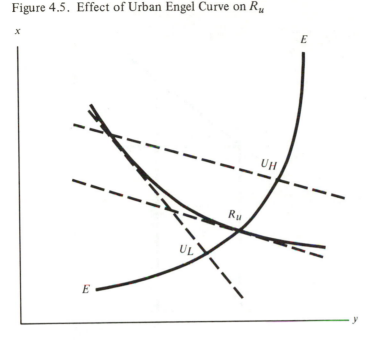

surplus that allows a specific estimate of $R_u$. The consumer surplus approach is to find a particular bundle of goods on the Engel curve that yields the same sum of the integrals of the demand curves for its goods as the bundle $R$. Assume that the utility function is additively separable and take linear approximations to demand curves. Then the Consumer Surplus equivalence condition is

$$P_{xu} \cdot x_u + P_{yr} \cdot y_u - \frac{(P_{yr} - P_{yu})\,(y_u - y_r)}{2}$$

$$= P_{yr} \cdot y_r + P_{xu} \cdot x_r - \frac{(P_{xu} - P_{xr})\,(x_r - x_u)}{2}. \qquad (10)$$

The condition is depicted in Figure 4.6. Whether these assumptions are a reasonable approximation depends upon the aggregates that have been adopted. If these assumptions are reasonable, $R_u$ can be inferred very easily because this approach is identical to taking a simple average of rural and urban prices. This can be seen when the triangle component of Equation 10 is rearranged as

$$\frac{(P_{yr} - P_{yu})}{2} \cdot (y_u - y_r)$$

and similarly for the $x$ term.

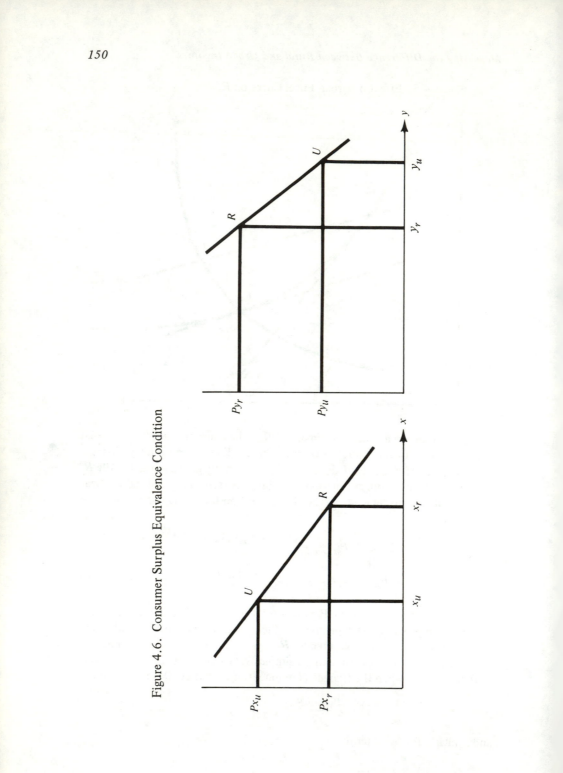

Figure 4.6. Consumer Surplus Equivalence Condition

To summarize the procedure, the first stage is to infer an urban living standard that offers the same valuation of income as the average rural living standard. Where relative opportunity costs differ in urban and rural areas, the simple average of the two has sufficient rationale in economic theory to be a reasonable guide to the ideal. Having arrived at the urban equivalent to the rural living standard, the second stage is to compare this with the living standard of particular urban groups. Urban relative prices will be used in this comparison.

So far rural and urban tastes have been assumed identical; this assumption is now relaxed. If tastes are heterogeneous, then there is no single set of weights to assign to items for the purpose of constructing a cost of living index. The weights adopted here will represent an average. Hence, a given rural-urban income differential can result in many patterns of labor allocation, depending upon the distribution of tastes. For example, if all rural inhabitants have a preference for goods that are cheap in rural areas and all urban dwellers have a preference for goods that are cheap in urban areas, then no migration need occur even if average real incomes diverge considerably. But if tastes are systematically biased, as in the example here, then the procedure suggested above will lead to an underestimate of rural living standards. This problem is illustrated in Figure 4.7.

The curves $I_R$ and $I_u$ show rural and urban preferences, respectively. The line $P_R$ is the rural budget constraint and the slope of the line $P_u$ shows urban relative prices. Point $R$ shows the chosen rural consumption bundle. The value, at urban prices, of the bundle of goods that would secure an identical level of welfare should be estimated. The previous method, based upon the assumption of identical tastes and knowledge of the urban Engel curve, $E_u$, has been to identify the bundle as $E$—the point on the Engel curve equal in value to $R$ at the average of rural and urban prices. However, with differences in tastes, the rural Engel curve at urban prices is not $E_u$ but $E_R$. Hence, if the use of the average of rural and urban prices is a reasonable approximation for knowledge of elasticities of substitution, the true equivalent bundle, $R'$, will have a higher value ($Y_t$) at urban prices than the estimated bundle ($Y_e$).

In order to arrive at $Y_t$ an estimate of $R'$ is needed. This requires either knowledge of the rural Engel curve at urban prices ($E_R$) or knowledge of price elasticities. Both possibilities have their merits and drawbacks.

Consider first the estimation of the rural Engel curve at urban prices. The obvious means of discovering this is from the expenditure pattern of rural migrants already in the city. However, this is subject to three qualifications, which prevent migrants in the city from being an accurate reflection of rural tastes. First, formal education probably changes tastes in favor of urban goods. Since migrants are disproportionately drawn from among the educated this will overstate the rural preference for urban goods unless the sample is

Figure 4.7. Effect of Rural and Urban Preferences

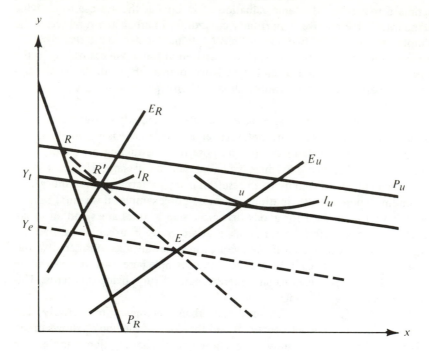

stratified by educational attainment. Second, the experience of urban living might change tastes in favor of urban goods. Psychologists claim to have discovered a systematic tendency for tastes to change in favor of whatever has been decided, so that the decision becomes justified even if it is initially incorrect. Third, those who migrate are inevitably a biased sample of the rural population, since those who most prefer urban goods are most prone to migrate.

The second approach is to estimate rural price elasticities. Rural expenditure surveys may reveal a stretch of the rural Engel curve (at rural prices). From this the income elasticities for urban and rural goods can be deduced. The relationship between price and income elasticities seems to be sufficiently reliable for an estimate of price elasticities to be made. In the absence of knowledge of the rural Engel curve, perhaps the best that can be done is to use the income elasticities from the relevant portion of the urban Engel curve, although this is obviously less satisfactory.

It may well be revealing to compare the resulting estimates of $R'$ that the two techniques yield. While little quantitative significance can be attached to the difference between them, the comparison might provide some qualitative "feel" for the importance of taste differences *within* the rural population as an explanation of migration.

Finally, once differences in tastes are accounted for, the notion of equal welfare becomes obscure. While bundles $R'$ and $U$ are equally valuable at urban prices, there is no clear meaning to the question "do they represent the same level of welfare?" although the question does have both a meaning and an answer when the comparison is between $R$ and $R'$, we should not worry too much that we cannot provide an affirmative answer to a question without a meeting. For reasons given above, urban prices are considered appropriate for income comparisons, and persons with equal incomes at urban prices are considered to be economically equal.

Finally, the appropriate level of aggregation of objectives and inputs is considered. The greater the extent of disaggregation, the worse will be the index number problem. There are two reasons for this. First, any aggregate will conceal rural and urban relative price differences between goods within the aggregate. Further, even if aggregate $A$ is relatively dearer at urban than at rural prices, some of the goods in $A$ are probably relatively cheaper. Hence the divergence between relative prices of aggregates will understate the average divergence between goods in different aggregates. Indeed, the aggregates can always be arranged so that relative prices are the same in rural and urban areas regardless of the divergence in relative prices of the underlying goods.

Second, the further the disaggregation, the greater the probability of encountering divergent relative prices for goods that are very close substitutes. For example, the elasticity of substitution between food and housing will be far lower than the elasticity of substitution between different types of food. For a given divergence in relative prices, the discrepancy between measurements based on rural and urban indices will be greater the higher the elasticities of substitution.

Now, a working definition of homogeneity of a good or objective is that all pairs of units have infinite cross elasticities of substitution. Hence, beyond a certain level of disaggregation, it becomes more appropriate to classify items as belonging to a common aggregate than to face the increasingly difficult index number problems that disaggregation poses. The criterion for the appropriate level of aggregation thus rests on the cross elasticities of substitution of the component goods. When elasticities are very high, a single aggregate is appropriate; when elasticities are very low, no index number problem exists anyway.

There is clearly no single "correct" level of aggregation. Beyond a certain stage, however, further disaggregation is not helpful—it artificially magnifies the index number problem and increases data requirements.

## Two Other Issues

### Shortages and Nonavailability

Implicit in the analysis as presented has been the assumption that the consumer can acquire as much of a good or objective as he demands at the same opportunity cost for each unit. Often, however, this is not the case because price controls, rationing, or poor distribution systems can lead to shortages. Since the incidence of such shortages is often more acute in rural than urban areas, a failure to make correct allowance for them biases comparative as well as absolute measures of income.

Consider the availability of a good that is subject to price control. If the price control is at all effective, it will shift consumption off the demand curve, as shown in Figure 4.8. It is assumed that $Q_1$ is purchased at the official price and that $Q_2 - Q_1$ is purchased at the market-clearing black market price. The price paid by the consumer is thus a weighted average of these two prices. However this understates the opportunity cost to the consumer, because time and possibly money will be used by the consumer in his efforts to make acquisitions at official prices. Indeed, marginal acquisitions at official prices should have opportunity costs equal to black market prices. Hence, the controlled price might be a very poor guide to the average opportunity cost of acquisitions. The black market price can be used as a step toward the opportunity cost of goods in short supply, but a different procedure is required when a good is simply unobtainable in a certain area.

At first sight, nonavailability might not seem to matter, if the opportunity cost criterion for valuing income is used. If $x$ is consumed in urban but not rural areas, why can it not be included in urban income at the urban opportunity cost? The fallacy here is that in rural areas, $x$ has a notional opportunity cost above the actual urban opportunity cost. Consider the case depicted in Figure 4.9.

Figure 4.8. Effects of Price Control

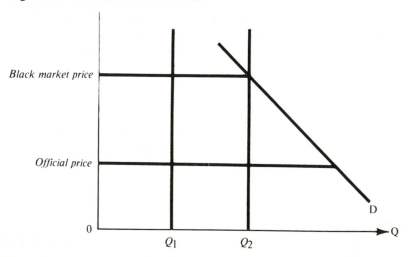

Suppose that the urban supply curve is $S_u$ and the rural supply curve is $S_r$. Urban consumption is $q_u$ and rural consumption is $q_r$. The price at which these quantities should be valued in estimating that urban living standard equivalent to the average rural living standard is the average of $P_u$ and $P_r$. Now suppose that the rural supply curve shifts up slightly to $S_r'$. The minimum rural supply now lies above the demand eliminating price $P_r'$. The difference in consumption at the urban price shows us that the relative living standard in the rural areas would appear to rise compared to the initial situation when it was valued at average prices; in actuality, it has fallen. In principle, when a good is not available, this zero consumption should be valued at the demand eliminating price and thus value the difference in consumption at the average of the notional rural and actual urban prices.

Thus, the problem in the case of nonavailability is to estimate the demand-eliminating price. There are two main approaches that can be adopted. One approach is to estimate the supply eliminating price of $x$ in the rural area. This will serve as an upper bound for the demand eliminating price. Since the urban price acts as a lower bound, a crude estimate of $P_r'$ is the average of $P_u$ and $P_r^*$.

The supply eliminating price is the minimum of three different estimates. First, estimate all the quantities of factor and material inputs needed to make the item in the urban area, and assign rural prices to these inputs. The only case in which theoretical problems arise with this method is that of economies

Figure 4.9. Case of Nonavailability

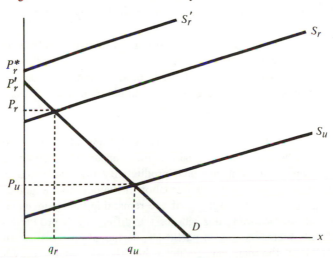

of scale, for demand might be insufficient in rural areas to support the urban-area production pattern. Second, estimate the cost of transporting the good from urban to rural areas and third, estimate the cost of travelling to the nearest available place of consumption. The minimum of these three estimates shows the least costly method of satisfying demand in the rural areas.

The other approach attempts to estimate the opportunity cost to the rural consumer of consuming the bundle of characteristics contained in $x$ by means of consuming other items. This involves reducing quality differences to a quantitative measurement of a few characteristics and has been analyzed in the first section of this chapter.

Which of these two approaches is adopted depends upon the nature of the unavailable good. If the good has reasonably close substitutes that are available, then the hedonic approach is to be preferred since it is a direct estimate of the demand-eliminating price. However, where there are no close substitutes, an attempt to price equivalent characteristics might well be spurious, and the supply-eliminating price will be more reliable.

## The Household and Transfer Payments

The assumption of household maximization of welfare underpins virtually the whole of the forgoing analysis. The delineation of the household in the social context of extended family systems is problematic. Unfortunately results can be sensitive to the above assumptions.

Four issues are considered to be both awkward and important:

1. Does an individual migrate to maximize the welfare of the whole rural family, or only his own welfare?
2. How should transfer payments made to the migrant by his urban relations be treated?
3. How should the higher future earnings of the children (possibly yet unborn) of the migrant be treated?
4. When comparing household heads of the same age, how should rural and urban families having different numbers of wives and children and different participation rates be treated?

Of these, the first question has received some attention, though it is probably not as important as might at first appear. The standard analysis is to infer from diminishing marginal productivity that the marginal product must be below the average product of labor. If the potential migrant consumes the average product, the welfare of the remaining family members will rise with migration. However, this ignores the difference in productivity of different family members and, in particular, participation rates less than unity. For example, if the marginal product is half the average, but only half of the family is economically active, then the migrant consumes only what he produces and family and individual maximization converge.

Generally, the estimate of the difference between the output and consumption of the potential migrant is unreliable, and the assumption of family motivation is unlikely, so that individual maximization seems a more useful assumption. However, where rural marginal product is known to be very close to zero, there might be a case for reconsidering this conclusion.

Transfers to the migrant by his urban relative pose problems that are amusingly intricate, as shown by three different motives of the donor: (1) an altruistic concern for the welfare of the recipient; (2) the status attaching to the financing of dependents; and (3) the avoidance of a family rupture, which a refusal would provoke. Gifts due to motives of the first type would seem to yield welfare to the donor; therefore, they should not be deducted from his income. Alternatively, the gift can be viewed as an intrahousehold transfer so that if it is part of the migrant's income it must be excluded from the donor's income. However, gifts of the second kind are unambiguously a purchase made by the donor. If both the Mercedes and the dependents are financed to achieve status neither should be excluded from the income of the donor. Finally, gifts of the third type might be viewed as an input into "family harmony," which is achieved by the urban donor's rural cousins without the same expenditure. In this case the gift should be deducted from the donor's income. Which of these options is adopted is clearly arbitrary. Perhaps motives (2) and (3) are equally plausible, so that one-half of gifts to distant relatives should be excluded from income.

There are two ways of treating the future earnings of children. First, in the absence of pensions, parents may regard their children as yielding an economic return in future income paid as gifts. Because of better access to education, and hence to good jobs in the town, children can be expected to earn more and make larger transfers. On this interpretation, the returns to migration should include the discounted stream of expected transfer payments from children. However, it is perhaps more plausible to view parents' aspirations for their children as being altruistic, the maximand being the joint discounted income of parents and children. This is not inconsistent with the treatment of the first problem. The household need not be a symmetrical concept; children may regard themselves as a household and thus maximize individually.

Finally, consider the comparison of income between households of different size. Typically, the migrant will become a household head sooner than his rural counterpart, though he marries later. His family may be smaller and have a lower participation rate. Total household income cannot validly be compared because of such differences. However, average household income is not a suitable alternative because, for example, consumption by young children will be less than consumption by the household head. Perhaps the most suitable approach is to stratify incomes by household size and then compare the mean rural and urban incomes within each group. These means can then be averaged, using as weights the proportion of the national population in each group. The result shows the income change that the typical family would experience by relocating.

## NOTES

1. The first section is a collaborative undertaking; the second section is primarily the work of Collier.

2. An alternative defense, that the influence of one error, which drives a number in one direction, is likely to be exactly offset by the influence of another error doing the opposite, is still weaker, as Morgenstern (1963) demonstrates:

> The notion that errors do cancel out is widespread and when not explicitly stated, it appears as the almost inevitable argument of investigators when they are pressed to say why their statistics should be acceptable. Yet any statement that errors "cancel," neutralize each other's influence, has to be proved. Such proofs are difficult and whether a "proof" is acceptable or not is not easy to decide. The world would, indeed, be even more of a miracle than it is if the influence of one set of errors offsets that of another set of errors so conveniently that we need not bother much with the whole matter.

3. See J. Harris and R. Sabot, Chapter 2, this volume.

4. The income of an individual or household can be monitored through acquisitions. Generally, for behavioral analysis, estimates of urban income use an earnings approach, making use of minimum wage rates and other wage data, while in rural areas where wage employment is less important, income is generally estimated via production. The acquisitions approach is favored because it can be applied in both rural and urban areas, improving the comparability of estimates, and because it allows a more sophisticated coverage of income.

5. Including items as quantities that should be prices results in double counting and hence an overestimate of income. The utility derived from a bus trip to the store solely to purchase oranges is entirely reflected in the expenditure on oranges.

6. That the line between intermediate and final goods is difficult to draw in the government sector is not an adequate justification for this inconsistency, as ambiguities also abound in the enterprise sector. For example, television and radio programs are household consumption items and thus ought to constitute final output and yet, because advertising expenses are

considered to be part of the production costs of enterprises financed by the sale of commercials, as is generally the case in the United States, expenditure on such entertainment is classed as intermediate. In other countries, where consumers directly bear production costs through the purchase of television and radio licenses or the government meets the expenses out of general revenue, these expenditures are classified as final.

7. Ruggles and Ruggles (1970).

8. This perspective suggests a more positive interpretation of the "demonstration effect" than the conventional one that is based not on interdependent preferences but on differences in access to information regarding new and more efficient products and services.

9. The strict specification is a little complex; although in most real situations the complexities will be unimportant, it is perhaps best to set down a precise definition. The problem is as follows. Suppose that there is some year, $t$, which is the year in which the man should migrate so as to maximize permanent income. Then, viewed from any year prior to $t$, say $t'$, the change in permanent income, termed "implicit saving," should include only the change in the income stream from $t$ onwards discounted back to $t'$. Any change in the potential urban income stream between $t'$ and $t$ is irrelevant because definitionally it cannot be sufficient to induce migration prior to $t$. However, $t$ itself is a function of the value of the change in permanent income. The solution to this is that $t$ must be defined as the first year in which it is true that no subsequent year $t^*$ can be found such that rural discounted income exceeds urban discounted income between $t$ and $t^*$ by a greater amount than implicit saving. Implicit saving is the reduction in urban income from $t^*$ onwards as a result of postponing migration from $t$ until $t^*$ all discounted back to $t$. This defines the optimal year for migration. Implicit saving should then be calculated as the change in permanent income subsequent to this date discounted back to the present as a result of postponing migration.

## BIBLIOGRAPHY

Becker, G. *Human Capital.* New York: Columbia University Press, 1975.

Harris, J., and Todaro, M. "Migration, Unemployment and Development: A Two-Sector Analysis." *American Economic Review* (March 1970).

Kravis, I., et al. *A System of International Comparisons of Gross Product and Purchasing Power.* Baltimore, Md.: Johns Hopkins University Press, 1975.

Lancaster, K. "A New Approach to Consumer Theory." *Journal of Political Economy* (1966).

Little, I. *A Critique of Welfare Economics.* Oxford: Oxford University Press, 1957.

Morgenstern, O. *On the Accuracy of Economic Observations.* Princeton, N.J.: Princeton University Press, 1963.

Nerlove, M. "Household and Economics: Toward a New Theory of Population and Economic Growth." *Journal of Political Economy* 82, no. 2 (1974).

Ruggles, N., and Ruggles, R. *The Design of Economic Accounts.* New York: Columbia University Press, 1970.

Stigler, G. "The Economics of Information." *Journal of Political Economy* 69 (1961).

Todaro, M. "A Model of Labor Migration and Urban Unemployment in Less Developed Countries." *American Economic Review* 59 (March 1969).

# 5
# Out-Migration, Rural Productivity, and the Distribution of Income

## G. EDWARD SCHUH

### INTRODUCTION

Economic progress entails all manner of changes in demand and supply—changes that induce many shifts in the allocation of resources. Our general conception of an economy experiencing economic development includes a vast amount of internal migration and many transfers of resources (both capital and labor) between sectors over time. Demand and supply changes also impose windfall gains and losses on labor (including management) and on owners of nonhuman resources.

Migration, both occupational and geographic, is generally viewed as a desirable characteristic of economic development and as a necessary condition for efficient allocation of resources in the context of changing demand and supply and for reasonably equitable distribution of income (because of its assumed role in reducing wage differentials among regions and occupations). Since labor is the most important factor of production because it usually accounts for roughly two-thirds of the cost of producing the flow of final goods and services, it is generally expected to bear the major burden of adjustment to the changing conditions of demand and supply. As will be argued in the conclusion of this chapter, however, there is no inherent reason why labor need bear the full burden.

Human resources have shown themselves to be highly mobile in the aggregate—witness the rapid urbanization of countries around the world in recent decades and the huge reallocation of labor from agriculture in such diverse countries as the United States, Argentina, and Brazil. Similarly, the large geographic shifts in resources that have occurred in many countries suggest a willingness of large parts of the labor force to pull up their roots and seek greener pastures elsewhere. It is puzzling, then, that the adjustment to sectoral and regional disequilibria has in many cases been slow, painful, and costly in terms of income forgone because of the persistence of the disequilibria.

Examples abound, but a few cases will illustrate the point. Per capita income in the Northeast of Brazil continues to lag behind the rest of the country despite an out-migration of labor both sizable and sustained. Per capita income in the U.S. South chronically lagged behind the rest of the country, despite a large out-migration from the region over a long period of time. Similar conditions have prevailed in southern Italy and parts of Mexico. And per capita income in Brazilian agriculture is little more than a third of that of the nonfarm sector, again despite large intersectoral and interregional flows.

The usual response of economists to this problem is to emphasize the equilibrating nature of the migration process and to argue that the solution lies in more of the same. The theme of this chapter, however, is that the length and the costs of this adjustment process are due in large part to certain neglected consequences of out-migration for the supplying region. In particular, geographic out-migration tends to remove critical resources from a region, while at the same time imposing on it sizable negative externalities. Consequently, although the private gains from migration may be high, the social costs to the supplying region may also be high. To these must be added the external diseconomies that eventually result from congestion in urban areas as migrants accumulate. Both the available theory and the results of empirical studies on the migration process suggest that these social costs of migration, too long neglected by economists (although not by politicians and policymakers), can be considerable. An appropriate policy response might involve a greater allocation of capital where the labor force is, rather than an almost exclusive reliance on shifts of labor to where the capital is accumulating as a result of market forces or government policy. This is not to deny the importance of sectoral or occupational mobility, nor to deny that some geographic mobility is both desirable and inevitable.

The analysis that follows draws on the rapidly growing literature on the brain drain, one of the few parts of the migration literature that has systematically addressed the consequences of out-migration for the supplying region or sector. Brain drain theory analyzes the consequences of migration within a general equilibrium trade model; the main extension of that model needed in the present context results from the need to give special attention to the terms of trade when considering sectoral and regional migration. Also windfall losses to a community experiencing rapid out-migration and the implications of these losses for the tax base must be considered. Relaxation of the assumption of perfect knowledge and foresight permits a more comprehensive analysis of the consequences of the outflow of human capital, and of the complementarities between human capital and technological change.

The analysis also draws on the considerable literature that has evolved in the attempts to understand both the agricultural transformation in the United

States and the complex and sizable migration processes in that highly mobile economy. The analysis also draws upon empirical experiences from Brazil and other Latin American countries.

The body of the chapter is in five sections. The first provides some background and discusses the importance of the problem. A review of relevant theory is presented in the second section, followed by a consideration of the different causes of out-migration and their differential impact on the factor markets. A selective review of some empirical research is then provided. The fifth section makes some suggestions for research that might serve as the basis for designing a more rational policy. The chapter ends with some concluding comments.

## BACKGROUND AND IMPORTANCE OF THE PROBLEM

The labor "surplus" has been a major focus of the post–World War II literature on economic development. A vast literature has evolved from W. Arthur Lewis' seminal article (Lewis, 1954), with sophisticated models formulated to explain how the excess labor in agriculture is transferred to the modern or industrial sector and to analyze the consequences of the transfer. The vitality of this literature was such that for a considerable period of time the potential importance of agriculture itself was forgotten, as was the importance of generating a commodity surplus[1] and its mobilization for development purposes.

The first challenge to this view questioned the proposition that labor was in fact in excess in agriculture. Numerous attempts were made to measure the amount of labor that could be withdrawn from agriculture without affecting output, and to test hypotheses about equilibrium or the lack thereof in the intersectoral labor market.[2] This research focused attention on the problem of seasonality in agricultural employment, and pointed to the intersectoral labor market as an important nexus of the problem. The labor market within agriculture was often found to work reasonably well.[3]

A major turning point in the literature occurred in the mid-1960s. Evidence accumulated that the industrialization-first development strategies that seemed to be a logical implication of the surplus-labor paradigm were producing disappointing results in terms of labor absorption as well as growth. Rapid rural-urban migration piled up in the large cities in the form of unemployed or underemployed masses living in the unsightly *favelas* of congested cities. A large literature on the employment problem evolved, and a number of world conferences on employment were held.

Parallel to these developments the world experienced its first post–World War II food scare in 1965 and 1966 as the monsoon failed on the Indian subcontinent, and the Soviet Union had a serious shortfall in agricultural production, as apparently did the People's Republic of China. This temporary scare caused policymakers and economists to turn their attention back to agriculture, recognizing its importance in feeding the burgeoning world population and also its usefulness as an employer of last resort.

Only a few years later came the misplaced euphoria of the so-called Green Revolution. To many it appeared that the food problem had been solved, and attention shifted to what were described as second and third generation problems—how to take advantage of the growing agricultural surplus and how to deal with what many believed was a serious equity problem resulting from the Green Revolution.[4] The euphoria was short-lived, however, as the initial impact of the Green Revolution waned rather quickly, and it became evident that there were no easy panaceas for the output problem. A renewed concern with world agriculture arose, together—perhaps for the first time—with a concern about the rural disadvantaged masses characteristic of so many low-income countries.

Serious efforts are now under way both by many individual countries and by international development agencies to strengthen world agriculture. If these results are successful, and there is no reason to believe that they will not be, the problem of labor adjustment out of agriculture will remain a major issue in the decade or decades ahead. The conditions of demand and supply for agricultural output and for the factors of production are such that the modernization of agriculture will require the transfer of large numbers of people from that sector to the nonfarm sector.

The efficiency of the transfer process will be an important determinant of how rapidly many countries will grow, how efficiently they capitalize on their investments in agriculture, and how equitably the benefits of the development process are distributed. In the United States, which now appears to be nearing the end of its agricultural transformation (Schuh, 1976), the transfer process has been unnecessarily wasteful of both human and physical resources (see President's National Advisory Commission on Rural Poverty [1967]). The desire of most low-income countries to collapse their development experience into a shorter period than that experienced by the advanced countries makes it almost imperative that they avoid such waste. The challenge to policymakers will be to accommodate the necessary adjustment problem as efficiently as possible. The professional challenge will be to understand better how the intersectoral labor market functions, the consequences of out-migration to the supplying region and sector, and those of in-migration to the receiving region and sector. This chapter, of course, is concerned with the consequences of out-migration to the supplying region and sector.

The burden of the argument is that, in general, insufficient attention has been given to the distinction between regional migration and sectoral migration, and to the contribution that "migration" of capital can play compared to migration of labor. More specifically, it will be argued that development policy, which attempts to promote sectoral mobility while at the same time reducing the need for regional mobility, will help to realize the gains from resource reallocation while avoiding the losses from regional out-migration. In effect, the gains from in-migration (the parallel of the losses from out-migration) will be internalized within the region. Moreover, such a development strategy may in fact accelerate the sectoral reallocation of resources, and thereby lead to a faster rate of economic growth.

## THE THEORY

The simple (naive) theory of factor migration argues that in a competitive economy resources will flow from regions (or sectors) where their returns are low to regions where their returns are high. The change in relative conditions of demand and supply in the sending and receiving regions is expected to be such that payment to the factor in the sending region rises while that in the receiving region declines. These adjustments are expected to continue until the factor's remuneration has been equilibrated.

In a simple two-factor world of homogeneous production functions of degree one, the initial disequilibrium in factor payments would be due to differences in capital/labor ratios—a high wage is associated with a high capital/labor ratio and a low wage with a low capital/labor ratio. Market forces would induce labor to flow to the high wage region and capital to flow in the reverse direction. These adjustments would improve the allocation of resources, leading to an increase in national income; a more equitable distribution of income would also result, in the sense that resources of comparable quality would receive the same remuneration in the different regions.[5]

Under more realistic assumptions, however, the analysis becomes a great deal more complex. The extent to which resource adjustment is equilibrating and whether it improves the situation in the supplying region (sector) are open questions. Moreover the time required for equilibration becomes an important issue. Perhaps the simplest assumption to relax is that of a given total supply of labor. In the long run the growth of the labor supply may differ among regions; if it grows faster in low wage regions, the rate of increase in the wage rate may be slow even with the expected inflow of capital. Similarly, once a difference in the production function is introduced and/or separate sectors of a region's economy are distinguished, the high wage region may experience a higher rate of capital accumulation than the other region. In that case, even though labor may be shifting to the high wage region, equilibrium may move further and further away.

### Implications of the Literature on International Migration

The literature on international migration, brain drain,[6] has analyzed the impact of out-migration on the supplying and receiving countries. Although it has not been extensively applied to the problem of migration within a country, authors such as Berry (1974) have recognized its applicability.

Perhaps one of the most surprising results from these models is that the supplying region is expected to incur a loss from out-migration even in the simplest of worlds. In particular, under a conventional neoclassical model of perfect markets, constant returns to scale, no external effects, and a two-factor production function with one product and with just one factor (labor) migrating in finite amounts, the individuals left in the region or sector after the emigration are worse off as long as the marginal physical product of labor is declining. The loss is due to the familiar "surplus" related to the fact that the intermarginal emigrants had contributed more to total product than the marginal unit, but all the emigrants were receiving a wage equal to the contribution of the marginal worker.[7] This result holds also in a two-product, two-factor model with only one factor (labor) mobile and with the supplying region not engaged in trade with the rest of the economy.

When the region trades with the rest of the economy under unchanged terms of trade (either because the region is relatively small in relation to the total economy, or because the country as a whole trades both products and is relatively unimportant in world trade), no loss occurs as a result of the emigration. Whenever changing factor proportions have not led to change in relative prices, the marginal product of each factor in terms of each good has remained constant, so the loss of surplus associated with a declining marginal physical product in the one-good case does not appear. If terms of trade can vary, however, the welfare of the nonmigrants is affected positively or negatively as the terms of trade improve or worsen, respectively. This term-of-trade effect might or might not outweigh any loss associated with the surplus noted above. This is, of course, an empirical question. The role of international trade is relevant here. If the economy is closed, the terms-of-trade effect of out-migration from agriculture could well be sizable, since the price elasticity of demand for agricultural products in the aggregate tends to be low and the supplying region (sector) may be benefited by the out-migration. If the economy is open and both products are traded, then the supplying region (sector) will at best be no worse off as a result of the out-migration. But in a one-sector case with the product price fixed by trade, the supplying sector can be worse off as a result of out-migration.

Another relevant extension is to situations where more than one factor migrates. In the one-product case, if migrants take with them any capital they own, then whenever the labor and capital leaving the supplying region or sector are not in the same proportion as in the premigration situation, per capita income of the remaining population decreases. In that singular case the nonmigrants are unaffected.[8] If migrants leave some or all of their capital behind (continuing to receive the corresponding remuneration), nonmigrants may gain if the wage/rental ratio rises and they are the "labor-intensive" group, or if the wage/rental ratio falls and they are the "capital-intensive" group. In this two-factor migration case the terms of trade may again be important. The presumption is that the terms-of-trade effect would be larger when both capital and labor emigrate than when only labor does.

The implications of emigration of a specific type of labor can be analyzed in a three-factor (one-product) model with labor differentiated into skilled and unskilled workers. The results are essentially those of the two-sector case. For nonmarginal migrations of either type of labor there would be the familiar loss of surplus. For a large region or a sector of the economy, however, the terms-of-trade effect could offset or more than offset this, making those left behind better off.

These results relate to a static framework, with the total stock of resources in the supplying and receiving regions (sectors) fixed and factor markets assumed to be competitive. For an overall gain to the supplying region, gains from a shift in terms of trade must more than offset the loss in surplus. Obvious instances where this will not occur include cases where the country trades in the product produced by the region or sector; cases where, although the supplying region is large, its product mix is about the same as that of the rest of the country; or cases where the migrants take up similar employment in another part of the country. (An example of the latter is the large amount of rural-rural migration in Brazil.) In short, migration can leave the supplying region or sector better off only if the country is autarkic, or the region is large and specializes in a product either not traded or produced in sufficient quantity to affect the price in world trade.

These static, competitive models have been extended in a number of ways. Imperfect factor markets (Bhagwati and Hamada, 1974) break the necessary equality between the income lost to a region or sector by migration and the wage that the (marginal) migrant earns. If, for example, labor is being paid more than its marginal product, the situation of those left behind would be improved by out-migration. Allowance for unemployment in the Todaro sense produces a new set of results. Recent dynamic models that concentrate on steady-state analysis (for example, Berry and Soligo [1969]) or that describe the transition of the economy outside the steady state (for example, Mishan and Needleman [1968]) tend to general conclusions rather similar to those of the static models.

Rather than focusing on any one of these, this analysis will extend in four directions of particular relevance to the process of out-migration from rural areas: capital losses incurred as a result of out-migration (drawing on Berry [1974]); education and skilled labor viewed in a somewhat broader framework than that cited above; shifts in the production function; and the role of government policy.

## Capital Losses and Induced Shifts in Labor

The discussion above has shown that, abstracting from terms-of-trade effects, the presumptive consequence of more than marginal out-migration is that those left behind would be worse off,[9] although the distribution of income would improve in the sense that labor's share would increase and the returns to labor would rise. Moreover, if capital migrates with the labor, those left behind would be worse off in all cases except when capital and labor leave in the same proportions as characterized the remaining population. But when the migrants own a disproportionately high share of total capital and leave it behind them, the capital/labor ratio will rise and, unless the terms-of-trade effect is large enough to cancel the increase in productivity,[10] the nonmigrants will benefit.

Berry (1974) correctly points out that the conditions under which the capital is left behind may be a key determinant of the welfare of those left behind. In principle the migrants either remove their capital physically, or sell it when they emigrate or soon after. As noted already, under simple neoclassical assumptions, joint labor and capital departure will have a negative impact on the nonmigrants in all cases except where the migrants owned an average amount of capital and thus caused no change in factor proportions. When the migrants retain ownership but leave the capital behind, the effect is usually negative unless their ownership of capital is substantial.

If the migrants sell their capital on terms advantageous to the nonmigrants these generally pessimistic conclusions can be modified (although an important exception for agriculture will be noted below). Berry notes that the price at which the capital is sold will depend on the propensity of the nonmigrants to hold wealth in general, the particular form of wealth in question, and the time span over which the migrants sell their capital. Assets differ a great deal in their liquidity, with certain capital goods used in agriculture being highly specific to that sector and having little salvage value in alternative uses. If the migrant is leaving the sector and wants to take his capital with him, he must sell the good for what it will bring. Similarly, there may be rather limited opportunities to transfer land from one sector to another, and certainly it cannot be transferred from one region to another. In general if the assets in question are relatively illiquid, then sale by the emigrants will lead to some decrease in their price; the decrease is greater the shorter the time during which the sales take place,[11] and it constitutes a gain to the nonmigrants, since in a sense some portion of the capital is being donated to them. The illiquidity can be a serious impediment to migration, since the potential migrant may be unwilling to incur such losses. The problem can be especially important in the case of acquired skills that have little value elsewhere.

The propensity of the migrants to retain physical capital will be determined in part by what Berry refers to as an "absentee differential," or the loss in returns (if any) associated with living in a region other than the one in which one's capital is located. If this differential is sizable, the migrant would be more willing to take his loss on illiquid assets, with the nonmigrants thereby benefiting. Many analysts believe that the "congestion" in the intersectoral labor market in the United States during the late 1950s was due to the farmers being caught in an investment trap (Johnson and Quance, 1972). The value of their physical and human capital was greater in agriculture than its salvage value in off-farm employment. The resulting "fixity" of the assets lowered incomes for everyone in the sector.

Recognition of this problem highlights the importance of the factor markets other than labor, both in facilitating the labor transfer and in determining the welfare of those left behind. With respect to land and acquired skills there are special problems. In countries such as the United States, where a wide range of capital market instruments is available and a viable credit market exists for the transfer of land, the migrants release their land to the nonmigrants, and disputes and controversy over the size distribution of land holdings do not arise. In other countries, where contrary conditions prevail, complicated by a greater desire to hold physical wealth as a protection against governments and unstable rates of inflation, the transfer does not take place as easily. Owners are reluctant to substitute other assets for land and become absentee landlords.[12] If the labor market should be clogged, as it often is in low-income countries, the struggle over land can become quite intense.

The specificity of skills, on the other hand, points up the importance of education and training programs as a means of facilitating the adjustment process. A difficulty arises, however, when the age selectivity of migration over the years has left a population of predominantly older people. Both the private and social rate of return to retraining programs may then be quite low because of the short pay-out period.

Before applying Berry's framework to the sectoral problem of agriculture, the price effects of output changes must once again be integrated into the model. If the demand for agricultural products is price inelastic, the benefits accruing to nonmigrants from the loss-sale of capital assets would be offset in part or in whole by the output effect. In other words, output would not be reduced as much if capital goods remained in agriculture at a lower price as if they were readily liquid so that the migrant could easily take them with him.

While the nonmigrants gain from the loss-sale of capital assets by migrants, they suffer a reduction in wealth from the lowered prices of those assets that they owned before. These price declines occur on the capital invested in the social infrastructure and in other sectors of a region's economy. If the out-migration from a region is sizable, the wealth loss incurred on such capital assets can be a sizable negative externality. Anyone familiar with the U.S. Midwest is struck by the number of dilapidated and abandoned buildings and other physical facilities whose value fell to the point where maintenance was no longer worth the cost.

To society as a whole, these declines in capital value may be bygone, but to the sector or region they are not. They reduce the wealth of nonmigrants of the present generation, possibly influencing also the rates of savings and consumption. And if local government services are financed from local property taxes, they can erode the tax base and induce a decline in public services supplied to the region.

Similarly, the out-migration from a region associated with the relative decline of a particular sector such as agriculture may induce a decline in employment in the service sector of the local economy. Of particular import here is the induced out-migration of such professions as doctors and dentists, or the decline in quality of such professionals as the decline in local population causes the better professionals to move on. The consequence of reduced service in these two particular professions could be a depreciation in the remaining human capital of the region, which is now unable to obtain adequate medical service. But the decline in other services can be important also. Such induced shifts of employment, together with the decline in wealth of those left behind, contributes to the snowballing effect, which can be one of the most significant impacts of population decline on a community.

To summarize, there are four different effects of out-migration on the supplying region. The first is the decline in the current income flows of nonmigrants associated with the traditional brain drain literature. The second is the effect on the price of capital assets sold by migrants to nonmigrants, as in Berry. The third is in the decline in market value of assets that do not change hands, which can induce a decline in the quantity and quality of local public services supplied to the region. And the fourth is the induced shift in service employment, which in the case of doctors and dentists may lead to a more rapid depreciation in the remaining stock of human capital in the region.

### Education

In a static framework with no externalities, as we have seen, the migration of human capital, either in the form of acquired skills or formal education, will normally leave those behind worse off, if the migrants have endowments of human capital above or below the average for the population. The nonmigrants are left no worse off only where the migrants take with them a capital endowment equal to that of the population average. We now broaden the analysis to consider externalities and also a dynamic framework in which the migrants' knowledge has value in decoding and using information.

First, it should be noted that formal education of the migrant may have been financed by those who are left behind, as when education is financed from the local tax base by means of a property tax or some form of income tax. Those left behind are then clearly worse off, even assuming no externalities, since in essence they are donating their capital to the migrant and to the region to which he moves. Two factors may mitigate this loss. Earnings from that capital may be remitted back to the supplying region, offsetting in part or in whole the original loss.[13] Although our systematic knowledge as to the amount of the remittances is rather limited, the data assembled by Michael Lipton (Chapter 6) suggest a rather mixed bag. In some cases the remittances are sizable, while in others they are fairly limited. Moreover, it is highly unlikely that the remittances will be in proportion to the contributions made in financing the education. Therefore, the personal and family distributions of income in the supplying region will be altered in any case.

A second relevant point is that in buying schooling collectively for their children, the parents of a community may be seeking the well-being of their children rather than of their school district as a regional entity. If that well-being can be increased by migration, the parents gain rather than lose. While this argument has a certain appeal in the context of the private and public expenditures that *parents* make on the education of their children, not all taxpayers have children, and those who do have children do not pay taxes in proportion to the number of their children. This disproportion is especially serious when the local tax is on local wealth. Further, there may be losses where creation of employment possibilities in the supplying region is a serious alternative to emigration, and preferable from the region's point of view. This point will be pursued later.

Consider next the case of externalities. It is generally believed that education contributes more to production than the individual is able to recuperate.[14] These externalities suggest a divergence between private and social benefits of education and are generally used as one of the justifications for public support of education.

To the extent that human capital leaves a region with the migrant, the supplying region will lose this externality, and the presumption that the non-migrants will be left worse off as a result of out-migration is upheld. However, in this case there may be a distinct difference between sectoral and regional migration. If the migrant changes his sector of employment but stays in the immediate vicinity, the externality would still be present.

Welch (1970) has recently focused on the contribution of education in enabling the worker to acquire and decode new information.[15] More specifically, he argues that there is a complementarity between education and the rate of technical change in an economy. A larger flow of new production technology increases the contribution of education since there is more information and knowledge to be decoded and applied in production. By the same argument, of course, a lack of education could cause the society to fail to realize the full potential of its investments in the production of new knowledge.

This theory has implications for evaluating the consequences of emigration at both the sectoral and regional level. It is now generally recognized that at the sectoral level the production and distribution of new production technology is an important source of growth for agriculture. If the better educated leave the agricultural sector, the social rate of return to investments in agricultural research would be lowered (abstracting from terms-of-trade effects), probably the optimal level of research expenditures would also be lowered, and the gains of nonmigrant beneficiaries of such research would thereby be decreased. Further, if the migrants had externalities through their pioneering of new technology, these would be lost.

Two important caveats are worth noting. First, a higher private rate of return to education under rapid technical change may keep the migration process from being selective in favor of the better educated. In fact, if there are Schumpeterian rents to be reaped from the technical change and education is the key to reaping them, it may be the less educated who are squeezed out of the sector or region and forced to migrate elsewhere, rather than the better educated who leave of their own volition to seek higher returns elsewhere. Second, substitutes for general education and on-the-farm decision-making capability exist in the form of publicly provided extension services. Although generally believed to be a less than perfect substitute for on-the-farm managerial skills, investments in an extension service may be one means of realizing the returns from the investment in new production technology.

### Differences in Production Functions

In conclusion, consider two additional factors in a dynamic context that may cause the supplying region to fall further behind the recipient region despite substantial out-migration: differences in production functions and in government policy.

If production functions shift at differential rates among sectors or regions, chronic imbalances can persist for a long period of time. This would be especially true if the sector whose product had a high income elasticity (creating a presumption that resources will have to be shifted to it) underwent slower technological change and was characterized by a relatively high price elasticity, so that failure of resources to move to that sector at an equilibrating rate would lead to a marked decrease in the relative price of the other product.

The increase in output from the adoption of the new technology in the progressive sector lowers the price of the product; if the price elasticity of demand for the product is less than one, this price effect will be larger than the productivity effect. This general equilibrium effect has been described in the case of U.S. agriculture by saying that the labor is squeezed out through the product market (Schuh and Leeds, 1963). The bias of the production technology is also important. In principle the bias could be such as to increase the demand for labor, as in the case of the improved-varieties-fertilizer package associated with the Green Revolution, or it could decrease the demand for labor.

### Role of Government Policy

Government policy also plays an important part in determining whether and at what rate the supplying region or sector catches up with the receiving region. This is especially important in agriculture since most governments, especially in the LDCs, discriminate against their agricultural sector by shifting the terms of trade against it through trade policy or other forms of government intervention. Unless this discrimination is offset by public investments in research and extension, the consequence is to shift both labor and capital out of the sector and to leave it in a debilitated form.[16] Unless labor is highly mobile, chronic imbalances can persist. If the sectoral discrimination also has a marked regional dimension to it, as in the case of the northeast of Brazil,[17] the consequences can be especially serious.

### The Different Causes of Out-Migration and Their Differential Impact on Factor Returns

The ultimate impact of out-migration on a region or sector depends in large part on government policy and on the proximate causes of the process. These relate to the basic demand and supply conditions of agriculture. The income elasticity of demand for agricultural products is lower than that for products from the nonagricultural sector. As a result, with a few exceptions in countries with unusual trade potential, resources have to be transferred out of the sector as development proceeds. Moreover, as per capita income rises, there is a presumption that the income elasticity of demand for agricultural products will decline.

A number of other factors reinforce this tendency, while at the same time causing the labor force to bear the brunt of the adjustment process. First, population growth rates tend to be higher in rural areas than in urban centers. In effect agriculture produces two products: agricultural output and a labor force for the economy. For the first, it is compensated; for the second, it is not—at least in countries where human capital cannot be sold. But the excess labor has to be transferred, and this alone will tend to cause wages in agriculture to lag behind those in the nonfarm sector. Note also that most land has only limited alternative uses, and if it is not used in agriculture it will be idle. Hence, as demand conditions change, there will be little adjustment in the stock of land used in agriculture, although land values may decline. Since the rate of return to capital will be high in the presence of technical change, the burden of the out-adjustment from agriculture must for the most part be borne by the labor force.

Now consider three paradigms of policy matrices. First, assume an absence of distortions in factor prices in the nonfarm sector, high investments in education in both the rural and nonfarm sectors, product prices that reflect true shadow prices, a reasonably high rate of technical change in agriculture (and in the industrial sector), and a nonfarm sector expanding at a rapid rate. In a closed economy the terms of trade would tend to shift against agriculture, unless the labor force were unusually mobile. Given the geographic "distance" that separates agriculture from the rest of the economy, however, the labor market is not likely to function perfectly. Incomes of farm people will lag behind those in the nonfarm sector even in this best of all possible worlds.

The decline in the terms of trade causes the benefits of technical change in agriculture to be widely diffused among the total population, however. The out-migration from agriculture causes factor proportions to change and therefore labor productivity to rise. Depending on the extent to which the new production technology is completely labor displacing,[18] the marginal value product of land can decline due to the decline in the terms of trade. If out-migration from agriculture is large, land values may actually decline, as may the share of income going to land.

In the second case, the economy is open and the small-country assumption applies. The results here will be somewhat different than the first case. The incentive for out-migration will not be as large since there will be no terms-of-trade effect. Consumers will receive the benefits of the technical change indirectly through a relative improvement in the trade position of the country, and an important share of the direct benefits of technical change will be capitalized into land values. Perhaps equally important, labor will tend to be *pulled* out of agriculture rather than *pushed* out by the terms of trade. Although farm incomes (at least labor earnings) are still likely to lag behind those in the nonfarm sector, they will not lag as much as in the previous case. Moreover, unless the new production technology is completely in the form of labor-displacing mechanization, the labor force will capture some of the benefits of the technical change.

Now consider the third case. Suppose, in marked contrast to the cases above, that in the nonfarm sector the government strongly subsidizes capital and raises wages by means of legislated minima set above equilibrium levels and by social welfare programs financed by payroll taxes. The combination of these two factors will induce a more capital-intensive production technology in the nonfarm sector. Assume further that the society severely underinvests in the education of its population, especially in the agricultural sector, and that it invests little or nothing in producing and introducing new production technology in the agricultural sector. The nonagricultural sector is protected by tariffs and other devices, but agriculture suffers discrimination by means of explicit export taxes, overvalued currencies, export quotas, and domestic price policies.

Under these conditions perhaps the first thing to note is that overall growth and development will be slower, even though it may have a rapid spurt for a short period of time. The distortions of factor and product prices create inefficiency, and resources in the agricultural sector, which may constitute the largest bundle of resources in the economy, are undervalued in relation to their true social productivity. Wage rates in the nonfarm sector may increase at a rapid rate because of the change in factor proportions and the protection conceded to that sector, but employment will increase slowly, and labor will be dammed up in the agricultural sector. Some out-migration from the agricultural sector will take place, however, although it will tend to create urban unemployment, thereby establishing an intersectoral equilibrium in the Todaro sense.

Because of the damming up of labor in agriculture, factor proportions will shift and real wages in that sector may actually decline as the marginal product of labor falls. The marginal product of land will probably rise, as will land values, this latter tendency being reinforced by the buildup of people who have no other source of employment. Although discrimination against agriculture through price and trade policy works in the opposite direction, the general tendency will be for the share going to land to rise, and for there to be a struggle over land.

The role played by new production technology and education in these alternative paradigms is important. Clearly, under a wide range of conditions the introduction of new production technology into agriculture will tend to be labor displacing. At the same time, however, it provides the means whereby labor productivity can be raised. If the labor market is not subject to large distortions, and the educational level of the rural labor force is raised, this raise will help realize an increase in productivity for the labor force remaining in agriculture.

It should also be noted that one reason absentee landlords can exist in many countries is that the production process is handled largely by custom and tradition. If new production technology is introduced into such a traditional agricultural sector, the importance of improved decision making will increase. This will tend to favor family farms, while at the same time it will increase the rate of returns to investment in education, increase the relative share accruing to educated or skilled labor, and perhaps lower the wage rate and the share accruing to unskilled labor.

To conclude, the impact of out-migration on the supplying region will depend importantly on the nature of development policy. If development policy focuses on investing in human capital and raising labor productivity, the wage rate of labor and its share can rise, even though the supplying region or sector *relatively* may lag behind the rest of the economy for a long period of time. On the other hand, if such investments are not made, and if the labor market is clogged by inappropriate government policy, not only may wage rates decline in the supplying region, but the share going to labor may decline in favor of land and the landowner.

## REVIEW OF SOME EMPIRICAL RESEARCH

The varied possible theoretical cases make it crucial to know a country's situation in order to predict the effects of migration from rural areas on those left behind. The literature on migration is vast and growing, but most of it focuses on the migration process per se, and very little on the effects of migration on the supplying or receiving region.

The present survey is of necessity brief and selective to focus on some of the key issues. Moreover, it concentrates primarily on the U.S. experience in an attempt to determine what might be learned from an economy that has experienced prolonged and sizable out-migration from its agricultural and rural sectors.

D. Gale Johnson (1960) made what was perhaps the first careful and rigorous analysis of the impact of reducing the farm labor force on output and labor earnings in the United States, over the period 1910–1914 to 1958–1959.[19] His analysis showed that output can increase, real farm prices can decline, and the value of the real marginal product of labor can simultaneously increase. He makes the case for out-migration from agriculture as a means of improving the earnings to labor ratio in that sector.

A study by James Maddox (1960) presents a detailed analysis of the costs of out-migration from agriculture, with special emphasis on the social costs. Maddox argues that the people who bear the costs of population shifts are often not those who reap the gains. In his view, the costs borne by the people who shift out of agriculture are not a serious burden to most of them. However, the farm families, educational institutions, and business firms left behind in the agricultural areas from which out-migration occurs bear a heavy share of the total costs associated with the movement of people out of agriculture. The nature and extent of these costs for a given area depend mainly on the size and speed of the out-migration from the area. Of four costs borne by those left behind on which Maddox focuses, three were already discussed in the theory section above: the costs (both private and public) of rearing and educating children (these costs will be local, of course, only if education is locally financed); the decline in capital values of fixed assets, both public and private; and the fact that many local businesses will go bankrupt or be forced to move to other areas. Maddox also cites the increase in per capita costs of maintaining essential public services for the smaller number of remaining residents. He feels that some of these costs will be serious only when off-farm migration is so large as to result in a decline in total community income or in the draining away of superior talent.

Maddox puts special emphasis on the loss that arises when farm families produce human capital, embodied in their children, from which they receive few financial returns. As discussed above, no simple quantification of this loss can be made since many of the payers may not care whether their children attain good incomes in the community or outside it. Some indication of a presumably upward biased or upper limit estimate of loss is possible, on the assumption that all costs of raising and educating the migrants are viewed by the local taxpayers as losses. Maddox's rough estimate of the export of human capital (so defined) in the period 1950–1958 is $1.6 billion per year. He considers only the direct costs of producing the child, and not the value in production of the human capital. Approximately 36 percent of the net decline in rural-farm population of 8.6 million people, which occurred during the 1940s in the United States, consisted of children under fifteen years of age at the beginning of the decade. Over 50 percent were under twenty years of age.

Income transfers from the children back to the parents help to offset part of the direct costs to the parents, as do the eventual moves of some parents to urban centers, but these flows are probably small compared to the outflow just cited. On net, farm and rural families contributed much of the stock of human capital for the nonfarm sector, and with little remuneration.

Taves' (1961) estimate of the potential outflow of human capital involved a broader look at the consequences of population loss from rural communities. If his logic is applied to the net annual rural-urban migration of 275,000 youth for the nation as a whole (during his reference period), the annual loss of human assets would exceed $5 billion. Estimated in terms of the cost of rearing a youngster to age eighteen ($20,000), the loss in human assets from out-migration (assuming that at least 50 percent of them spend their productive years outside the community) amounts to approximately $1 million a year for a community of 3,000 with a contributory agricultural population of another 1,000. If the transfer of economic potential is evaluated on the basis of the earning potential of the out-migrants, a much higher figure of over $27 billion a year emerges for the total rural-urban youth migrants. At an estimated $2,500 per migrant per year over a forty-year earning period, the potential earning loss to a community of 3,000 population would be $5 million each year.

Taves judged that the dependency and social costs that would have to be borne by the community if the youths did not migrate would be even larger. Clearly, he presumed that no productive alternative employment could be created for them locally, an assumption to which we take exception.

The export of human capital from rural areas is not, of course, unique to the United States. In a study of rural poverty in Brazil we have found that the sample in the Northeast was made up primarily of the remnants of what at one time must have been a vital population (Patrick and de Carvalho Filho, 1975). The *average* age of the sample is substantially above the life expectancy for Brazil. Formal schooling among the remaining population is almost non-existent, and reading and writing skills are extremely limited. It seems plausible to expect that this group has been harmed by the outflow. Devising development policies for them is quite a challenge; were the emigrants still there, these less-prepared individuals might benefit from considerable externalities.

Taves made the important point that the causes of the out-migration are important in evaluating its consequences. He noted that out-migration may be the relief valve that reduces certain existing strains and stresses if a community is already in disequilibrium. If the community is not already in disequilibrium or decline, however, he argued that the out-migration may itself lead to a decline, which may feed on itself and persist for a long time. Hence, in his view, the impact on the local community will be different depending on whether the migration is a consequence of an existing disequilibrium or an exogenous shock to a system already in equilibrium or near-equilibrium.

In another study of the economic aspects of population decline, Raup (1961) examined the issue of whether economies of scale imply unavoidable problems for rural villages in the United States. He concluded that there are no compelling technological reasons why marketing and supply functions cannot be performed efficiently on a relatively small scale. He argued further that if the small town is technologically obsolete, this obsolescence is most probably a consequence of the failure to develop external services and institutional structures adapted to small-town needs, particularly in credit, planning, and research. The decline of the small town during the decade of the 1950s has been further hastened by the absence of mortgage credit available for residential construction. Government guaranteed loans were available only in the large urban centers.

Raup also emphasized the impairment of the local tax base as a consequence of out-migration, with the decline in population leading to a collapse of rural nonfarm land values. During the 1950s there was a relative and absolute decline in property values in many of the small rural towns of the United States, despite continually increasing farm land prices. This erosion of the tax base curtails locally provided public services, further encouraging out-migration.

Of particular interest is Gardner's (1974) attempt to test the impact of out-migration from agriculture on the incomes of those left behind. Using cross-sectional data (state observations) for the 1960–1970 period, he found that faster rural-farm population decline was associated with faster growth of rural-farm income, while bearing no clear relation to growth of nonfarm rural incomes. In a simple regression he found that rural nonfarm incomes grew more rapidly the faster the farm population fell. In a more complete specification of the model, however, the coefficient of farm population decline is not statistically significant, independent of whether he used state or county observations.

Both Johnson's (1960) and Gardner's (1974) analyses suggest that out-migration from agriculture is equilibrating—the incomes of those left behind do rise. Few studies have addressed the more ambitious questions of whether a different pattern of development might have led to a more rapid adjustment, or whether aggregate gross national product for the economy as a whole might have grown more rapidly with an alternative migration process, in which, for instance, geographic migration was less and sectoral migration as a result was greater.

More conventional forms of capital frequently emigrate with labor, and this has implications for the length of the adjustment process. Ruttan (1966) has argued that in the United States an important share of capital leaves agriculture through the labor market, with the member of the family who stays on the farm buying out his brothers' and sisters' shares. In cases where a strong terms-of-trade effect might occur (such as a closed economy) this transfer of capital may accelerate the adjustment process by slowing down the rate of growth of agricultural output. On the other hand, if the terms of trade are relatively inflexible, the transfer of capital along with labor can stretch out the adjustment process since it retards the shift in resource proportions required to raise the productivity of labor.

It has been argued (Schuh, 1974) that there are also strong interactions between the land market and the migration process. To the extent that labor markets are clogged and labor is dammed up in agriculture, land values will tend to rise, other things being equal. The landowning potential migrant can realize this capital gain only by selling his land to others. At some point the rise in land values may provide the incentive for him to sell his land and leave the sector. This will permit reorganization of the remaining resources, and the migrant will have the capital gain to live on until he makes adjustment to employment elsewhere. Similarly, mechanization, which gives rise to pressures for farm enlargement, can cause land values to be bid up and in the same way provide incentives to migration.

The studies referred to so far have dealt with sectoral emigration, primarily in relation to U.S. agriculture. Greenwood's (1975) survey of the more general U.S. migration literature notes, among other things that it is the younger, more skilled, and better educated population groups that tend to migrate, leaving behind an older and less well trained group. Such selectivity may be debilitating to a *region,* as suggested by the cases of the U.S. South, the Northeast of Brazil, the South of Italy, and certain regions of Mexico. A region may lose the very resources that could reestablish its vitality, together with the conventional capital migrants take with them.[20] An equilibrium may eventually be reached, but the length of time required can be long and the resources left in the region may be underutilized from a social standpoint.

One body of literature discusses the impact of migration on the relative per capita income of receiving and sending regions. (It must be emphasized that this is not the same issue as the impact on those who stay behind.) Almost twenty years ago Myrdal (1957) argued that migrants tend to be in the most productive ages, and that migration widens the gap in per capita income between the advanced and the poorer region. Okun and Richardson (1961), however, showed that it is impossible on theoretical grounds to predict the effect of internal migration on inequality. Borts (1960) made a careful empirical analysis of the equalization of returns and regional economic growth in the United States as well as the conditions under which geographic migration could be equilibrating. For the three periods he considered—1919–1929, 1929–1948, and 1948–1953—per capita income among states converged only in the latter period. Interstate migration occurred, as expected, from low to high wage areas in all three periods, but the migration did not produce a convergence in earnings. Capital grew more rapidly in high wage states in two of the three periods considered, casting doubt on the hypothesis that low wages are a major influence on capital movements. And Borts concluded that product demand has a strong influence on the relative movements of capital and on the increase in wages. In his view this is the chief reason why wage convergence failed to appear in two out of the three periods considered.

Borts ignored the selectivity of migration, which could also explain why capital does not flow into the low-income regions; the best components of the labor force, with their skills and invested human capital, may be flowing out. The migration process may then be self-perpetuating, up to a point. Interestingly enough, there seems to be a general consensus in the literature that internal migration increases an economy's growth rate by achieving a more efficient allocation of resources.

This brief survey of some of the available literature, taken together with the lack of empirical work on the suggestive theoretical models presented in the previous section, suggests that a great deal of additional research will be needed to adequately understand the economic *consequences* of migration, as contrasted to the migration process per se, or what happens to the income of the migrant. Before turning to a discussion of these research implications, some of the tentative policy implications that both the theory and the available empirical results suggest will be discussed.

Perhaps the most important point is that migration in general is a response to normal growth processes, which require the reallocation of resources among activities as demand and supply conditions change. Interferences with this reallocation should generally be resisted, since they are likely to reduce aggregate output. On the other hand, in a growing economy, resource mobility should be facilitated and a reduction in the cost of transfer among activities should be an important part of any optimal policy.

At the same time, it may be that a more even spatial dispersal of economic activity might lead to a more efficient pattern of growth. Government policy often plays a major role both in the retardation of particular regions and in the concentration of economic activities in selected regions of a country. A better understanding of the implications of regional economic concentration may suggest that such policy is misguided.

It is also recognized that the participation of a geographic area in a larger political entity with a common currency can be deleterious to the region.[21] One solution, of course, is for the region to become an independent political entity and so have its own currency and an appropriate exchange rate. This was Leff's (1972) suggestion for the Northeast of Brazil. More practical solutions include subsidies to migration through retraining programs and other policies, and publicly induced flows of capital into the region, as Brazil has tried to do during this last decade in the Northeast.

The two key problems faced by policymakers with respect to migration are the transfer of labor out of agriculture as the economy develops, which in the past has usually meant the concentration of this labor in large urban centers, and the large geographic areas bypassed by the development process for one reason or another. These two situations require government assistance, if for no other reasons than the size, scope, and political implications they have. Other sectoral and regional adjustment problems will tend to be of smaller scope.

A policy of industrial decentralization, which amounts to an attempt to make capital more mobile and to channel it in the appropriate directions, can contribute to the solution of both the above problems. In the case of the rural-urban migration process, such a policy would provide a means of retaining the human capital and skills in the immediate area—in effect internalizing the externalities. The outflow of conventional capital would also be retarded or stopped, and the local tax base would remain strong.

Critics of such a strategy have for the most part rested their case on static efficiency arguments that ignore externalities. When the negative externalities of migration on both the sending and receiving regions are recognized, however, it may well be that a country could rationally expend considerable funds to decentralize its economic activities. Clearly, the goal should not be to erect barriers to geographic mobility for their own sake but rather to recognize the negative externalities associated with regional out-migration and to use regional economic policy to internalize these externalities. Subsidies and fiscal incentives can rationally be provided to decentralize industrial activity and to attract it to low wage areas. The gains could be considerable. Transfer of resources out of agriculture might be substantially increased since migration distances would be considerably shortened. Capital losses would be reduced or precluded. The allocation of human capital might be more efficient both in relation to the unskilled labor force and in relation to conventional capital. And, finally, a more nearly optimal rate of investment in human capital might be induced, since communities would be able to capture the returns to such investments. This in turn would lead to a higher rate of economic growth in its own right and could also facilitate the intersectoral migration.

Although the data do not uniformly support the proposition, the evidence from the United States,[22] and to a lesser extent from Brazil (Nicholls, 1969; Rios, 1969; and Katzman, 1974), suggests rather strongly that under a wide range of conditions, local industrialization makes for more efficient factor markets serving agriculture. More efficient factor markets, in turn, promote a rapid rate of modernization in agriculture and a reduction in the disparity in per capita income between the agricultural and nonagricultural sectors.

The moral to the story, of course, is that a proper strategy for promoting overall economic growth and agricultural development involves exploiting the positive interrelations between agriculture and other economic sectors. These interrelations can more easily be exploited if the industrial activities are dispersed geographically. Since governments widely intervene to promote industrialization, there is no obvious reason why they should not give some attention to the location of that industrialization. Doing so may make for more efficient labor markets, for a more rapid rate of productivity growth in agriculture, and for a higher rate of economic growth in the aggregate.

Although a more neutral government policy might substantially reduce observed tendencies to locational concentration, except in those cases where a fixed exchange rate among regions impedes an appropriate shift in the terms of trade, there is evidence from the U.S. experience that the rate of return to subsidized location can be quite high. Moes (1962), Rinehart (1963), and Saltzman (1964) examined private income and employment changes caused by subsidized location of a new plant. Moes reported average annual rates of return of 500 percent from subsidies to 130 industrial firms in Wisconsin, 800 percent for the Mississippi Balance Agriculture with Industry program (BAWI), and 900 percent for an Illinois industrial subsidization experience. Rinehart measured the impact of 22 firms on ten communities under three assumptions about the duration of the income stream from the new plant and the amount of subsidy paid. The annual rates of return ranged from 119 percent to 1,140 percent, depending on the assumptions used. Similarly, the benefit/cost ratio in Saltzman's study of industrialization in eighteen Oklahoma communities averaged 24 to 1.

Schaffer and Tweeten (1974) studied the economic effects of industrial development in five communities in eastern Oklahoma. They noted that generating jobs locally allows farmers to continue farming part-time, which is a gain in national income. They concluded that, in the short run, location of industrial plants in rural areas is beneficial to both the local community and nation. In the long run, retaining the population in rural areas through low wage industries could in their view have adverse effects on national income, but they concluded that the "long run" is so distant for the plants in question that bringing such jobs to rural people appears consistent with national economic efficiency over time. Their important caveat, however, is that it is neither possible nor desirable to bring jobs to every rural community, and that continued efforts to assist human resource development and mobility are very important.

Various other studies have found negative results from subsidized industrial location, validating the caution with which Schaffer and Tweeten draw their conclusions. Crecink (1970), for example, examined a Mississippi firm that failed after four years of operation despite financial assistance from public agencies. And Wadsworth and Conrad (1965) showed that estimates of community benefits based on plant payroll alone are often exaggerated. Policies designed to decentralize the industrialization process and to take it into areas of surplus labor require the use of discretion and should not attempt to preserve every community. So managed, it appears that the social benefits from a relative decentralization might be substantial.

## SOME SUGGESTIONS FOR RESEARCH

Out-migration from agriculture generally involves geographic as well as sectoral mobility. The theme of this chapter has been that geographic out-migration may impose sizable negative externalities on the supplying region, such that the migration may not be equilibrating or may require an inordinate amount of time to produce an equilibrium. The selectivity of migration can cause the incomes of nonmigrants to lag behind the rest of the economy and may prevent productivity from increasing in accord with the proportions of modernized theory. Some important areas requiring further research are as follows:

1. Careful evaluation of the consequences of out-migration, both sectoral and regional, on factor proportions and on the earnings of labor in the

supplying region and sector. Perhaps the most serious deficiency is in broad-based studies of the consequences of regional migration.

2. Identification and measurement of the externalities associated with out-migration. Only limited attention has been given to either the sectoral or regional dimension of this problem.

3. Study of factor market interactions. It is necessary to understand better how the land and labor markets interact, as well as how the capital and labor markets interact.

4. Identification and measurement of the flow of human capital associated with the flows of labor.[23]

5. Analysis of the interactions of technical change and selectivity of migration. It was hypothesized that rapid technological change may reverse the usual selectivity pattern of migration. If so, the policy implications are important.

6. Evaluation of the role of scarcity of labor as an inducement to technical change, and the conditions under which labor constraints may limit the adoption of production technology. This subject was discussed only tangentially in this chapter, but an interpretation of agricultural development gives considerable attention to it (Hayami and Ruttan, 1971).

7. Assessment of the effect of trade policy on the incentives to resource flows, with special emphasis on its effect on price relatives.

8. Evaluation of the role of credit and trade policy and social welfare programs in creating imperfections and distortions in labor markets.

9. Identification and measurement of external pecuniary economics from resource adjustments, especially as a consequence of technical change in agriculture.

10. Evaluation of the efficiency of subsidies and fiscal incentives as a means of obtaining optimal location of industry and other economic activities in light of externalities.

Research in areas such as those above will help to construct a more general theory of migration; available theory tends to neglect the externalities that are more clearly seen from a general equilibrium approach to the problem. A by-product of these efforts will be implications for the optimal geographic and occupational dispersion of human capital, an important problem about which very little is known.

## CONCLUDING COMMENTS

Migration performs an important function in the development process by facilitating structural change and helping to keep the difference between sectoral and regional incomes within bounds. Moreover, migration tends to have a beneficial effect on those migrants who can successfully make the adjustment.

However, although migration may ultimately be equilibrating, it is not without its costs. Geographic mobility in particular can impose sizable external diseconomies on both the supplying and receiving region. Moreover, it can drain critical resources from the supplying region so that the adjustment to the new equilibrium takes a very long time—perhaps a generation or more.

The main theme of this chapter is that a distinction should be made between regional migration and sectoral transfer in shaping migration policy. Sectoral movement should be encouraged and facilitated to accommodate the changing conditions of demand and supply as development proceeds. However, a decentralization and dispersion of the industrialization process may reduce the need for geographic mobility and at the same time lead to a more socially desirable allocation of resources. The key issues include how much capital flows with the labor as it migrates, the empirical significance of the externalities associated with high-quality labor, and whether the combined migration of human and conventional capital cause self-generating adjustments that go beyond a social optimum.

Migration, of course, is not necessarily a response to general economic differences among regions, but rather to personal opportunities. In that sense one might argue that not too much attention should be given to regions, in contrast to people. But two points seem pertinent. First, the political process or the relevant political entity is typically defined for a geographic area, and second, government funds are allocated on this basis. Hence, practically speaking, areas are important. But more importantly, the above analysis is not so much a concern with areas per se as with the people in those areas. The externalities that the analysis addresses affect the *people* in the areas, not the areas as such.

## NOTES

1. Commodity surplus is referred to in Nicholls's (1963) sense. Some authors, such as Ranis and Fei (1961), did consider an agricultural surplus to be an important variable in the model, but they tended to neglect the importance of policy directed to increasing the surplus.

2. For a survey, see Kao, Anschel, and Eicher (1964).

3. Perhaps the classic article in this regard was by Hopper (1955).

4. Walter Falcon addressed most of the pertinent issues in his 1970 paper before the American Agricultural Economic Association (Falcon, 1970).

5. The ethical implications of this more "equitable" distribution of income should not be taken too seriously, for all of the obvious and well-known reasons. Moreover, labor flow in the case posited would not necessarily

improve the personal or family distribution of income, since an improvement would depend on the distribution of capital by income levels in the labor-losing and labor-gaining regions.

6. For an excellent survey of this literature, see Bhagwati and Rodriguez (1975). The rest of this section draws mainly on that paper.

7. For a treatment of this proposition, see Berry and Soligo (1969).

8. For a discussion, see Berry and Soligo (1969).

9. This applies even though average incomes in the region or sector could rise if those leaving had received less than average income.

10. It should be noted that when the price elasticity of demand for the product is highly inelastic, this can easily occur.

11. This decline in price is reinforced by a decline in the demand price for capital goods as a result of emigration, since the decline in the labor/capital ratio implies a decline in the marginal productivity of capital, other things being equal.

12. It is unfortunate that so little attention has been given to the development of alternative, secure forms of holding wealth as an alternative to land reform, or even as a means of bringing it off. The advent of monetary correction (indexation) and the introduction of new capital instruments in Brazil in the mid-1960s led to sizable shifts of capital out of land and apartments to these new instruments.

13. Recognition of this fact in the context of the brain drain has led to suggestions that a tax be imposed on the emigrant to be remitted to the supplying country. See Bhagwati and Hamada (1974).

14. For a penetrating discussion of the externalities associated with education, see Weisbrod (1964).

15. Welch (1970) used this model to explain the failure of the rate of return to investments in education to decline in the U.S. economy, despite a phenomenal increase in the average level of education between 1940 and 1960, and with it a major shift in the proportion of the total stock of capital in the economy made up of human capital.

16. The contrast between the state of São Paulo and the rest of Brazil is interesting in this regard. Similarly, the contrast between a country like Brazil and the United States is also insightful.

17. Baer (1964) was the first to call attention to the regional discrimination inherent in Brazil's trade and development policy. For a more recent update, see Martin and Schuh (1976).

18. Mechanical technology, for example, tends to be labor displacing while having very little effect on output.

19. Johnson's (1960) analysis deals with sectoral adjustment, and says little about the problem of regional adjustment, or the case in which both regional and sectoral adjustments are involved in the resource transfer. More important, he assumes that resources are homogenous, and neglects any possible selectivity in the migration process.

20. In the case of the Northeast of Brazil, the problem has been further aggravated because the trade policy that discriminated against agriculture in

effect discriminated particularly against the Northeast. As a result, there was a sizable net transfer of capital from the Northeast to the higher-income South during an important part of the post–World War II period. This transfer was primarily a result of a policy-induced shift in the terms of trade against the region. See Baer (1964), and Martin and Schuh (1976).

21. For a discussion of the problem of an optional currency area, see Mundell (1961).

22. For a survey and evaluation, see Schuh (1969).

23. For a careful discussion of the conceptual problems and data requirements, see Bowman and Myers (1967).

## BIBLIOGRAPHY

Baer, W. "Regional Inequality and Economic Growth in Brazil." *Economic Development and Cultural Change* 12, no. 3 (April 1964), pp. 268-285.

Berry, R. A. "Impact of Factor Emigration on the Losing Region." *The Economic Record* 50, no. 131 (September 1974), pp. 405-422.

Berry, R. A., and Soligo, R. "Some Welfare Aspects of International Migration." *Journal of Political Economy* 77, no. 5 (September/October 1969), pp. 778-794.

Bhagwati, J., and Hamada, K. "The Brain Drain, International Integration of Markets for Professionals and Unemployment: A Theoretical Analysis." *Journal of Development Economics* 1, no. 1 (June 1974), pp. 19-42.

Bhagwati, J., and Rodriguez, C. "Welfare Theoretical Analysis of the Brain Drain." *Journal of Development Economics* 2, no. 3 (September 1975), pp. 195-222.

Borts, G. H. "The Equalization of Returns and Regional Economic Growth." *American Economic Review* 50, no. 3 (June 1960), pp. 319-347.

Bowman, M. J., and Myers, R. G. "Schooling, Experience, and Gains and Losses in Human Capital Through Migration." *Journal of the American Statistical Association* 62, no. 319 (September 1967), pp. 875-898.

Crecink, J. C. *Rural Industrialization: Case Study of a Tissue Paper Mill in Pickens, Mississippi.* Agricultural Economics Report no. 189, Economic Research Service, U.S. Department of Agriculture, September 1970.

Falcon, W. P. "The Green Revolution: Generations of Problems." *American Journal of Agricultural Economics* 52, no. 5 (December 1970), pp. 698-710.

Gardner, B. L. "Farm Population Decline and the Income of Rural Families." *American Journal of Agricultural Economics* 56, no. 3 (August 1974), pp. 600-606.

Gisser, M. "Schooling and the Farm Problem." *Econometrica* 33, no. 3 (July 1965), pp. 582-592.

Greenwood, M. J. "Research on Internal Migration in the United States: A Survey." *Journal of Economic Literature* 13, no. 2 (June 1975), pp. 397-433.

Grubel, H., and Scott, A. "The International Flow of Human Capital."

*American Economic Review* 54, no. 2 (May 1966), pp. 268–274.

Hayami, Y., and Ruttan, V. W. *Agricultural Development, An International Perspective*. Baltimore: Johns Hopkins University Press, 1971.

Hopper, W. "Allocative Efficiency in a Traditional Indian Agriculture." *Journal of Farm Economics* 47, no. 3 (August 1955), pp. 611–624.

Johnson, D. G. "Output and Income Effects of Reducing the Farm Labor Force." *Journal of Farm Economics* 42, no. 4 (November 1960), pp. 779–796.

____. *World Agriculture in Disarray*. London: Fontana/Collins in association with Trade Policy Research Centre, 1973, Chapter 9.

Johnson, G. L., and Quance, C. L. (eds.). *The Overproduction Trap in U.S. Agriculture*. Baltimore: Johns Hopkins University Press, 1972.

Johnson, Harry. "Some Economic Aspects of the Braindrain." *Pakistan Development Review* 3 (1967).

Kao, H. C., Anschel, J., and Eicher, C. K. "Disguised Unemployment: A Survey." In Carl Eicher and Lawrence Witt (eds.), *Agriculture in Economic Development*. New York: McGraw-Hill Book Company, 1964, pp. 129–144.

Katzman, M. T. "The Von Thuenen Paradigm, The Industrial-Urban Hypothesis, and the Spatial Structure of Agriculture." *American Journal of Agricultural Economics* 56, no. 4 (November 1974), pp. 683–696.

Kenen, P. B. "Migration, the Terms of Trade, and Economic Welfare in the Source Country." In J. Bhagwati, et al. (eds.), *Trade, Balance of Payments and Growth*. Amsterdam: North Holland, 1971, pp. 238–260.

Leff, N. H. "Development and Regional Inequality in Brazil." *Quarterly Journal of Economics* 84, no. 2 (May 1972), pp. 243–262.

Lewis, W. "Economic Development with Unlimited Supplies of Labor." *Manchester School of Economic and Social Studies* 22 (May 1954), pp. 139–191.

Maddox, J. G. "Private and Social Costs of the Movement of Rural People Out of Agriculture." *American Economic Review* 50, no. 2 (May 1960), pp. 392–402.

Martin, M., and Schuh, G. E. "Brazilian Trade Policy and Its Impact on the Regional Distribution of Income." Mimeo. Paper presented at the Annual Meetings of the American Agricultural Economic Association, College Station, Pennsylvania, August 15–18, 1976.

Michael, R. R. "The Effect of Education on Efficiency in Consumption." Occasional Paper 116, National Bureau of Economic Research, New York: Columbia University Press, 1972.

Mishan, E. J., and Needleman, L. "Immigration: Some Long-Term Consequences." *Economia Internazionale* 21, nos. 2 and 3 (1968), pp. 281–300 (Part A); pp. 515–524 (Part B).

Moes, J. E. *Local Subsidies to Industry*. Chapel Hill: University of North Carolina Press, 1962.

Mundell, R. A. "A Theory of Optimum Currency Areas." *American Economic Review* 51, no. 4 (September 1961), pp. 657–665.

Myrdal. G. *Economic Theory and Underdeveloped Regions.* London: Duckworth, 1957, p. 27.

Nicholls, W. H. "The Agricultural 'Surplus' as a Factor in Economic Development." *Journal of Political Economy* 71, no. 1 (February 1963), pp. 1–29.

___. "The Transformation of Agriculture in a Semi-Industrialized Country: The Case of Brazil." In Erik Thorbecke (ed.), *The Role of Agriculture in Economic Development.* National Bureau of Economic Research, New York: Columbia University Press, 1969.

Okun, B., and Richardson, R. W. "Regional Income Inequality and Internal Population Migration." *Economic Development and Cultural Change* 9, no. 2 (January 1961), pp. 128–143.

Patrick, G., and de Carvalho Filho, J. J. *Low-Income Groups in Brazilian Agriculture: A Progress Report.* Station Bulletin No. 79, Agricultural Experiment Station, Purdue University, Lafayette, Indiana, April 1975.

President's National Advisory Commission on Rural Poverty. *The People Left Behind.* Washington, D.C.: U.S. Government Printing Office, 1967.

Ranis, G., and Fei, J.C.H. "A Theory of Economic Development." *American Economic Review* 51, no. 4 (September 1961), pp. 534–565.

Raup, P. M. "Economic Aspects of Population Decline in Rural Communities." In Earl O. Heady (ed.), *Labor Mobility and Population in Agriculture.* Ames: Iowa State University Press, 1961, pp. 95–106.

Rinehart, J. R. "Rates of Return on Municipal Subsidies to Industry." *Southern Economic Journal* 29 (April 1963), pp. 297–306.

Rios, P. L. "The Impact of Industrialization on the Agricultural Sector of Minas Gerais." Unpublished Ph.D. thesis, Iowa State University, 1969.

Ruttan, V. W. "Agricultural Policy in an Affluent Society." *Journal of Farm Economics* 48, no. 5 (December 1966), pp. 1100–1120.

Saltzman, D. R. *Economic Case Studies of Community Sponsored Efforts to Develop Industry.* Small Business Administration, Management Research Summary MRS-205, Tulsa, Okla.: Tulsa University Department of Commerce and Industry, April 1964.

Schaffer, R. E., and Tweeten, L. G. *Economic Changes from Industrial Development in Eastern Oklahoma.* Bulletin B-715, Agricultural Experiment Station, Stillwater, Oklahoma: Oklahoma State University, July 1974.

Schuh, G. E. "Comment," in Thorbecke, Erik (ed.) *The Role of Agriculture in Economic Development.* National Bureau of Economic Research, New York: Columbia University Press, 1969.

___. "The Exchange Rate and U.S. Agriculture." *American Journal of Agricultural Economics* 56, no. 1 (February 1974), pp. 1–13.

___. "The New Macroeconomics of Agriculture." *American Journal of Agricultural Economics* 58, no. 5 (December 1976).

Schuh, G. E., and Leeds, J. R. "A Regional Analysis of the Demand for Hired Agricultural Labor." *Papers and Proceedings of the Regional Science Association* 11 (December 1963), pp. 295–308.

Schultz, T. W. "A Framework for Land Economics—The Long View." *Journal of Farm Economics* 33, no. 2 (May 1951), pp. 204-215.

\_\_\_. "The Education of Farm People: An Economic Perspective." In P. Foster and J. R. Sheffield (eds.), *Education and Rural Development.* World Book of Education 1974. London: Evans Brothers, 1973, pp. 50-68.

\_\_\_. "The Value of the Ability to Deal with Disequilibria." *Journal of Economic Literature* 13, no. 3 (September 1975), pp. 827-876.

Schwartz, A. "On Efficiency of Migration." *Journal of Human Resources* 6, no. 2 (Spring 1971), pp. 193-205.

Sjaastad, L. A. "The Costs and Returns of Human Migration." *Journal of Political Economy* 70, no. 5, part 2 (Supplement, October 1972), pp. 80-93.

Taves, M. J. "Consequences of Population Loss in Rural Communities" in *Labour Mobility and Population in Agriculture,* Centre for Agricultural and Economic Adjustment. Ames, Iowa: Iowa State University, 1961.

Todaro, M. "A Model of Labor Migration and Urban Unemployment in Less-Developed Countries." *American Economic Review* 59, no. 1 (March 1969), pp. 138-148.

Wadsworth, H. A., and Conrad, J. M. "Leakages Reducing Employment and Income Multipliers in Labor Surplus Rural Areas." *Journal of Farm Economics* 47, no. 5 (December 1965), pp. 1197-1202.

Wallace, T. D., and Hoover, D. M. "Income Effects of Innovation: The Case of Labor in Agriculture." *Journal of Farm Economics* 48, no. 2 (May 1966), pp. 325-336.

Weisbrod, B. *External Benefits of Education.* Princeton, N.J.: Industrial Relations Section, Princeton University, 1964.

Welch, F. "Education in Production." *Journal of Political Economy* 78, no. 1 (January/February 1970), pp. 35-59.

# 6
# Migration from Rural Areas of Poor Countries: The Impact on Rural Productivity and Income Distribution

## MICHAEL LIPTON

### INTRODUCTION

Migration from rural areas means the departure of individuals or households for more than a week or so from the small, primarily agricultural communities in which they live. The migration can be for a harvest or for life; to cities or to villages; for marriage, for work, or for study. Much of this migration is missed in empirical research. Rural surveys usually omit households totally removed from the village, as well as individuals resident too long elsewhere to be regarded by their relatives (the respondents) as household members. Urban surveys, on the other hand, miss rural-rural migrants. Because many types of work have to be drawn together although their aims and methods are different, the following analysis of migration may seem like casual empiricism. The hypotheses of this chapter are, however, asserted with more confidence than the evidence perhaps warrants, in the hope of provoking the collection of better data to test them.

The impact of migration depends on the numbers involved, the duration of absence, the effect of both absence and possible return on migrants and their home communities, and the concentration of migrants' origins in a few places or classes. Rural migration is defined here as the ratio at an average time of year (if one could measure it) of the members of a rural community residing elsewhere to the population of the community before they left, net of corresponding immigrants. I argue (pp. 198–201) that this ratio is much smaller than is usually thought, being susceptible both to statistical overstatement and to forces reducing it. However, since net rural emigration is concentrated on particular areas, groups, and seasons, a small national flow can considerably redistribute resources among and within rural communities, and between rural and urban areas. Most neoclassical economists would expect voluntary population movements to cut inefficiency and inequality (pp. 201–02): an expectation belied by most recent experience, almost certainly intrarurally, and probably for the economy as a whole (pp. 208–15). This is not to say that migration is irrational or fails to raise the migrant's own income; such statements are seldom true of regions of any size.

Rural-urban migration might affect four aspects of rural output: per worker, per man-hour, per efficiency-weighted unit of rural labor, or per unit of price-weighted total factor inputs.[1] Initially, we make the following assumptions:

1. Migrant/nonmigrant ratios are identical for all rural age groups in both sexes at each level of education and income ("balanced migration").[2]
2. Emigrants are all exactly self-supporting—no remittances flow either way between city and country.
3. Emigrants and remaining villagers have identical community indifference maps between income and leisure.
4. The average product of labor over the range of plausible variation in labor inputs due to migration is constant in face of such variation.

Under these assumptions, the community of remaining villagers has no reason to alter its labor input after migration. For all ages and both sexes, rural labor input and rural population fall in the same proportions as rural output, by assumption 4 above. Hence rural output per worker, man-hour, and efficiency unit of rural labor do not change. If land is cheaply extensible and capital negligible, land goes out of cultivation as migrants withdraw. Since the worst land is given up first, more land falls idle than in proportion to the fall in work force. With a Laspèyres price-weighted index for inputs including land, total factor productivity therefore increases—if perhaps somewhat spuriously—following emigration even on these extreme homogeneity assumptions.

Even given that the first three assumptions above are true, in 95 percent of the rural Third World the average product of labor is not constant, because new land is scarce or costly to bring under the plough. Thus assumption (4), constant average product of labor must give way to the normal neoclassical assumption (4') that as work force (such as balanced migrant work force) is withdrawn, the marginal and average product of labor increases. Hence emigration as such raises the rural output per worker and per man-hour at first. The villagers, however, respond to the incentive—more marginal physical product (MPP) for the labor of peasants and more marginal value product (MVP) and hence wage for the labor of employees—by raising labor input per villager. Especially in the peak season, therefore, some mixture of tired man-hours by established members of the work force and inexperienced man-hours by new members is added to the work applied. This pushes down rural output per worker and per man-hour, and one can easily specify sufficiently high price-elasticities of supply of effort, combined with sufficiently low output-elasticities with respect to extra effort of falling quality, so that the rural output per worker and output per man-hour end up lower than before emigration. Such specification is not very plausible, however, and its analog with regard to rural output per efficiency unit of rural labor is even less so, because measurement of labor input in efficiency units eliminates the apparent fall in labor productivity resulting from the rising share of man-hours contributed by the old, the young, and women. As for rural output per unit of price-weighted total factor inputs, assuming a rise in rural output per man-hour even after responses to incentive, a rise in total factor productivity would follow if output rose faster (or fell more slowly) than other factor inputs. A rise in output per unit of land is less certain once we replace the constant average produce assumption with the assumption that average product increases as labor is withdrawn. After emigration the amount of cultivated land might fall more slowly than output even though labor input fell faster than output, not only when this constituted a profit-maximizing procedure on one-season production functions, but even otherwise; for example, if land scarcity, or conflicts, or high rehabilitation costs made farmers unwilling to give up cultivating areas they might need later on.

So, under assumptions (1), (2), (3), (4'), emigration very probably raises rural production per efficiency unit of labor; somewhat less probably per worker and per man-hour; and, less confidently but still plausibly, per unit of total factor inputs. If capital is introduced as a factor of production, confidence in the conclusion is reduced even further. But for policy purposes it is much less important to deal with this and to model the increased complexity than to point out that the neoclassical edifice collapses once we pause to consider the plausibility of assumptions (1) to (3). As for (3), even given (1), emigrants almost certainly prefer income over leisure more than nonemigrants at any constellation of prices and wages. They are more willing to take risks, and to incur current costs, in order to find new ways of replacing leisure by income at old rates, or old ways of doing so at higher rates. They are also more likely to possess the organizing skills that enable an enterprise to transform inputs into income effectively. By leaving the rural sector the migrants possessing these attributes reduce the rate at which those who remain can transform inputs into outputs. This counterbalances, and may outweigh, the favorable effect of migration on rural prodctivity via (4').

The impact of dropping the assumption that emigrants are all self-supporting is unclear; it increases the indeterminancy of the effect of migration on rural productivity in all four aspects of rural output. If migrants send in substantial net remittances, the remaining villagers can achieve a given level of living with less income and effort, and are thus encouraged to substitute leisure for effort. With imperfect rural capital markets, however, such remittances might be needed if villagers are to pay for physical capital, and thus to embody in it technical progress that would certainly raise rural output per worker, per man-hour, and per efficiency unit of rural labor, and probably per unit of price-weighted total factor inputs too. If villagers send out remittances to support migrants, both effects are reversed. The sparse evidence, shown later in this chapter, suggests that *net* remittances are quite small relative to village income; are concentrated on richer village households unlikely to suffer from capital constraints; and tend to be little used to finance investment, except in house building and in such items as tractors to replace absent migrants from other social classes. The net effect of dropping the assumption that emigrants are self-supporting on the impact of emigration upon rural total factor productivity, then, does not look very promising.

When we consider the plausibility of assuming balanced migration and the effects of dropping it, the frailty of a priori neoclassical reasoning—from emigration via rising MPP of rural labor to rising rural productivity—becomes very clear. As we shall see, in the really poor rural areas of Africa and South and Southeast Asia, rural emigration is overwhelmingly concentrated among young men, it over-represents the educated, and it is probably bipolar with respect to income and status, concentrating on the fairly high and the fairly low. One need not despair of eventually encompassing these complexities in a formal model, but their destructive effect on the expectation of rural productivity gains based on balanced emigration, in the simplistic model with the neoclassical assumptions (1)-(4'), is clear. The next task is to examine the evidence before engaging in more a priori theorizing.

Even if the evidence of the impact of emigration on rural areas leads to gloomy conclusions, such emigration is not necessarily nonrational from the migrants' standpoint; indeed, they expect, rightly in most cases, to raise their own incomes. Nor does it mean that their migration should be impeded, adding imprisonment to the other rural disadvantages and ignoring the possible benefits of mobility for *urban* growth. No, the implications are rather that since development almost certainly implies steady labor transfers out of agriculture (and since most expectations of efficient labor absorption by rural industry are probably misplaced), governments should stop allocating investment and incentives in ways that encourage excessive, premature, and therefore disappointing labor transfers. Accordingly, investment and incentive biases against the rural sector must be corrected, and labor-replacing activities from tractors to tower cranes must cease to be subsidized through cheap foreign exchange, investment allowances, and tax holidays.

Moreover, market distortions, misincentives, and maldistribution all mean that any positive gain in rural or national productivity as a result of migration (observable at market prices) is reduced at "appropriate" prices and may become negative. Market distortions almost always assist monopoly and cartel formation more in the concentrated, articulate, capital-intensive parts of the urban sector than in any parts of the rural sector. Consequent high urban output prices, assisted by easier urban unionization, raise urban wages relative to rural wages, pulling in more migrants at market prices than would be the case at standard accounting prices and producing a larger urban share of a higher GNP. Misincentives that are caused by public policy have similar effects (Lipton, 1977). Very unequal distribution of income encourages higher, and usually urban, production of nonfoods—especially durable consumer goods and luxury houses. Production of these goods requires more migration than would occur if incomes were more equal.

One other consideration militates against any productivity gains from urbanization. Rural migrants to towns incur 5 to 20 percent higher living costs (Chatterjee and Bhattacharya, 1969; Knight, 1971) because of the higher urban cost of food and shelter, transport to work, and related services.[3] Hence the "force" of any net productivity gains induced by net migration— the welfare impact of the extra output due to relocation of persons—is reduced, as it is also by the transport and training costs of migration itself.

Turning to the impact on income distribution, the two major issues are whose income distribution is affected and which dimensions of that distribution are affected. Much of this chapter will be devoted to explaining why migrant streams are so structured that—contrary to the expectations of marginal analysis (Hoselitz, 1972; Stiglitz, 1973)—their movement worsens overall distribution among remaining rural persons, among remaining rural persons plus migrants, and between village and town. The impact on distribution among townspeople is little known, though if these are the most unequal to begin with, this impact may have the greatest moral importance. It is certainly complicated: new migrants are unlikely to be as desperate as the last batch of failed migrants; they are younger and stronger than average townspeople, but also poorer and less literate; they may well drive urban wage rates down but urban employment rates up. And many observers would claim that gains from migration in shaking once immovable barriers to equal *opportunity*—age, sex, social hierarchy—could outweigh the increased inequality in other areas.

The central argument here emerges from a cross-section analysis of migration data from several hundred village studies (Connell et al., 1976).[4] The argument is that there are two main types of migrant, tending to come from similar types of village, but polarizing the impact on the rural sector through their different backgrounds, migrant behaviors, and prospects, so that inequalities within (and probably among) villages increase, contrary to neoclassical expectations.

The following "ideal type" of high-migration village is probably not far out, although it stretches the available evidence past its intended limits.

Such a village has relatively unequal distribution of land, a high proportion of landless laborers, and probably a low land/man ratio. The village is relatively literate and has good urban contacts, being fairly near a road and a town (but not so near that people commute to work or school instead of migrating), and it has access to information and influence through previous migrants to the town. Yet it also has many poor people—landless or minifarmers—whose migratory search for outside income is different in nature from that of better-off migrants.

Two main migrant streams flow from such a village. The deficit farmers and landless laborers—though seldom the *very* poorest, who cannot afford the initial cost of movement—tend to be pushed out; they would not be pushed out, however, if inequality in the village were less. The sons of the bigger farmers—though seldom the biggest, who must guard their assets and who have enough for all their sons to prosper rurally—tend to be pulled out, assisted in bearing costs of urban education or urban job search by the bigger rural surpluses generated by village inequality.

Thus "push" and "pull" migration are twin children of inequality in the same sort of village, but they are also sources of new inequality. The push migration of the poor is, at first, individual rather than family-linked in motivation. It takes the migrant short distances towards doubtful, dwindling, and imprecise prospects in the informal urban sector, or (more importantly and increasingly) in the rural sector; it involves mostly illiterates; and, because it fails to generate much extra income or skill, it eventually tends to drive the whole household to quit the rural community of origin, in what is increasingly becoming a wandering drift across the countryside in search of work. The pull migration of the better-off, on the contrary, aims—often over long distances—at a selected town, either to obtain education or to exploit the higher urban-rural income differentials to which earlier education has given access. It is linked to family requirements as articulated by the head of the household and tends, therefore, to generate income, skills, knowledge, or remittances useful to the family as a whole.

To the extent that migration conforms to the above highly simplified picture, it increases rural inequality. It does so *within* villages, because pull migration allows the better-off to advance as a group, while push migration (though individually usually better than the alternative) weakens the poor and sets some of their potential leaders roaming the countryside without a base.[5] Migration worsens inequality *among* villages because, inasmuch as it confers net benefits, a few villages reap benefits from successive migrations, whereas remote and "backward" (albeit more equal) villages seldom hook onto the chain of successive movements, contacts, and information through which migratory traditions are transmitted in a community. And, since migration is supposed to be a process that cures inefficiency by reducing inequality (sending migrants, whether doctors or farm laborers, where scarcity makes their incomes unusually high), its failure to reduce inequality suggests a failure to cure inefficiency.[6]

But what is the evidence? First, among the forty-odd villages with strictly comparable data sets (chiefly in North and West India), over two-thirds of the variance in individuals' rates of migration can be associated with *either* only push factors—high man/land ratios, low yields, and indices of intravillage inequality—*or* only pull factors—cash cropping, sale of produce, nearness to town, and literacy rate (Connell et al., 1976; Dasgupta and Laishley, 1975). Typically the push factors are collinear but the pull factors vary independently. The two are clearly at work together in one group of villages and absent together in another group.

Second, for *household* migration between survey and resurvey, in fourteen villages of Northeast India some 30 percent of variance is associated with differences in one inequality indicator alone—the proportion of land owned by the top 10 percent of households (Connell et al., 1976). In two districts of Bihar the lowest and highest income groups showed the highest propensity to migrate (Sovani, 1965). Ivory Coast data also suggest two types of migrant—"the illiterate, unskilled migrant laborer, who remains rural-orientated," and "the high-aspiring, village-abhorring, would-be permanent towndwellers" (Joshi, 1973). In eleven villages in Nepal, emigration was highest (McDougal, n.d.) in two polar gorups: villages with most landlessness and least irrigated land, and villages with the opposite features.

Evidence exists, not only for the general proposition that the same villages expel better-off pull migrants *and* worse-off push migrants, but also for the specifics, such as education. In Colombia (Haney, 1965), Brazil (Sahota, 1968), and Liberia (Riddell, 1970), rural-rural movements have been associated with the illiterate poor, and rural-urban movements with the better-educated less poor. The link between education and planned trial migration to a particular city where work is sought has been noted in Latin America (Bourge, 1967) and prerevolutionary China (Yang, 1959). High propensities to migrate have been associated with *both* illiteracy *and* high education in San Salvador, and associated age-specifically with high education in Ghana (Caldwell, 1969; Foster, 1965), Kenya (Todaro, 1971), and the Philippines (Hart, 1971). Three percent of the illiterates born in the households of sixteen North Indian villages had migrated—11.5 percent of those with primary education, 9 percent with middle, and 20 percent with secondary; the "dip" at middle level is statistically significant at 5 percent (Connell et al., 1976).[7] The "educated to the big city, illiterate to rural areas or small towns" pattern has been validated in Tanzania (Sabot, 1972), Thailand (Sakdejayont, 1973), and the Philippines (Hart, 1971). African and Polynesian evidence suggests that uneducated poor migrants must learn by doing through step migration, while the better-informed and better-off can make straight for the goal, thus lowering the costs of migration (Allen, 1969; Baxter, 1973; Amin, 1974). Finally, migration for education—with its heavy costs, uncertain outcome, and delayed returns—is inevitably linked to higher income. However, in our Indian case study the villages with relatively high student migration were, in general, those that also featured high labor migration from the poorer classes (Connell et al., 1976).

## SCALE AND IMPACT OF MIGRATION

In a situation of gross intrarural inequality, really promising forms of migration, like any new technology or opportunity not specific to the poor, will be taken up initially by the better-off,[8] who "saturate" the new prospect with fewer units of effort, leading to less output-per-unit from that prospect. However, it is true that permanent and net rural-urban migration remains marginal in the poor countries of Africa and South and Southeast Asia, partly because of the unexpectedly slow shifts of workers out of agriculture. A regression function for LDCs in the 1960s linking share of work force in agriculture with income per person, taking into account information about income growth in the 1960s, would predict much more rapid industrialization of the work force than has actually happened (Kuznets, 1971). In India, despite such unfounded assumptions as that "the agricultural population will drop to 55 percent by 1980-85 as against 70 percent in 1950-55" (Bansil, 1971), the agricultural population has stayed obstinately around 70 percent from 1931 to 1971 (Krishnamurthy, 1972). Indeed, for 1950-1967, as many countries recorded a significant rise in agricultural shares of work force as recorded similar falls, both in Africa (six each) and in South and Southeast Asia (four each) (FAO, 1970).

Sustainable net urbanization depends on lowering the agricultural share of the work force. Corresponding to the data in the last paragraph, therefore, *gross* rural-urban migration in the 1950s was only 3 percent of rural population in South Asia, 6 percent in Southeast Asia and 7 percent in Africa (Jolly, 1971). Though analyses of the 1971 census are incomplete, it is clear that the rates fell in the 1960s and will probably continue to fall, as argued below. In China, even the absolute urban share of population fell in the 1960s (Piotrow, 1971). From 1951 through 1971, Calcutta's population grew more slowly than that of rural West Bengal (Lubell, 1973). At the 1961 census, only 4.2 percent of Indians were rural-born townsmen, while 1.1 percent were urban-born villagers, so that net rural-urban migrants were perhaps 15 percent of townsmen, but below 4 percent of villagers; at least half of even this small net migration was temporary in intention (Bose, 1971). Similarly low figures apply to Pakistan (Afzal, 1971).

The myth of mass rural-urban migration is fostered by three statistical illusions. First, a city, physically expanding with natural increase, often "swallows" villages without changing their character, as in the Philippines (McGee, 1971). Second, natural increase pushes many communities across arbitrary urban-rural borderlines: in Peru between 1940 and 1961, population grew by 51 percent, but in places with over 20,000 people, population grew by 220 percent; one-quarter of this 220 percent was due to such border-line crossing, another third to natural increase of the 1940 urban population, and about another tenth to natural increase of subsequent migrants, leaving less than half due to migration as such (Harris, 1971). Similar calculations are possible elsewhere. Third, two nearby villages, expanding with natural increase, may become contiguous and thus acquire the status of a single community above the urban border line.

Further natural misinterpretations lead observers to overstate the *permanence* of trends in migration. In many poor countries, temporary migration has for centuries been a "rite of passage" from adolescence to adulthood (International Development Research Center, 1973; Lea, 1964; Riddell, 1970; Bedford, 1973). The proportion of villagers involved in townward migration will rise with the proportion of late adolescents in the population, even if no age group alters its propensity for (or duration of) migration. This adolescent proportion has indeed been increased by the fall in child mortality, particularly the selective impact of malaria eradication on the death rates of children under age eight. But *temporary* migration—which is what has thus risen—has different, fewer, and cheaper policy implications, especially for urban social provision, than permanent migration. As age structures stabilize, rural proportions of late adolescents will fall, bringing life cycle townward migration rates down again; meanwhile the over-45s will have become a growing share of *urban* populations, and their return migration will further depress total *net* townward migration rates. Thus there is net urban-rural migration in this group in Ghana (Caldwell, 1969) and elsewhere in Africa (Byerlee, 1972), and retirement probably creates similar patterns in New Guinea (Salisbury and Salisbury, 1972) and Bombay (Zachariah, 1968).

The sex ratios of recent streams of migrants also cuts the scale of urbanization in the long run. Migrant streams in Asia and Africa are overwhelmingly male. They are large compared with the urban population, but small compared with the still rural 65–90 percent of the population. Hence huge sex imbalances appear in childbearing age groups in towns, but small or no imbalances in rural areas (Lipton, 1964). Recent UN *Demographic Yearbooks* show the following typical male/female ratios for age groups 15–44: Ghana, 1,176 urban and 895 rural; Kenya, 1,696 urban and 832 rural; India, 1,253 urban and 1,000 rural; and Pakistan, 1,428 urban and 1,020 rural.[9] Also, family planning has more impact in towns: the family planning programs may enjoy economies of scale; program spending per person is higher; and average levels of education mean that people are more receptive. Therefore, birthrates in urban areas fall well below rural rates. (So do deathrates, but not enough to compensate.) Hence any improvements in the allocation of labor that may be generated in neoclassical fashion by townward migration are offset by reverse demographic "allocations" brought about by the migration itself.

Economic mechanisms also tend to choke off rural-urban migration, and hence the capacity of migration to affect rural production and income distribution. First, rising marginal costs affect many urban services, notably water, sewage, urban transport, and fire and police protection. These costs affect individuals rather than firms, whose average costs, at least in India, seem to fall as city size increases to 200,000–250,000, and to stabilize thereafter (Wellisz, 1971; Berry, 1971). Second, city expansion raises land prices for both homes and amenities; new immigrants increasingly rely on urban moneylenders or on relatives with spare space. Third, past immigration—plus the disappointing growth of urban demand for labor—increasingly induces settled workers to organize job protection against future immigrants.

Traditional rural-*rural* marriage migration, often based on village exogamy (Bose, 1971), still exists in quantity, as does emigration from *some* villages, notably in Central Africa and Papua New Guinea (Connell et al., 1976). However, for forty North Indian villages surveyed in 1955–1970, student and working migrant absentees averaged only 4 percent of village populations (Connell et al., 1976) (total household emigration was not covered). Most microeconomic evidence does not suggest massive, net, system-changing rural migration for major areas or classes in many poor countries. This is confirmed by the national demographic considerations already mentioned. Moreover, the falling birthrates of the late 1960s and early 1970s in many poor countries will, as neonates grow up into peak migration age groups (15–25), depress national average urbanization rates.[10]

On some groups and areas, however, the concentrated impact of rural emigration is large. The long-established "catchment areas" for mines and plantations, especially in Africa, and the recent large streams of rural-rural migration from eastern Uttar Pradesh to the "wheat revolution" areas of the Indian Punjab, spring to mind. More systematically, concentration is associated with proximity to towns and main roads. In Colombia, Papua New Guinea, and (for student migrants) India, for villages not very far from towns, distance is *positively* and significantly linked with migration (Schultz, 1971; Connell et al., 1976; Lea and Weinard, 1971; Salisbury and Salisbury, 1972). Time-series studies of catchment areas are not available, but one would expect rural areas 5–20 miles from the centers of urban attraction to send out migrants first and to do so increasingly as information spreads through the rural community. As potential migrant sources in this area are exhausted, the main belt of attraction would move out to 20-35 miles. A complex mixture of gravity-flow and infection models is indicated by the mixed metaphor. In any event, net emigration from rural areas, small on a national scale, concentrates upon different places as time passes—as well as on particular groups—so that its impact can be large on a local scale.

## REGIONAL EFFECTS OF MIGRATION AND THE BELIEF IN EQUILIBRIUM

Can more by said about the regional impact of migration? Most studies are insufficiently recent, or have been done in the wrong place, so that they cannot illustrate any impact of high-yielding grain varieties and associated inputs. Nevertheless, there is apparent (though, in fact, "ecologically fallacious") support for the equilibrating hypothesis that migration corrects localized poverty and locally low labor productivity because people with underprivileged living standards will vote with their feet against regional biases. Where land is scarce, man/land ratios correlate significantly and positively with various measures of migration in Polynesia (Walsh and Trlin, 1973), Turkey (Ministry of Village Affairs, 1965–1968), Chile (Shaw, 1974), Andean America as a whole (Preston, 1969), and Pakistan (Rochin, 1972). The few counter-examples are in areas where land is plentiful and migrants seek capital to expand the land frontier with cash cropping (Bedford, 1973); or are due to differences in land quality—plentiful but bad land can also produce equilibrating, push emigration (Brookfield, 1960; Cisneros, 1959); or are due to time-series effects in that *past* high emigration is linked to reduced current man/land ratios (Baxter, 1973; Essang and Mabawonku, 1974). Thus, while our Indian case study emphasizes the many causes of migration, the key role of high man/land ratios provides consistent encouragement to the optimistic, equilibrating view of migration.

Such a view is nevertheless fallacious. To argue from the point that "poor villages expel more migrants" to the point that "poor villagers are likeliest to migrate" is to commit a classic "ecological fallacy" (Dasgupta and Laishley, 1975). In fact, it is seldom the poorest who migrate and more seldom who migrate successfully. This study reveals only two clear positive associations *at farm level* between man/land ratios and emigration, and six clear negative associations. In the sample of forty North Indian villages, only 5 percent of the working migrants came from households with agricultural labor as a primary occupation, though these households accounted for 19 percent of those in the village (Connell et al., 1976). Where the landless do migrate, it is increasingly the unplanned migration of despair, uprooting the whole household and degenerating into a wandering search for work.

What invalidates the plausible neoclassical hypothesis that rural emigration in LDCs will reduce inequalities by opening new chances to the poorest, and in the process will raise output? In a sense, to answer that question—to decide why the move north and west by the U.S. southern Negroes since 1930, for all its limitations a powerful solvent of racial and regional inequality, has few and weak analogies in today's Third World—is to define underdevelopment. This is in large part a lack of the skills, information, and access to capital that permits the workers of the United States or Europe to respond in mobile fashion to economic opportunity. Rural emigration in LDCs is of two types: that in which better-off countryfolk use their surpluses (accumulated education,[11] cash, or other assets) to buy into the urban scene, with its prospects of further accumulation; and that in which the poorer (but seldom the poorest) villagers seek to make up for the land deprivation, high rents, and labor-replacing technologies associated with the concentration and use of surpluses by the better-off in their villages of origin.

## WHY EQUILIBRATION FAILS: MIGRANT CHARACTERISTICS

Almost everywhere, migration concentrates on villagers aged 15–30 years: 60 percent of individual adult migrants were aged 15–24 years in our forty North Indian villages compared to 30 percent of remaining village adults; similar disproportions are found in most LDCs. Since gerontocracy contributes so largely to intravillage inequality (Hill, 1972), is not the concentration of outside prospects on young people a welcome escape into both greater equity and less arbitrary decision making? Probably not often, for a number of reasons. First, migration takes away the young with more "get-up-and-go"; men aged 15–25 years are often the most significant agricultural innovators (Rogers and Svenning, 1969),[12] so their departure removes the main *economic* claim of younger people to challenge the gerontocracy (apart from implying that rural enterprise suffers and rural-urban inequality is increased). Second, *politically*, if such potential leaders are removed, the older men left behind are strengthened, and with them inequalities due to age. Third, the better-off fathers, whose abilities to finance education and job search and to use urban contacts are likely to produce more successful migrant sons, have more to offer to, and hence more social control over, those sons than the poorer fathers (Dahya, 1973; Wilkie, 1973). Thus the richer villagers are more likely to gain from their sons' migration. But—whatever the side effects and complications[13]—young men, the dynamic and strong element in village society, dominate migrant streams. Their movements do not fit into a pattern of escape by the poorest and weakest villagers, nor do they seem likely to benefit village innovativeness or equality.

The sex structure of migrant streams—overwhelmingly male in Asia and Africa (Connell et al., 1976)—works in the same direction as the age structure:

chances of migration do not go to those with the lowest opportunities. But there is one major difference: if the village's number of youth is depleted, the village gerontocrats gain; but if the village's supply of working males is depleted, a weaker group, the village women, may gain. The female work force/population ratio rose significantly with migration rates in our North Indian sample (Connell et al., 1976); this can well lead to the formation of more female-headed households and farms. Resistance to women's new role after migration is common, but migration raises the issue, even if it cannot be seen as a sufficient cause of women's rural emancipation (McEvoy, 1971; Riddell, 1970; Baxter, 1973; de Gonzales, 1961). Unfortunately, job discrimination means that women require more education than men to achieve a similar rise in migration rates (Hart, 1971), so that highly gainful migration will likely continue to be biased toward men. Women's rewards come, if at all, in the villages the men leave. Yet the selection against women in migrant streams again contradicts the expectation that the worst-off villagers will "vote with their feet" and reduce inequality through emigration. Inasmuch as men are likelier than women to move, because men enjoy higher lifetime income differentials between city and country, who can argue that the effect on output in LDCs is mainly due to genuine differences in marginal productive capacity? And who could claim that women in Asia and Africa are tied to the rural home mainly because their urban-rural income differential is lower than that of men?

Though age and sex characteristics of migrants do not necessarily prevent rural-urban migration from contributing to national production and equalization, they do prevent it from doing so within the areas of origin. That is because, although the expected yearly income gap between country and city is highest for young men, the older rural people, especially the women, are likely to be the least "productive" (at prevailing prices) and often the poorest.[14] Hence the worse-off are less likely to gain directly from migration.

Similarly, more education (which goes with higher initial rural income) means more rural-urban migration, and again the better-off gain most. Among migrants, more education obviously means more absolute urban and rural earnings, and hence a greater *absolute* income differential from movement; there appears to be, moreover, a greater *proportionate* differential in most studies, in that the private rate of return to total education in developing countries usually rises with its amount (Psacharopoulos, 1973). Conversely, only after considerable sacrifice, in the form of costs (including opportunity costs) incurred to secure education, are the private returns likely to justify the whole exercise of education-for-emigration (Caldwell, 1969; Wyon and Gordon, 1971). Hence the better-off—who can raise money, incur risk, and accept long time horizons—are the likeliest to make the sacrifices from which high subsequent benefits from education can flow. The concentration of high-yielding, "educated" migration upon the better-off is demonstrated by the way successful migrants finance the emigration-for-education of younger siblings (Sardar Patel Agro-Economic Research Centre, 1971; Simon, 1966; Moock, 1976; Anderson, 1972), a process for which there is evidence from India, the Philippines, and Kenya. The rise in migration with education lowers the proportion of educated persons in the rural work force—probably inefficiently, since that proportion is already so much lower than the urban that the marginal *social* product of education is likely to be higher in the village. (Even "irrelevant" education enhances literacy, numeracy (sometimes), and above all capacity to handle a system dominated by the qualified, the clerical, and the urban.) In Delhi University around 1957-1963, 22.2 percent of the students came from rural areas, while at most 7.5 percent returned to rural areas (Khusro, 1967; Rao, 1961).

Status also affects the impact of migration on rural income and its distribution, though much less clearly and probably less negatively than age, sex, or education. Where migration is a "rite of passage" to mature status, it can confirm village hierarchies (Hill, 1972; Bedford, 1973; Connell et al., 1976). One might expect the adult male dominance in migrant streams to lower the supply of labor relative to demand in the rural underclass—the laborers, peons, and Harijans. On the other hand, the potential leaders of this underclass are also its most likely emigrants; educated migrants transfer their *demand* for service labor townward; and migrant remittances to better-off families can sometimes buy capital to replace stroppy laborers! In India, artisan castes tend to leave the rural sector less than either high castes or laborers (Connell et al., 1976).

The external costs of rural skill drain must fall overwhelmingly on the countryside (and the external benefits on the initially richer, more unequal towns). It may be objected that if one skilled baker leaves one village, the supply of services to replace him—from his brothers, from bakers in nearby villages, from do-it-yourself housewives—is probably quite price elastic. But if skilled persons as a whole leave villages as a whole, their effective replacement is a major problem; their rewards will rise (and quality fall) and intra-village inequality between skilled and unskilled will grow. As for unskilled workers, their substantial *random* rural emigration might perhaps help those who stay to raise wage rates. But selective emigration of bright, young, male unskilled workers deprives those who stay of potential leaders and leaves them less able to take the risks of organizing for higher incomes.[15]

## WHY EQUILIBRATION FAILS: THE MIGRATION PROCESS

Perhaps the most important relevant characteristic of the migration process is its cost. In one study, *movement costs* appeared to influence migration propensities more than income expectations (Connell et al., 1976). These costs are likely to rise with distance, either greatly curtailing the migration prospects of the rural poor, or reducing the average benefits of migration to them by requiring risky and disruptive step migration (Speare, 1971). High *urban food and housing costs*[16] can deter family migration among the poor, imposing on the working migrant a costly pattern of regular return. There are also the *costs of the education* required to obtain access to particular job markets outside the village; *information costs,* likely to be higher for the illiterate, contactless, or inexperienced; and *"psychic" costs* of cultural disruption, likely to bear hardest on those who speak only a local dialect, cannot read, and have few urban contacts. Sure costs now for doubtful benefits later must discourage the poor from migration, since they are relatively risk averse.

To understand how the flow of information about migration can hamper the poor and steer the gains to the rich, it is useful to interpret migration to a new source of jobs (or training) for a village as a form of innovation. Diffusion of innovations in a community usually follows a standard leader-follower pattern, with the medium-rich shouldering the initially high subjective risk of adoption and unconsciously exhibiting success to their poorer and more risk-averse neighbors, who then innovate in their turn (Rogers and Svenning, 1969). If information about migration were similarly diffused—not just for acquisition but for effective utilization—all might be well. The acquisition process, however, is overwhelmingly through relatives and friends (Lewis, 1967; IDRC, 1973; Rempel, 1971; Godfrey, 1973), who often control hiring also (Sardar Patel Agro-Economic Research Centre, 1970; McEvoy, 1971); this plainly favors the early migrants—usually the better-off—who can pass on information to younger siblings for "chain migration" within a family or peer group.[17] Formal, written information about urban prospects is also better among the more prosperous (Yeshwant, 1962).

The utilization of any innovation tends to favor early "leader" adopters, who are the first to get onto the rising income-time curve of "learning by doing." The bias is especially severe for migration, however, and in ways that illustrate its dissimilarity from such innovations as improved seeds. The early migrants know sooner about, can afford to go to, and hence use up opportunities in more attractive destinations and jobs—leaving the rest for the poorer "followers." For instance, the deterrent effect of distance declines with education in Venezuela (Levy and Wadycki, 1974) and Kenya (Rempel, 1971)—yet education, access to information, income, and the ability to take on the risks and costs of being the "leader" are obviously interrelated.

So the better-off can more easily bear the costs of high-yielding migration, and can more readily acquire information to reduce those costs. The resulting chain migration favors the family that is an early "adopter" of migration. It also favors the early-adopting village, where views about prospects are most likely to be intelligently optimistic, because they have not yet been depressed by large migrant flows. "Later" villages are more likely to suffer—increasingly so as their chain migration proceeds—from the fact that supernormal opportunities for economic gain are likely to be "overshot" and become subnormal for want of information that equilibrium has been reached (Richardson, 1959). Further, while expected lifetime income differentials greatly affect migration flows (Todaro, 1969), earlier migrants will protect their new urban jobs, reduce their income variance, and raise their expected lifetime income at the expense of later migrants, actual and potential.[18] The general raising of job qualifications by employers, as migrant supply rises relative to demand, will also prove a handicap to later migrants and their villages. Differences in migration rates, which may seem to be ethnically specific (Rempel, 1971), are in reality usually due to the "echo effects" in particular villages or communities of initial success followed by chain migration (Sabot, 1972; Connell et al., 1976). Perhaps the only feature of chain migration supporting the belief that migrant flows reduce intrarural inequality and remove village workers of relatively low productivity is that, according to evidence from Nigeria, Mexico, and India (Upton, 1967; Wiest, 1970; Pathare et al., 1972), migration rates are higher in larger families, and ceteris paribus[19] such families are likely to be poorer and to feature lower marginal value products of farm effort.

The features of the migration process discussed in this section tend to confine the more promising, self-advancing forms of migration to better-off villagers (though often from villages with low average income per person). This is clearest for the distance, and hence nature, of migrant movement. Rich and poor rural families put their toes in the water in different ways. The richer family sends one well-prepared member far afield to test the prospects, perhaps as a student, doctor, or engineer. His remittances finance similarly distant moves by younger brothers. Where the rich thus chain, the poor only step, and not so far; the poor fail to reach the metropolis (or, having reached it, to get past its peripheral slums) because they cannot meet the cost of surmounting the intervening obstacles, or because they cannot afford to pass up intervening opportunities.[20] This helps explain why complete household migration (while generally very low) is usually highest among landless laborers, while individual migrants usually retain rural land (Vidyarthi, 1969) or other assets.

Prospects distant from a particular village favor its better-off residents, who know enough and can afford and risk enough to seek out remote chances of work or training. *Among* villages, however, this is much less clear. If the famous "laws of migration" (Ravenstein, 1885, 1889), with their implicit gravity-flow model, applied, they would be "amplified" by chain migration to increase the advantages of villages near a city. However, to some extent modern transport outdates these laws.

## WHY EQUILIBRATION FAILS: THE IMPACT
## OF ABSENCES ON THE VILLAGE

The emigration of strong, enterprising, innovative, respected young men from the village is likely to require their replacement by others in the work force and "entrepreneur force," especially in peak seasons. Innovations, usually capital using, may also be required to replace their labor and enterprise. To what extent are output-maintaining adaptations to migrant absence possible, in the long run and in the short run? Which types of adaptation are desirable? Can the development process accommodate the need for adaptations to migration-induced lowerings of labor/land and labor/capital ratios, even though the growth of the work force and the shortage of capital should be inducing *higher* ratios? Is such accommodation possible despite the growing sense that recent development has involved unduly low ratios?

Several migration patterns have been found to reduce adjustment problems in the village: regular weekend return by small, part-time family farm entrepreneurs in the Philippines (Hart, 1971) and Japan; off-season movements with peak-season return (Bedford, 1973); or work in nearby places, especially in the informal sector, facilitating quick return if needed (Bienefeld, 1974). More important, because more generally applicable, are the determinants of adaptability in the village itself: an extended family or kinship structure that eases labor bottlenecks, as found in parts of Liberia and Nigeria (McEvoy, 1971; Riddell, 1970); existing or potential cooperative labor structures to achieve the same ends, as found in parts of Liberia, Polynesia, and elsewhere (McEvoy, 1971; Johnston, 1967); willingness to bring women and children into the work force (Gallin, 1966; McGee and Drakakis-Smith, 1973; Cohen, 1965; Anderson, 1972); innovations such as new crops or varieties, which permit the spreading of labor peaks and may even increase *total* (while reducing *seasonal*) labor input (Sansom, 1970); or possible shifts to less effort-intensive crops (McEvoy, 1971; Cohen, 1965), to pasture (Dussauze-Ingrand, 1974), or to labor hiring (Dussauze-Ingrand, 1974; Essang and Mabawonku, 1974; Friedland, 1971). Conversely, unwillingness or incapacity to make such adjustments leads, in some sense, to the failure of emigration to leave sustainable conditions in the communities of origin: massive male absences in parts of Papua New Guinea have caused reversion from settled village agricultures to gathering communities living off wild sago (Brookfield, 1960). Where women cannot replace migrant men, either migration or family structures tend to break down (Goddard, 1973; Baxter, 1973; de Gonzalez, 1961).

The most striking feature of those (relatively few) rural areas that are much affected by townward migration is their age structure. Edward Schuh reported, in discussion, that a substantial number of villages in areas of Northeast Brazil much affected by migration showed an average age of fifty-seven. That is an extreme case, of course;[21] in some of the rural areas demographic adaptions to migration—falling birthrates (Oliver, 1973; Connell et al., 1976), or delayed marriage (Doughty, 1968; Khuri, 1967)—ease the task of women in replacing absent male migrants as workers and entrepreneurs and are economically, though possibly not psychologically, desirable in themselves.[22] The socioeconomic adaptations to migration are harder to evaluate: more and harder work by women and children will be needed to replace absent young men; extra women's work, especially if seasonally concentrated, can endanger the health, nourishment, and care of babies before as well as after childbirth; and extra children's work may stunt growth and detract from schooling. "In Duidui village, Guadalcanal, at the season of peak out-migration, 3- to 6-year-olds, the elderly, and the infirm were all obliged to carry water, prepare vegetables, supervise infants, and keep the village swept and weeded" (Connell et al., 1976; Cohen, 1965). A shift from family to hired labor[23]—while perhaps increasing the power, employment, wage, or prestige of the laborers—reduces the incentives to heavy and efficient labor input, especially if many of the supervisors are women, who may not easily command the respect of laborers used to taking instructions from men. Places with long agricultural seasons (culminating in continuous cropping) (Miracle and Berry, 1970), or with sharp seasonal peaks in labor demand, are most vulnerable to strain in adapting to migration; yet such places are not necessarily able to retain potential migrants and are often unattractive to them, either absolutely or compared to opportunities elsewhere.

Migration from a farming family, or in substantial quantities from a village, reduces labor/land and labor/capital ratios, encouraging the migrant's family, village, or former employer to save labor, unless all factors are perfectly mobile. To the extent that the migrant is able to feed himself and need not be supported by remittances, the reduction in demand for output also causes his family's land (if not sold) to be worked less labor intensively. If the family seeks to replace the migrant's lost output, it tends to do so through extra nonlabor factors, especially if a shift from family to hired labor involves increased costs, through supervision, credit for wages, or simply reduced average labor productivity. The latter reduction will also be involved in responding to the emigration of young male labor by a shift to labor by females, children and older workers. If that shift takes place within the family, where the proportionate productivity reduction is seldom fully matched by proportionate reduction in the marginal (caloric) cost of effort, it further encourages the search for labor-replacing farm methods.

The quest for high total factor productivity via labor replacement after a working relative has migrated is socially maladaptive, especially in the medium run, while rural work force is growing much faster than other, scarcer (but artificially underpriced) factors of production. If the short-term private acts of labor saving are reversible—an adjustment toward less labor-intensive annual or seasonal crops, an altered seasonal pattern, or a change in the balance of current inputs—little or no harm is done. Three types of damaging, lasting adjustment must be mentioned, however. First, "high-migration" families or villages sometimes shift from labor-intensive field crops to pasture, tree crops, or continuous cropping. Such shifts are costly to reverse[24] as population grows (or as failed migrants return); these shifts, unless they induce dense root-crop cultivation, also reduce calorie output per acre. Second, where individual migration is concentrated among richer families in poorer villages, such families can well respond to its effect on farm income by land purchase,[25] expanding the extensive frontier, concentrating land further, and again raising the land/labor ratio and the thrust toward labor-saving techniques. Third, substantial and *expected* long-term loss of labor often leads to purchases of big items of labor-replacing capital, notably tractors, especially when supported by remittances, as in the Indian Punjab, Libya, and Vietnam (Hilal, 1969; Sansom, 1970). These adaptations, as much for social and political reasons (demonstration effects, acquisition of subsidy) as for economic ones, are not easily reversed if migrants return or population grows; and their effects are not confined to the few families or places genuinely needing to replace labor.

## WHY EQUILIBRATION FAILS: REMITTANCES

There are two objections to relying on remittances to save the argument for rural-urban migration as a cause of intrarural or rural-urban equalization. First, total net remittances are very small compared with rural income in the great majority of villages; indeed, they are often negative. Second, positive remittances go disproportionately to the better-off; *townward* migrants, especially the remitters, and above all the international remitters who send back really big sums, are seldom from the poorest village groups (Vidyarthi, 1969).

Except when a survey aims to select a unit of study to which remittances are important, remittances turn out to be a surprisingly small[26] share of annual rural income. In twelve Northwest Indian villages they averaged 6.5 percent, ranging from 0.1 percent to 39 percent. In eleven Southeast Indian villages the average was 1.3 percent, ranging from 0 to 8.4 percent (Connell et al., 1976). Similarly small proportions are reported from Thailand (Keyes, 1966) and Malawi (Beize, 1971; Van Velsen, 1960). There are exceptional villages, in urban or mine-recruiting peripheries or with international contacts, where shares are higher (Connell et al., 1976); but these low figures are probably normal.

Yet international migrants from Pakistan, Mexico, and Monserrat send back over half their earnings (Dahya, 1973; Hancock, 1959; Philpott, 1970);

rural emigrants from Turkey remitted 15 percent of income but saved a further 24 percent, much of it presumably to be brought home on return as cash or goods (Paine, 1974). Even among intranational rural-urban migrants, evidence from India, Kenya, Nigeria, and Thailand suggests that over half remit, and that the amounts are typically 20 to 35 percent of earnings (Connell et al., 1976; Johnson and Whitelaw, 1972; Adepoju, 1974; Sakdejayont, 1973). Remittances that are low in relation to total village income, but high in relation to individual urban earnings (and a fortiori to average rural income), suggest low townward migration rates and imply great concentration of remittance benefits upon migrants' families.

The suspicion that this is "unequalizing" within the village is reinforced by evidence from the Cameroons, Papua New Guinea, Guatemala, and Liberia that rural-rural migrants—who usually come from poorer households than other migrants—are less likely to remit, and when they do remit they send smaller proportions of income (Ardener, Ardener, and Warmington, 1960; Dakenye, 1967; Schmid, 1967; Riddell, 1970). This is confirmed by some urban studies of persons sending cash to rural areas. For instance, in Dar-es-Salaam, 24 percent of self-employed workers, but 46 percent of wage earners, remitted, and the former group was characterized by lower incomes and other features suggesting that fewer of its members came from better-off rural households (Bienefeld, 1974).

If remittance income goes disproportionately to better-off villagers, that is bad for intrarural equality, but could be good for production, provided their higher marginal propensity to save[27] outweighs the tendency of bigger farmers to have lower output per unit of extra capital (caused by lack of family labor and hence high internal cost of effort and supervision). There is not much systematic evidence on the use of marginal income derived from remittances, and indeed the fungibility problem renders this topic difficult to study. However, the impact on national (as opposed to individual) savings of remittance income is probably not very high. This is because the village's better-off families, who receive most remittances, would have been able to borrow if they had wanted to exploit investment opportunities. It is the investment plans of the village poor that are likely to be constrained by finance.

Recipients seem to use remittances first to pay off debts incurred in financing migration or preparing their sons educationally for the move (Dahya, 1973; Hopper, 1957). Second priority goes to consumption; everyday needs often absorb 90 percent or more of a village's remittances (Johnson and Whitelaw, 1972; Adepoju, 1974; Caldwell, 1969); furthermore, conspicuous consumption out of remittance income is often used to reinforce status (Dussauze-Ingrand, 1974; Doughty, 1968; Simon, 1966)—high payments for bride-price (Mayer, 1971; Baxter, 1973; Hayano, 1973) and more luxurious house building (Hart, 1971; Lewis, 1970; Mfwangavo, 1969) are examples of this. Third, much "chain migration" rests on education financed by remittances from older siblings (Simon, 1966; Moock, 1975; Anderson, 1972; Sardar Patel Agro-Economic Research Centre, 1971). Sometimes such use of funds comprises genuine investment in socially productive human capital, but often it is private rather than social saving—raising the saver's income at the expense of other people, with no net gain to gross national product—since the "investment" it finances is in human pseudocapital: the acquisition of paper qualifications, which increase the qualifier's prospects of income only by reducing nonqualifiers' prospects by the same amount (and which steadily escalate as the army of the "educated" jobless grows). Investment is only the fourth priority for remittances, and it is often used outside the village; in mere capital transfer rather than capital creation (notably by purchase of land) (Dahya, 1973; McEvoy, 1971); to hire workers (e.g., for irrigation maintenance) where once family labor was used (Dussauze-Ingrand, 1974; Boeder, 1973; Friedland, 1971; Lasaga, 1972); or for labor-replacing mechanization rather than the generation of extra output or the better use of scarce land inputs.

The origin—rural, urban, or foreign—of the consumer goods or investment goods obtained by remittances is relevant to their impact on rural welfare. The demonstrably urban nature of many remittances in kind (Sakdejayont, 1973; Caldwell, 1969; McFarlane, 1972; Skinner, 1965; Hayano, 1973; Salisbury and Salisbury, 1972; Riddell, 1970), as of goods brought back by returning migrants, changes rural tastes toward consumer durables and goods that meet old needs in new and costly ways (McFarlane, 1972; Simon, 1966) (from breast milk or cows' milk to tinned baby food, for instance). This not only reduces the demand for rural products, but also, by raising the cost of living, reduces the "force of productivity" to increase welfare, just as the higher food costs incurred by urban migrants do (p. 195).

Fungibility renders somewhat risky all attempts to associate particular sources of extra cash (such as remittances) with particular changes in spending behavior. However, this rather depressing picture of remittances doing little for the base village's investment—and even what little is done tending to conserve traditional values (Ahiauyo-Akakpo, 1974) and status at the expense of efficient production—is drawn from three aspects of the logic of rural emigration itself.

First, if the village offered high-yielding outlets for the investment of surpluses, these surpluses would have been invested there initially, not used to finance migration away from potential prosperity, unless (Stark, 1975) the family needed to reduce risk by diversifying its income-earning portfolio or to save above a "threshold" to finance big and indivisible investments. Second, a well-off family[28] that has lost migrants—usually sons, and often its eldest son—may need to preserve its status in the village by using remittances for what are *socially* fairly unproductive investments (buying land, hiring "client" workers, building a mosque) against the risk that the family's possible non-continuity will lead other villagers to lose respect for it. Third, bigger *and* better-off farm families are most likely to expel migrants *and* to receive substantial remittance per migrant. Such large families, with some monopsony power in local factor markets and with rising supervision costs, will tend to use remittances to replace absent workers, i.e., to select among productive investments those that reduce labor/land and labor/capital ratios, and that therefore have socially excessive capital/labor and land/labor ratios as compared with available alternative investments.

Remittances, then, are unlikely to do much to reduce rural poverty, either by financing productive and labor-intensive investments or by being sent directly to the rural poor. International migrants feature both high earnings and a high propensity to remit, but come mainly from better-off educated groups. Poor rural migrants, to other rural areas or to the urban "informal sector," earn much less and have lower propensities to remit. Since remittances in kind cannot correspond to spending in the village—not even indirectly if such town-made goods as transistor radios are involved—there is little prospect that they may create demand for the labor services of the rural poor.

In some ways, however, poorer people and poorer villages can gain from remittances. First, like the propensity to migrate, remittances per migrant seem to increase with the size of the nuclear family (Caplan, 1970).[29] Second, in our Indian sample, remittances per villager were significantly higher in villages with high landlessness and high female and child labor rates (Connell et al., 1976). Third, remittances per capita are higher for poorer villages (Caldwell, 1969)—though emphatically not for poorer villagers (Anderson, 1972; Hart, 1971; Sardar Patel Agro-Economic Research Centre, 1970)—so that circulation of *cash* remittances within the village may in part trickle down to some of its *working* poor.

The limited capacity of remittances to increase productive, labor-intensive investment is further reduced, and their impact on income distribution complicated, by reverse flows—remittances out of the village to support migrants while they undergo education or job search. They would fall still further if (as is hardly ever done) we netted out the villagers' other costs: educating family members to prepare them for successful migration (including opportunity-costs of the student's forgone labor); paying interest to cover the delay between such costs and "in-remittances"; and tending sick or pregnant migrants during their recuperation in their home village—a service seen by some (Pye, 1969) as helping "development" by obviating the need to divert urban surpluses from industrial investment to medicine.

Yet even crude reverse remittances, without discounting forward to allow the fact that they usually precede direct flows, are substantial. Of nine villages in Tamilnadu with available data, four are *net* out-remitters; in all the Indian villages with data, out-remittances ate up a large share of gross in-remittances (Connell et al., 1976). In five Nigerian villages, out-remittances plus migrants' education costs far exceeded in-remittances (Essang and Mabawonku, 1974).[30] In India, the level of out-remittances from a village is significantly related to the number of student migrants (Connell et al., 1976). At the risk of an ecological fallacy, one may conclude that out-remittances could well reduce the inequality associated with in-remittances—the better-off get more from their relatives' migration, but they pay more for it too. This interpretation is backed up, though not proved, by the fact that "out-remittances are [significantly] higher relative to in-remittances in villages with higher [average] income" (Connell et al., 1976).

Another concept of reverse remittances has probably never been netted out. Indian data (Bose, 1971) suggest that for every three rural-urban migrants at any moment there is one urban-rural migrant. If, as often happens, the latter has retired to his farm after a successful urban career, he is likely to remit to his children in the town. (The "failure return migrant" seldom leaves children in the town.) Such remittances, minus reverse flows, should also be deducted from net rural receipts from rural-urban migrants, especially as return migration is a consequence of initial migration.

## WHY EQUILIBRATION FAILS: RETURN MIGRATION

Most evidence, then, suggests a negative impact of rural emigration on *rural* productivity and equality. Does the return of migrants reverse that negative impact? There is some evidence that it does. However, there are several objections: the tendency of return migrants to be the old, the sick, and the unsuccessful; the contradiction between equalizing effects and productive effects of return, and (analogously) between external benefits and catalytic action from it; and the frequent irrelevance to rural advance of the skills and attitudes acquired by migrants during their absence.

In Ghana, about two-thirds of rural-urban migrants intend to return on retirement or old age, and about four-fifths do—but most leave their (productive) children in the town (Caldwell, 1969). For older age groups, return migration exceeds urban flow in many countries in Africa and around Bombay in India (Byerlee, 1972; Caldwell, 1969; Zachariah, 1968). With a given cash flow, reverse migration for retirement imposes care of the old as a cost on the initially poorer rural sector, increasing rural-urban inequality, and reducing any net benefit from migration to the village's potential productive surplus.[31] Return migration in sickness and pregnancy has similar effects. Of course, advocates of industrialization at great speed and almost irrespective of short-run costs to rural people may welcome this process as a method of making villagers bear "social-security" expenses that would otherwise erode the urban surplus (Pye, 1969).

Four factors accentuate the pressure on townward migrants to return home unless they succeed quickly in the town (Lipton, 1964): rising urban rents, congestion, and squalor; the growing difficulty of finding a home or job for migrants without urban relatives; the migrants' consequently increasing subservience to the urban moneylender; and growing resistance to migrants by their employed, often unionized, competitors. Against a background of job expectations rendered overoptimistic by the growth of the supply of urban labor relative to the demand, these factors steadily raise the proportion of migrants failing to achieve their job targets (Conroy and Stent, 1970; ILO, 1971) and returning home because of that failure. This pattern has been identified "from China to Peru" (literally), taking in Ghana, Liberia, Mexico, Papua New Guinea, and Sri Lanka (Fiendt and Browning, 1972; Freidland, 1971; Hafer, 1971; ILO, 1971; Salisbury and Salisbury, 1972; Peil, 1960; Yang, 1959; McEvoy, 1971). Plainly, if return migration is concentrated on those who cannot get or hold urban jobs—and who return to the village with a sense of inferiority—it is unlikely to help rural productivity. If successful migrants stay in the town, while failures return to the village, then the private and external benefits of *both* sets of decisions are largely urban, while the private and external costs fall largely on a rural sector that starts off poorer and with a lower incidence of the skills and dynamism "successful" migrants often embody.

There are exceptions to this "failure" pattern of permanent return. Some migrants return because they have achieved what they wanted in the town; or because their new skills are useful in the rural areas; or because—perhaps owing to capital accumulation out of their own remittances—opportunities in the home village have improved. Return migration of successful migrants is likely to reinforce intravillage inequality; since they are likely to return only to villages with growing opportunities, they probably also reinforce intervillage inequality; but they do enhance rural productivity. Conversely, an unsuccessful town migrant's return probably harms rural productivity, but—since he seldom comes from the poorest rural strata, which have little to offer a returnee—promotes equalization, since it tends to impose burdens on the better-off in the village.

Hence return migration, like most industrial investment but unlike most agricultural investment, involves conflict between efficiency and equality: the same action is unlikely to advance both aims. A similar conflict occurs between two smaller-scale desiderata of return migration: that it have enough impact to change the village; and that it provide external benefits to others. Unless the benefits of return migration can be internalized to the returning migrant or his family—and, often, unless they can be internalized as status gain within the traditional hierarchies the migrant respects—he will either not move or not return. Often, therefore, the returning migrant's family remains the only one in a village to absorb the innovations he returns with (Wiest, 1970); or the family has to leave the village because the traditional farm system cannot incorporate the innovations (Mfwangavo, 1969), or perhaps because the climate is physically unsuitable for them (Miracle and Berry, 1970); or the family simply uses new skills to climb old ladders (Bailey, 1960; Ahiauyo-Akakpo, 1974).

As some of these responses suggest, learned skills are often not relevant. The prospects for new agricultural skills, learned from rural-*rural* migration, are better (Hayano, 1973; Sexton, 1972) but, since it is poorer migrants who generally engage in such movements, they are less likely to bring back funds to acquire capital, which limits their capacity to generate "embodied" technical change. Nonfarm skills, learned outside the village, usually prove too capital intensive, too environmentally specific, too advantageous in cities, or otherwise unlikely to be productively applied in the villages (Caldwell, 1969; Alvarez, 1967). There is, however, no doubt that "cosmopolitan education" (Rogers and Shoemaker, 1971), external contacts (Sexton, 1972), and language skills (Hayano, 1973), acquired through migration, prove valuable on return in initiating innovation.[32] The prospect of rural gains from return migrants mainly depends on such general considerations, rather than on benefits from particular skills.

## SOME CONCLUDING REMARKS

This chapter, based heavily on work by colleagues (bibliographical and analytic work by Connell [1976]; statistical interpretation of Indian data by Dasgupta and Laishley [1975]), has set out the rural microevidence on the impact of migration, absence, remittance, and return. The story is surprisingly gloomy. The objections set out to the equilibrating theory of migration—objections inherent in the nature of migrants of high-migration villages and of the scope, costs, and limits of the movement process—have force; but it is surprising that they seem to produce such unhappy results, which almost totally "overpower" the rags-to-riches, perfect-information, people-do-what-they-want-and-gain-from-it model. This is partly because, given rapid change in job qualifications and rapid growth of work force, increasing disappointment is built into imperfectly informed job markets; partly because the better-off can most readily and most "informedly" incur costs for risky future benefits; and partly because it is perfectly consistent to claim, as in this chapter, that on average the migrant gains from migration, but the village left behind loses.

It would be out of place to speculate at length about the policy and research implications of the above. The material is fragmented, and it has been deliberately pushed to, or perhaps past, its interpretable limits. This chapter closes with two general points about policy, one negative and one positive: an observation about efficiency-equity conflicts, and the identification of a major research need.

It would be nonsense, and probably evil, to respond to the disappointing results of migration by restricting it. Migration is chiefly a response to deep-seated inequalities and rigidities, which push out those of the poor who can muster a few scanty resources for the move and pull out the better-off (who have seized most of the community's surplus but cannot, within their place of residency, use it to improve their income or status substantially). Rural emigration is a response also to decades of public policy biased, in both investment allocation and price manipulation, against agriculture. The response may worsen rural poverty, and intrarural and rural-urban inequality. But the response reveals the *migrants'* preferences; probably on balance enriches them; and enables more poor people to share, however dimly, in the artificial light of biased urban development. To imitate Russia in the 1890s (or South Africa today), by adding to discrimination against the rural poor laws to keep them where they are, is neither sensible nor just. Policy must concentrate on removing the factitious causes of rural emigration; on enabling those left behind in the rural sector to recover their costs and forcing the urban sector to pay for its benefits; and on identifying "better" and "worse" migration—encouraging the former, and discouraging the latter.

Blocking the safety valve is no good, but how can the flow of steam be rationalized? It helps little to provide more urban jobs, to which more than proportionately increasing numbers of villagers will flow (Todaro, 1969, 1975), thereby increasing the drain of rural leadership and skills without improving the urban situation. Rationalization of migrant flows requires more rational policies toward agriculture. In LDCs, with typically 70 percent of the work force and 50 percent of output, agriculture barely gets 20 percent of investment (and even that often enriches mainly urban contractors and labor-saving large farmers), despite its general association with two to three times as much extra output as the nonfarm sector, even at prevailing prices (Szczepanik, 1969). These prices are often so turned against farmers as to take from them 50–60 percent by value of their sold output, and hence of the derived labor that produced it (Lewis, 1970; Lipton, 1977). Consequently, there are so few rural resources, and the value of their product is so depressed, that, once rural power has diverted income to the better-off, there is little left for the rural poor. The rich also find rural opportunities severely limited and the ablest, rich and poor, are therefore induced to migrate. Meanwhile the general failure to implement land reform, and the enormous difficulty of getting benefits to the rural poor in its absence, increase intravillage inequality and further swell the migrant streams. Moreover, the nature and location of education, and of jobs providing big income gains to the educated, favor the cities; rural families bear the cost of educating migrants from whose education the village can reap few benefits external to the migrants' own families. Measures redressing urban bias, intravillage (though not necessarily intervillage) inequality, and divergences between paying and gaining community (such as those caused by location of school and work), will reduce rural-urban emigration, probably in its less desirable forms.

The problem of development theory and policy regarding the conflict between efficiency and equality has two aspects. First, many activities (steel production and tractor farming, for instance) feature genuine economies of scale in production or administration. Second, in agriculture—where there is usually no such conflict and where *with a given technology* small farms usually exploit land and capital most intensively—social pressures direct resources, even if intended for efficient use by the poor, into generally less efficient use by the rich. In one policy area after another—irrigation water, cooperative credit, improved rural power and communications, or subsidized fertilizer—the big and labor-replacing units manage to get most of the resources intended (at least verbally) for the labor-intensive rural poor. Migration, while neither a technology nor an input, is also more accessible to those who have resources and access to networks providing benefits, and can get information and borrow money to incur acquisition costs. Such people seize most of the scarce opportunities for really successful migration.

There seem to be three ways to try and correct such inequities of access. They are, in increasing order of hopefulness: to cover costs and fill gaps specific to poor users of irrigation, migration routes, or whatever; to devise technologies specific to poor people, such as grain storage systems that are cost effective only for small amounts of grain; and to redistribute "power," or command over assets linked to power. In the area of migration, these three ways would be expressed, respectively, in such measures as rural labor exchanges and loans to permit the acquisition of simple skills usable elsewhere; transport to, and temporary rented homes in, remote *rural* areas with different seasonal labor peaks; and redistribution of control over rural land and capital, which would reduce both migration and the maldistribution of such rural benefits as it may bring.

This chapter has concentrated on "rural-end" evidence; some of the pessimism might be reduced if the impact on urban areas (and on individual migrants) were stressed. Unfortunately, research into migration is seldom designed to provide a complete picture of the effects on output and income distribution. A major research need is for *parallel* studies, with control groups, of recipient and originating areas in the migration process. Ideally, one would start by looking at an urban area and a rural area that were major recipients of migrants. Then two or three villages sending out substantial numbers of persons to each area would be identified. Next, "otherwise similar" (words requiring careful definition) places that sent out and received far fewer migrants would be determined. The income paths of migrant and non-migrant individuals and communities would then be contrasted. Only research of this nature, preferably in several countries, will enable us to reach a full evaluation of the size and distribution of benefits and costs from rural emigration. That full evaluation would be less bleak than the "rural-biased" picture painted here. This partial evaluation certainly cannot justify antimigratory policies. Yet it does suggest strongly that past and present policies are producing frustrated migrants, unintended damage, and few prospects that migration will often benefit the places of origin.

## NOTES

1. Weights for measures of output per worker, for age-groups by sex, are obvious, if, when an adult male member of another group 1, 2, 3 . . . works an $x$-hour day, the adult male produces $k_1$, $k_2$, $k_3$ . . . times as much output as the other worker, where the $k$'s are constants whatever the value of $x$; matters are more complicated if this assumption is badly awry. Weights for output per unit of total factor input are usually market prices; the effect of using "appropriate" prices, i.e., prices adjusted for market distortions, and for "desirable" income-distribution and derived patterns of demand, for inputs is considered in the first part of this chapter.

2. This assumption is necessary (except in degenerate cases), though not sufficient, for migrants and non-migrants to have identical preferences for leisure. Its breakdown is what most damages the optimistic neoclassical taxonomy regarding the effects of migration. But the assumption of balanced migration is really no more plausible (though it is less flagrantly non-neoclassical) than the assumption of constant average product, which has to be relaxed to generate that taxonomy.

3. These costs are, of course, largely internal to the migrants themselves; but some are reflected in higher money-wages (and hence apparently higher value added) for their outputs.

4. However, except for China (almost unrepresented) and Polynesia (overrepresented), the sample of villages surveyed in Connell et al. (1976) is distributed among regions very similarly to the rural population of the developing world. India has about half of both, excluding China.

5. In discussion Joseph Stiglitz added the interesting suggestion that, to the extent that informal social security (income sharing) transfers income from rich to poor within a village more than in a city, bipolar process of rural-urban migration, by shifting both potential donors and potential recipients to the less-integrated urban sector, increases inequality both rurally and nationally. Nationally, this is consistent with the evidence that urban inequality generally

exceeds rural. All this is pretty comparative-static, and "dynamic" economic critics might object that the urban-rural wage gap would be much higher in the absence of townward migration; but that objection may place more faith in price-inelastic urban or rural labor supply than the facts (labor forces growing at 3 percent yearly; imported technology bringing labor-saving technical "progress") justify.

6. It should be stressed that this evaluation, brief, and title are largely confined to the impact of migration, principally *townward* migration, on rural income, distribution, and hence economic welfare. If the impact on urban welfare, and the increasingly important role of rural-to-rural migration, were considered, the balance-sheet would be more favorable. Moreover, for all its faults, urbanization does represent an attempt by some villagers to escape from urban bias by joining it. The policy implication is not to ban or restrict townward migration but to correct the misallocations and misincentives that currently, and artificially, reduce the relative appeal of rural life and work.

7. This particular bipolarity may apply only where poverty is so severe that many villagers, including next-to-poorest ones, who are most prone to push migration, cannot afford even primary education because of the opportunity cost of forgone income from child labor. Paul Schultz, in discussion, pointed out that empirical work in several countries where poverty is not quite so extreme (Venezuela, Colombia, and Tunisia) showed a propensity to migrate that increased linearly with number of years of education, and Richard Sabot (1972) has verified a linear relationship in Tanzania. The ongoing National Migration Survey in Botswana, being supervised by John Harris, will be a test case, because migration is substantial and locally differentiated, while boys are denied primary education on opportunity-cost grounds fairly high up the income-scale in some regions only (see Smith [1977]).

8. To the extent that early migrants "use up" a limited number of urban job opportunities, whereas subsistence farmers can follow earlier innovators without much damage from coming late, townward migration is a type of innovation that seems especially likely to show a prolonged, perhaps permanent, initial period in this sense.

9. Paul Schultz pointed out, in discussion, that this shortage of potential wives increasingly deters young men from migrating to town for long periods.

10. This point is due to Paul Schultz. Mark Leiserson pointed out, in discussion, that the fact that the rate of true, net, permanent rural-to-urban migration in Africa and in South and Southeast Asia is small doesn't mean that the impact is unimportant but that it takes longer to become important. However, this in turn means that the effect of such migration upon key variables is reduced relative to that of other, often also cumulative, explanatory variables. Migration has less of an impact on man/land ratios than is usually believed, as compared with the impact of salinity or double cropping on these ratios. Likewise it has less of an impact on the rural poor's chances of getting less poor than does agricultural change or different rates of natural increase.

11. It is noteworthy that, among Indian villages, yield-per-acre is significantly and positively correlated with *student* migration.

12. In correspondence, Walter Elkan suggests that this applies principally to those young men who are returning migrants; this hypothesis, which awaits testing, would improve the impact of migration-plus-return on the village. But would not the young potential innovators, if migration were less appealing, innovate more in the villages instead?

13. Paul Schultz points out a very important complication, in need of modeling, but too complex to develop here. Much intravillage inequality depends on the family's stage of development through its "life cycle": marriage, young children to support, older children supporting parents, death of one parent. The cost of educating migrants (usually sons), and the benefits from remittances, if any, do not of course appear randomly over this life cycle. That distribution can greatly affect the impact of migration on inequality.

14. This is fully consistent with the effect of migration in strengthening the village gerontocrats—a small, relatively well-off subset of elderly villagers.

15. In other words, even if unskilled labor shows low price-*elasticity* of supply in an area (so that random migration of unskilled workers would raise its wage substantially along a *given* supply-of-labor curve), the selective migration of labor leaders must lower the *plasticity* of supply of labor: its capacity so to organize that the whole supply curve rises over time.

16. Moreover, the better-off gain more from the fact that "urban" goods (e.g., refrigerators) are cheaper to own and run in cities, and lose less from the fact that food is more expensive, for a bigger proportion of their income is spent on urban goods and a smaller proportion on food. (See Srinivasan [1974].)

17. In India, the urban "informal sector" resides largely in single-caste, often single-village or kin-group, neighborhoods; the members of each neighborhood, obviously, favor their would-be migrant kin by supplying information about promising prospects for work, housing, or loans in the city. Since many places and kin-groups are unrepresented in the city, and since first-comers acquire cumulative advantages, the informal sector is not conducive to the equal spread, among potential migrants from country to city, of access to urban opportunities.

18. Again, note the contrast to the myth of an easily entered informal sector (because it is unfragmented and nonprotectionist); see note 17.

19. However, this is not a clear ground for hope as regards the effect on poverty. In most surveys, family size is highly correlated with landholding size, both per household and per person.

20. My characterization of the "step migration" of the imperfectly informed rural poor as risky, disruptive, and costly is not intended to deny that their strategy, given their initial situation, is optimal; it is intended only to imply that the public provision of better information (including negative information) about intervening opportunities has high social benefits, and that without such information, it is seldom the rural poor who gain much from migration.

21. So is Botswana, where one in three adult male workers is abroad, with

similarly extreme effects on rural age structure.

22. They are partly offset by higher deathrates, both because those left behind are in more "death prone" demographic groups than are the males aged fifteen to thirty who in Africa and Asia dominate migrant streams, and because rural medical care is depleted by the drain of actual and potential medical personnel to the towns. See Lipton (1977).

23. Itself, incidentally, a confirmation that migration is chiefly from landed rather than landless households.

24. Trees or bushes have to be uprooted, and often the land must be reclaimed (by a season under an appropriate grass) before cereals can again be profitably sown. Reversion from pasture involves peasants in capital losses when they try to sell their beasts at the same time, cutting the price.

25. A more hopeful, though probably quite rare and usually temporary, alternative is for poor immigrants from other rural areas to replace the emigrant village workers. However, the immigrants are usually unorganized, vulnerable, and very ill paid (Epstein, 1973), so that intravillage inequality falls. Where, as in the Punjab, the (seasonal) "replacement workers" remain scarce enough to command decent wages, *they* are exposed to rapid replacement; remittances from successful rural-urban migrants are used by their families to buy reaper-binders instead of rural-rural replacement labor!

26. This is especially true when we recall that all the data discussed in this paragraph are for remittances gross of the reverse flow of rural-to-urban in-remittances.

27. This is, of course, the conventional one-round view of the saving-spending choice. The overall MPS becomes less important, and the hope of a good production impact weaker, if we analyze successive "rounds" of spending and saving with the matrix multiplier. (See Lipton [1977], ch. 10.)

28. A well-off family is the only sort likely to get major remittance income.

29. However, this is not a clear ground for hope. (See note 19.)

30. D. Byerlee (1972) points out that work in progress in Sierra Leone, and perhaps elsewhere in Africa, shows the migrants' kin already in the urban informal sector as a more important source of support than rural relatives during early postmigration unemployment (but surely not during education?). See also Colclough (1975) for evidence that, in urban Botswana, remittances to and from rural areas are in approximate balance.

31. One alternative, to support retired migrants at the higher (urban) living costs, is even costlier for the village than to support them after return to the village. More likely options for the retired migrant—dependence on support from kin in the urban informal sector or (as in Sri Lanka or the cotton mills of Ahmedabad, India) on some form of social security—transfer the costs to the urban sector.

32. Walter Elkan, in correspondence, suggests that skills acquired in the urban "informal sector" may add more rural earning power to the returning migrant—at least per unit of cost—than skills acquired in formal employment.

## BIBLIOGRAPHY

Adepoju, A. "Rural-Urban Socio-Economic Links: The Example of Migrants in SW Nigeria." In S. Amin (ed.), *Modern Migration in Western Africa.* London: Oxford University Press, 1974.

Afzal, M. "Migration to Urban Areas in Pakistan." In International Union, *Contributed Papers,* 1971.

Ahiauyo-Akakpo, A. "L'impact de la Migration sur la Société Villageoise: Approche Sociologique (Exemple Togo-Ghana)." In S. Amin (ed.), *Modern Migration in Western Africa.* London: Oxford University Press, 1974.

Allen, B. J. "Markets, Migrants and the Mangaians." In I. G. Bassett (ed.), *Pacific Peasantry; Case Studies of Rural Societies.* Palmerston North, New Zealand: New Zealand Geographical Society, 1969.

Alvarez, J. H. *Return Migration to Puerto Rico.* Berkeley: Institute of International Studies, University of California, 1969.

Amin, S. (ed.). *Modern Migration in Western Africa.* Studies presented and discussed at the Eleventh International African Seminar, Dakar, April 1972. London: Published for the International African Institute by Oxford University Press, 1974.

Anderson, J. A. *Social Strategies in Population Change: Village Data from Central Luzon.* New York: Southeast Asia Development Advisory Group, 1972.

Ardener, E., Ardener, S., and Warmington, W. *Plantation and Village in the Cameroons: Some Economic and Social Studies.* London: Published for the Nigerian Institute of Social and Economic Research by the Oxford University Press, 1960.

Bailey, F. "An Oriya Hill Village II." In M. N. Scinivas (ed.), *India's Villages.* London: Asia, 1960.

Bansil, P. C. *Agricultural Planning for 700 Millions.* Lalvani, Bombay: 1971.

Baxter, M.V.P. *Migration and the Orokaiva.* Papua New Guinea: Department of Geography, University of Papua, 1973.

Bedford, R. D. *New Hebridean Mobility.* Canberra: Australian National University, 1973.

Beize, T. W. (ed.). *Masambanjati: A Sample Farm Management Survey.* Zomba: Ministry of Agriculture and Natural Resources, 1971.

Berry, B.J.L. "City Size and Economic Development." In L. Jakobson and V. Prakash (eds.), *Urbanization and National Development.* Beverly Hills, Calif.: Sage Publications, 1974.

Bienefeld, M. A. *The Self-Employed of Urban Tanzania.* Brighton: Institute of Development Studies, 1974.

Boeder, M. L. "The Effects of Labor Emigration on Rural Life in Malawi." *Rural Africana* 20 (Spring 1973).

Bond, C. *Women's Involvement in Agriculture in Botswana.* London: Overseas Development Institute, 1974.

Bose, A. "Migration Streams in Modern India." In International Union, *Contributed Papers,* 1971.

Bourge, S. C., et al. *Factions and Faenzas: The Development Potential of the Checrao District, Peru.* Ithaca, N.Y.: Andean Community Research and Development Program: Cornell University, 1967.

Breese, G. (ed.). *The City in Newly Developing Countries, Readings on Urbanism and Urbanization.* Englewood Cliffs, N.J.: Prentice-Hall, 1969.

Brookfield, H. C. "Population Distribution and Labour Migration in New Guinea." *Aust. Geog.* 7, no. 6 (1960).

Byerlee, D. *Research on Migration in Africa: Past, Present and Future.* African Rural Employment Paper No. 2. East Lansing: Department of Agricultural Economics, Michigan State University, 1972.

Caldwell, J. C. *African Rural-Urban Migration: The Movement to Ghana's Towns.* London: C. Hurst, 1969.

Caplan, L. *Land and Social Change in East Nepal: A Study of Hindu-Tribal Relations.* Berkeley: University of California Press, 1970.

*Census of India, 1961.* Vol. 10, pt. 6, no. 1. Delhi: Kunkeri, 1966.

Chatterjee, G. S., and Bhattacharya, N. "Rural-Urban Differences in Consumer Prices." *Economic and Political Weekly* 17 (May 1969).

Cisneros, C. "Indian Migration from the Andean Zone of Ecuador." *America Indigena* 19 (1959).

Cohen, A. *Arab Border Villages in Israel.* Manchester, U.K.: Manchester University, 1965.

Colclough, C., et al. *Survey of Three Peri-urban Areas.* Botswana: Central Statistical Office, Gaborone, 1975.

Connell, J., Dasgupta, B., Laishley, R., and Lipton, M. *Migration from Rural Areas.* Delhi: Oxford University Press, 1976.

Conroy, J. D., and Stent, W. R. "Education, Unemployment and Migration." *Search* 5, no. 1 (November 1970).

Dahya, B. "Pakistanis in Britain." *Race* 14, no. 3 (January 1973).

Dakenye, R. B. "Labour Migration in New Guinea." *Pacific Viewpoint* 8, no. 2 (September 1967).

Dasgupta, B., and Laishley, R. "Migration From Villages: An Indian Case Study." *Economic and Political Weekly* (September 1975).

Doughty, P. L. *Huaylas, an Andean District in Search of Progress.* Ithaca, New York: Cornell University Press, 1968.

Dussauze-Ingrand, E. "L'emigration Sarakollaise." In S. Amin (ed.), *Modern Migration in Western Africa.* London: Oxford University Press, 1974.

Epstein, S. *South India: Yesterday, Today, Tomorrow.* London: MacMillan, 1973.

Essang, S. M., and Mabawonku, A. F. *Determinants and Impact of Rural-Urban Migration: A Case Study of Selected Communities in Western Nigeria.* African Rural Employment Paper No. 10. East Lansing: Department of Agricultural Economics, Michigan State University, 1974.

Fiendt, W., and Browning, H. L. "Return Migration: Its Significance in an Industrial Metropolis and an Agricultural Town in Mexico." *International Migration Review* 6, no. 2 (Summer 1972).

Food and Agriculture Organization (FAO). *The State of Food and Agriculture 1970.* Rome: FAO, 1970.

Foster, P. *Education and Social Change in Ghana.* London: Routledge and Kegan Paul, 1965.

Friedland, A. B. "An Ethnographic Study of San Mateo Almondoa." Ph.D. dissertation, University of California, Los Angeles, 1971.

Gallin, B. *Hsin Hsing, Taiwan: A Chinese Village in Change.* Berkeley and Los Angeles: 1966.

Goddard, A. D. *Population Movements and Land Shortage in the Sokoto Close-Settled Zone, Nigeria.* Liverpool, U.K.: Department of Geography, University of Liverpool, 1973.

Godfrey, E. M. "Economic Variables and Rural-Urban Migration: Some Thoughts on the Todaro Hypothesis." *Journal of Development Studies* 10, no. 1 (October 1973).

de Gonzalez, N.L.S. "Family Organization in Five Types of Migratory Wage Labor." *American Anthropologist* 63, no. 6 (1961).

Hafer, R. F. "The People up the Hill: Individual Progress without Village Participation in Pariamarca Cajamarca, Peru." Ph.D. dissertation, University of Indiana, Bloomington, 1971.

Hancock, R. H. *The Role of the Bracero in the Economic and Cultural Dynamics of Mexico.* Stanford: 1959.

Haney, E. B. "The Economic Organization of Minifundia in a Highland Community of Colombia." Ph.D. dissertation, University of Wisconsin, Madison, 1965.

Harris, W. D., Jr., in collaboration with H. L. Rodriguez-Camilloni. *The Growth of Latin American Cities.* Athens: Ohio University Press, 1971.

Hart, D. V. "Philippine Rural-Urban Migration." *Behavioural Science Notes* 6, no. 2 (1971).

Hayano, D. "Individual Correlates of Coffee Adoption in the New Guinea Highlands." *Human Organization* 32, no. 3 (Fall 1973).

Hilal, J. M. *Family Marriage and Social Change in Some Libyan Villages.* M. Litt. thesis, University of Durham, 1969.

Hill, P. *Rural Hausa: A Village and A Setting.* London: Cambridge University Press, 1972.

Hopper, D. "The Economic Organization of a Village in North Central India." Ph.D. dissertation, Cornell University, Ithaca, 1957.

Hoselitz, B. "The Role of Cities in the Economic Growth of Underdeveloped Countries." In D. Wall (ed.), *Essays in Economic Development.* Chicago: Chicago University Press, 1972.

International Development Research Center, *Town Drift.* 1973.

International Labor Organization (ILO). *Matching Employment Opportunities and Expectations, A Programme of Action for Ceylon.* Geneva: ILO, 1971.

International Union for the Scientific Study of Population. *Contributed Papers of the Sydney Conference Australia, 21st to 25th August, 1967.* Canberra: Australian National University Press, 1971.

Jakobson, L., and Prakash, V. (eds.). *Urbanization and National Development.* Beverly Hills, Calif.: Sage Publications, 1974.

Johnson, G. E., and Whitelaw, W. E. "Urban-Rural Income Transfers in Kenya." Nairobi: Institute of Development Studies, 1972.

Johnston, K. M. *Village Agriculture in Aitutki.* Wellington, New Zealand: Cook Island, Department of Geography, Victoria University, 1967.

Jolly, A. R. "Rural-Urban Migration: Dimensions, Causes, Issues and Policies." In R. Robinson (ed.) *Prospects for Employment Opportunities in the Nineteen Seventies.* (Papers and Impressions of the 7th Cambridge Conference on Development Problems.) London: HMSO, 1971.

Joshi, P. *Migration Urban Employment Problems: A Study of the Ivory Coast.* Oxford: Oxford University, Institute of Economics and Statistics, 1973.

Keyes, C. F. "Peasant and Nation: A Thai-Loo Village." Ph.D. dissertation, Cornell University, Ithaca, New York, 1966.

Khuri, F. I. "A Comparative Study of Migration Patterns in Two Lebanese Villages." *Human Organization* 26, no. 4 (1967).

Khusro, A. M. *A Survey of Living and Working Conditions in the University of Delhi.* London: Asia, 1967.

Knight, J. B. "Measuring Rural-Urban Income Differentials." Brighton, U.K.: Institute of Development Studies, 1971.

Krishnamurthy, J. "Working Force in 1971 Census." *Economic and Political Weekly* 15 (January 1972).

Kuznets, S. *Economic Growth of Nations: Total Output and Production Structure.* Cambridge, Mass.: Belknap Press of Harvard University Press, 1971.

Lasaga, I. *Melanesians' Choice: A Geographical Study of Tasimboko Participation in the Cash Economy, Guadal Canal, British Solomon Islands.* Canberra: Australian National University, 1972.

Lea, P.A.M. "Abelan Land and Sustenance." Ph.D. dissertation, Australian National University, Canberra, 1964.

Lea, P.A.M., and Weinard, H. C. "Some Consequences of Population Growth in the Wosera Area." In N. W. Ward (editor), *Population Growth and Socio-Economic Change.* Canberra: Australian National Press, 1971.

Lewis, R. K. "Hadchite: Emigration from a Lebanese Village." Ph.D. dissertation, Columbia University, New York, 1967.

Lewis, S. P. *Pakistan: Industrialization and Trade.* London: Oxford University Press, 1970.

Levy, M. B., and Wadycki, W. "What is the Opportunity Cost of Moving? Reconsideration of the Effects of Distance on Migration." *Economic Development and Cultural Change* 22, no. 2 (January 1974).

Lipton, M. "Population, Land and Diminishing Returns to Agricultural Labour." *Bull. of the Oxford University Institute of Economics and Statistics* 26, no. 2 (May 1964).

_____. *Why Poor People Stay Poor: Urban Bias in Developing Countries.* London: Temple Smith, 1977.

Lubell, H. "Urban Development and Employment in Calcutta." *International Labour Review* 108, no. 1 (July 1973).

McDougal, C. "Village and Household Economy in Far Western Nepal." Tribhuvan University, Kathmandu, n.d.

McEvoy, F. D. "History, Tradition and Kinship as Factors in Modern Subo Labor Migration." Ph.D. dissertation, University of Oregon, Eugene, 1971.

McFarlane, A.D.J. "Population and Economy in Central Nepal: A Study of the Gurungs." Ph.D. dissertation, University of London, London, 1972.

McGee, T. G. "Catalysts of Cancers? The Role of Cities in Asian Society." In L. Jakobson and V. Prakash (eds.), *Urbanization and National Development.* Beverly Hills, Calif.: Sage Publications, 1974.

McGee, T. G. and Drakakis-Smith, D. W. "Sweet and Sour Source." *Geographical Magazine* 45, no. 11 (August 1973).

Mayer, P. *Townsmen or Tribesmen.* Capetown: Oxford University Press, 1971.

Mfwangavo, A. Y. "Population Pressure on Land in Kisanjieri Village." *Journal of Geographical Association of Tanzania* 5 (December 1969).

Ministry of Village Affairs, *Kuy Evanter Etudierine Gore*, Vols. 1–26, Ankara, 1965–1968.

Miracle, M. P., and Berry, S. S. "Migrant Labour and Economic Development." *Oxford Economic Papers* 22, no. 1 (March 1970).

Moock, J. K. "Pragmatism and the Primary School." Mimeo. Nairobi: Institute of Development Studies, 1976.

Oliver, D. L. *Bougainville: A Personal History.* Honolulu: University of Hawaii Press, 1973.

Paine, S. *Exporting Workers: The Turkish Case.* Cambridge: Cambridge University Press, 1974.

Pathare, A., et al. "Seasonal Migratory Agricultural Labourers." *Indian Journal of Agricultural Economics* 27, vol. 4 (1972).

Peil, M. "Ashiaman: Eyesore and Opportunity." *Legon Observer* 5, no. 18 (August–September 1960).

Philpott, S. D. "The Implications of Migration for Sending Societies." In R. F. Spencer (ed.), *Migration and Anthropology,* Seattle: 1970.

Piotrow, P. *Population and Family Planning in the People's Republic of China.* New York: Victor-Boston Fund, 1971.

Preston, D. A. "Rural Emigration in Andean America." *Human Organization* 28, vol. 4 (1969).

Psacharopoulos, G., assisted by Hinchliffe, K. *Returns to Education: An International Comparison.* Amsterdam: Elsevier Scientific Publication Company, 1973.

Pye, L. S. "The Political Implications of Urbanisation and the Development Process." In G. Bresse (ed.), *The City in Newly Developing Countries, Readings on Urbanism and Urbanization.* Englewood Cliffs, N.J.: Prentice-Hall, 1969.

Rao, V.K.R.V. *University Education and Employment.* New Delhi: Institute of Economic Growth, University of Delhi, 1961.

Ravenstein, E. G. "The Laws of Migration." *Journal of the Royal Statistical Society* (June 1885 and June 1889).

Rempel, H. "Labour Migration into Urban Centers and Urban Unemployment in Kenya." Ph.D. dissertation, University of Wisconsin, Madison, 1971.

Richardson, G. B. *Information and Investment.* Oxford: Oxford University Press, 1959.

Riddell, J. C. "Labor Migration Among the Ghannah Mano of Liberia." Ph.D. dissertation, University of Oregon, Eugene, 1970.

Rochin, R. I. "Inter-Relationships Between Farm Environment, Off-Farm Migration and Rates of Adoption." Purdue University, Lafayette, 1972.

Rogers, E., and Shoemaker, F. F. *Communication of Innovations, A Cross-Cultural Approach.* New York: Free Press, 1971.

Rogers, E., and Svenning, L. *Modernisation Among Peasants, The Impact of Communication.* New York: Holt, Rinehart and Winston, 1969.

Sabot, R. H. "Education, Income Distribution and Rates of Urban Migration in Tanzania." Dar es Salaam: Economic Research Bureau, University of Dar es Salaam, 1972.

Sahota, G. S. "An Economic Analysis of Internal Migration in Brazil." *Journal of Political Economy* 76, no. 2 (1968).

Sakdejayont, Y. *Village Life Near Bangkok.* Kyoto, Japan: Centre for S.E. Asian Studies, Kyoto University, 1973.

Salisbury, R. F., and Salisbury, M. E. "The Rural-Oriented Strategy of Urban Adaptation." In American Ethnography Society, *The Anthropology of Urban Environments,* 1972.

Sansom, R. L. *The Economics of Insurgency in the Mekong Delta of Vietnam.* Cambridge, Mass.: M.I.T. Press, 1970.

Sardar Patel Agro-Economic Research Centre, *Rampura* Village Study No. 15, Vallabh Vidyanagar, 1970.

____. *Umedpur* Village Study No. 17, Vallabh Vidyanagar, 1971.

Schmid, L. J. "The Role of Migratory Labor in the Economic Development of Guatemala." Ph.D. dissertation, Universtiy of Wisconsin, Madison, 1967.

Schultz, T. P. "Rural-Urban Migration in Colombia." *Review of Economics and Statistics* 53, no. 2 (1971).

Sexton, J. D. "Education and Innovation in a Guatemalan Community: San Juan la Laguna." Latin American Center, University of California, Los Angeles, 1972.

Shaw, R. P. "Land Tenure and the Rural Exodus in Latin America." *Economic Development and Cultural Change* 23, no. 1 (October 1974).

Simon, S. R. "Changes in Income, Consumption and Investment in an Eastern U.P. Village." Ph.D. dissertation, Cornell University, Ithaca, 1966.

Skinner, E. P. "Labor Migration Among the Mossi of Upper Volta." In H. Kuper (ed.) *Urbanisation and Migration in West Africa.* Berkeley and Los Angeles: University of California Press, 1965.

Smith, C. "Factors Affecting Primary School Attendance in Botswana." Mimeo. Ministry of Finance and Development Planning, Gaborone, 1977.

Sovani, N. V. *Urbanisation and Urban India.* London: 1965.

Spear, A. "Urbanisation and Migration in Taiwan," Working Paper no. 11, Population Studies Center, University of Michigan, Ann Arbor, 1971.

Spencer, R. F. (ed.). *Migration and Anthropology.* Seattle: 1970.

Srinivasan, T. N. "Resources from the Rural Sector." *Economic and Political Weekly.*

Stark, O. "Utility, Technological Change, Surplus and Risk: The Micro-Economics of Rural-To-Urban Migration of Labour in Less Developed

Economies." Ph.D. dissertation, University of Sussex, Brighton, 1975.

Stiglitz, J. "Alternative Theories of Wage Determination and Unemployment in LDC's." Mimeo. Nairobi: Institute of Development Studies, 1973.

Szczepanik, E. "Size and Efficiency of Agricultural Capital Formation in Developing Countries." *Monthly Bulletin of Agricultural Economics and Statistics* (December 1969).

Todaro, M. P. "A Model of Labor Migration and Urban Unemployment in LDC's." *American Economic Review* 59, no. 1 (March 1969).

____. "Education and Rural-Urban Migration." Paper presented at a Conference on Urban Unemployment in Africa, Institute of Development Studies, University of Sussex, Brighton, 1971.

Upton, M. *Agriculture in South-West Nigeria: A Study of the Relationship Between Production and Social Characteristics in Selected Villages.* Reading: Department of Agricultural Economics, University of Reading, 1967.

Van Velsen, J. "Labour Migration as a Positive Factor in the Continuity of Tonga Tribal Society." *Economic Development and Cultural Change* 8, no. 3 (April 1960).

Vidyarthi, L. P. *Cultural Configuration of Ranchi.* Delhi: Indian Planning Commission, 1969.

Wall, D. (ed.). *Essays in Economic Development.* Chicago: Chicago University Press, 1972.

Walsh, A. C., and Trlin, A. D. "Niuean Migration." *Journal of Polynesian Sociology* 32, vol. 1 (1973).

Ward, N. W. (ed.). *Population Growth and Socio-Economic Change.* Canberra: Australian National Press, 1971.

Wellisz, S. W. "Economic Development and Urbanization." In Jakobson and Prakash, *Urbanization and National Development.*

Weist, R. "Wage Labor, Migration and Household Maintenance in a Central Mexican Town." Ph.D. dissertation, University of Oregon, Eugene, 1970.

Wilkie, R. W. "Toward a Behavioural Model of Peasant Migration: an Argentine Case." In R. N. Thomas (ed.) *Population Dynamics of Latin America, a Review and Bibliography.* East Lansing, Mich.: Conference of Latin Americanist Geographers, 1973.

Wyon, J. B., and Gordon, J. E. *The Khanna Study: Population Problems in the Rural Punjab.* Cambridge, Mass.: Harvard University Press, 1971.

Yang, C. K. *A Chinese Village in Early Communist Transition.* Cambridge, Mass.: 1959.

Yeshwant, T. S. "Rural Migration—A Case-Study." *Agricultural Situation in India* 17, no. 6 (1962).

Zachariah, K. C. *Migrants in Greater Bombay.* London: 1968.

# 7

# Conclusion:
# Some Themes and Unresolved Issues

## RICHARD H. SABOT

Although none of the contributions that appear in this book was conceived as a piece of the larger design they now form, several broad, closely interwoven strands of thought can nevertheless be traced in their diverse subject matter. These themes stand out against the detailed analysis, which ranges from the intrafamily distribution of income and its influence on migration to the costs for nonmigrants of externalities generated by out-migration. The most prominent theme is the importance of arriving in a more rigorous way at assumptions about the structure and efficiency of labor markets and of then making these assumptions explicit. Much current discussion of such central issues of development economics as growth, distribution, labor utilization, and planning is based on unexamined assumptions about labor markets, although these issues are highly sensitive to changes in the underlying model of the labor market. A corollary theme stresses the gaps in our knowledge of interactions between employers and sellers of labor services, which loom large in most developing countries, and the need for an enlarged program of applied labor market research to fill those gaps. The discussions of shadow pricing, urban unemployment, and the rural consequences of migration provide obvious illustrations of these themes.

"The theory of shadow prices is well established. What we know less about is the scope for their use in different kinds of economy and the directions in which it matters most whether market prices are superseded by shadow prices." So concluded A. Cairncross in an essay on "The Limitations of Shadow Prices"[1] in which he also bemoaned the lack of attention economists pay to such issues as whether shadow prices can be consistently applied by semiautonomous local authorities responsible for investment decisions when market prices provide a strong incentive not to do so; the difference in practice that shadow pricing makes to the ranking of projects; and, more generally, the social returns from the substitution of shadow for market rates. Stiglitz's discussion of the sensitivity of shadow wages to differences in labor market conditions makes it clear, however, that feasibility of implementation is not the only constraint on the effectiveness of shadow pricing as a tool for increasing allocative efficiency.

The crudeness of the process of estimation of the shadow wage in the appraisals of most existing projects, together with evidence that the rate of social profitability is quite sensitive to the level of the shadow wage, could be interpreted as support for a skeptical view of the usefulness of cost-benefit analysis, at least with regard to labor-intensive enterprises. But the issue is not simply whether or not to shadow price. Rather, Stiglitz's discussion in Chapter 1 bears directly on the issue of the "optimal" amount of background economic work for estimating the shadow wage. The more detailed the specification of the model of the labor market and the more accurate the estimates of parameters and relevant elasticities, the greater the confidence in the estimates of shadow wages derived from such a model and the greater the costs of obtaining them. To estimate a highly detailed model of the labor market can take years and requires large scale sample surveys to generate the relevant data, generally not available from conventional statistical sources. In many countries the most significant cost is likely to be the opportunity cost of employing extremely scarce highly skilled manpower on a large-scale program of applied labor market research.[2]

The judgment to date, based on the assumption that the structures of labor markets in developing countries are relatively simple and readily apparent, has been that even casual observation by a trained eye would yield a reasonably accurate estimate of the opportunity cost of labor, more accurate at least than the market wage; detailed research would only alter this estimate slightly. By emphasizing that labor markets are far more complex than previously believed, Stiglitz suggests a reconsideration of this judgment. Casual observation would not be a sufficient basis, not even for the most sophisticated economist, to arrive at estimates of the variety of variables to which Stiglitz shows the opportunity cost of labor to be sensitive. The implication is that the optimum level of background research lies rather closer to a comprehensive program of labor market research, and that to protect the integrity of such procedures, where projects are labor intensive, it may be necessary to eschew quick and dirty methods of estimation.

Governments may be under pressure to respond to a symptom of inefficiency in the allocation of labor, such as unemployment, not just by shadow pricing but by intervening directly in the labor market so as to counteract the cause of the problem, or to compensate particular groups who bear the brunt of the costs it imposes on society. Estimated rates of urban unemployment in developing countries frequently exceed levels that trigger major remedial government actions in industrialized economies, and definitional biases are, on balance, likely to be in a downward direction. Time series evidence to support assertions that rates have been increasing is sketchy, but there is little doubt that due to rapid urbanization the number of unemployed workers has increased markedly. This has resulted in many countries adopting make-work schemes, imposing direct controls on migration, or in other ways intervening in the labor market in response to political pressures. However, assessments of the resource costs (aggregate output forgone) and welfare costs (deprivation suffered by individuals directly affected) of open unemployment tend to be exaggerated because the relationship between the composition and cost of surplus labor is ignored and, more fundamentally, because of the common tendency to abstract from the precise nature of the inadequacies of the labor market that give rise to the problem. It is assumed that since the costs of leaving workers unemployed are high in industrialized countries, they must be high in developing countries also.

Where unemployment is due to labor market segmentation, output forgone is measured roughly by earnings in the low-income segment of the labor market. If marginal product there is low, then aggregate resource costs will generally be low also. Consistent with estimates of costs of allocative inefficiency in other markets, the resource costs of urban unemployment of this type are unlikely to exceed 1-2 percent of gross national product. By contrast, where unemployment is due to deficiency of demand, output forgone per idle labor force participant is higher and aggregate costs have been measured to be 10-15 percent of gross national product, and more in some cases. In the absence of a formal social security system, the loss of income through unemployment in industrialized countries would significantly reduce consumption because workers without much accumulated wealth, but with family responsibilities, are a high proportion of the unemployed. In developing countries the welfare costs are lower, not because the unemployed have a greater store of assets on which they can draw, but because these costs are shared by family members who have jobs, and because sectors in which incomes are flexible are available as employers of last resort.[3] The implication of this relationship between causes and costs of a symptom of labor market inefficiency, stressed by Harris and Sabot, is that casual examination of unemployment and other aggregate statistics may be inadequate to properly assess the costs and benefits of direct interventions. Such an assessment may require at least as much background research and as detailed a specification and estimation of a labor market model as does the estimation of shadow wages.

Similarly, Lipton clearly demonstrates that the consequences of migration may vary dramatically with the structure of the labor market within which migrants are moving. If interactions between sellers and employers of labor services conform to the neoclassical perception of perfect markets, it is implausible to conceive of some subgroups of the source area population benefiting disproportionately from migration. By contrast, in segmented labor markets the spoils—high wage jobs—tend to go to migrants able to finance a perhaps lengthy period of search. Whether the ability to finance job search is a significant constraint on the mobility of some subgroups, but not on others, may in turn depend on such factors as the wage elasticity of demand for labor in urban informal sectors and the extent to which employment in such sectors reduces the efficiency of search for high wage jobs. Thus, without background research on the labor market, an accurate assessment of the distributional consequences of migration flows induced by a policy intervention such as a regional development program may not be feasible.

The issues brought out in the chapters of this book emphasize the need for microeconomic applied research and for the insights that come from perceiving the operation of general and abstract principles in concrete and particular circumstances, even at the cost of breadth of coverage. Though many areas for research are proposed, one receives markedly more attention, and the discussion of it sets a theme of the book, considered in the next section of this chapter; in the last section some of the other suggestions for research are noted.

## THE MEASUREMENT AND DETERMINATION OF WAGES

An unchallenged assumption in all of these chapters is that differences in the price of labor among regions and sectors provide the principal incentive for mobility of economically active members of the household. No doubt is cast on the effectiveness of the decentralized price system in mobilizing labor to meet new and growing demands, or on the desirability of the economic growth and change in the structure of production, which create the need for reallocations. Nevertheless, distortions in these incentives bear most of the blame for such socially undesirable consequences of reallocation as urban unemployment and an increased skew in some dimensions of the distribution of income. The payment of higher wages to some workers than to others with the same skills, simply on account of their sector of employment, is the labor market pathology most frequently relied on to explain symptoms of inefficiency in the allocation of labor and evidence of distributional consequences of reallocation that run counter to neoclassical predictions. The centrality of the process of determining the price of labor, arguably the most important price in the economic system, to nearly all the significant labor market issues, and our ignorance regarding this process in developing countries, are recurrent themes in these chapters.

One hypothesis is a focus of attention. An unappealing aspect of most segmentation models is that they rely on what Stiglitz calls "the black box" of exogenous constraints on factor pricing. A negative relationship between wages and the cost of employing labor provides an alternative explanation for segmentation within the framework of an unfettered market. Urban employers may voluntarily raise wages above the minimum at which they can fully staff their enterprises because by so doing they increase worker productivity or decrease the costs of hiring or training their labor force.

Stiglitz shows that the social opportunity cost of employing an additional worker is not highly sensitive to the determinants of the intersectoral wage gap. However, without an economic explanation for the wage gap, segmentation models are intellectually incomplete. Moreover, the social costs of unemployment vary with the determinants of the gap as do optimal remedial policies. Where institutional factors segment the labor market, the costs of unemployment may appear low as a proportion of gross national product, or when compared with costs in industrial societies. Nevertheless, in absolute terms they may be quite high, particularly when calculated over a long period; to governments of poor countries the prospect of increasing national output without increasing the stock of productive resources would understandably be appealing, particularly when elimination of the wage gap would also improve the distribution of income. However, where the wage gap is the result of a wage-productivity relationship and decreasing wages lower worker productivity, then an $x$-efficiency cost must be set against the benefits derived from the elimination of segmentation and unemployment and the consequent improvement in allocative efficiency. Where an institutional intervention is the cause of segmentation, government policies that succeed in unfettering the labor market should be sufficient to achieve an optimal allocation of labor. Where a wage-productivity relationship is the cause, such institutionally oriented policies clearly are inadequate; on the contrary, increased government intervention in wage determination in the form of a detailed income policy will be necessary to eliminate the wage gap.

There have been few attempts to test the hypothesis, perhaps because it is rather difficult to do so, as discussion revealed. A positive association between wage increases and productivity increases is a necessary condition for confirmation of labor cost minimization as the cause of labor market segmentation. However, such an association does not specify the direction in which the causal relationship between the two is running. Wage increases could follow productivity increases deriving from nonwage sources. Indeed, the structure of the manufacturing industry in developing countries suggests that an independent rise in productivity would make employers less resistant to pressures for wage increases. High capital/labor ratios mean that wage costs are a small proportion of value added and that quite significant wage increases may have only a small impact on total costs. Moreover, many large-scale, capital-intensive enterprises operate behind tariff barriers that allow them to pass on costs to consumers as higher prices. It is necessary to assess the contribution to the increase in productivity of such factors as shifts toward more productive enterprises, changes in technology, and improvements in management or organization. If these are shown to be unimportant, so that there is a reasonable presumption that rising productivity is not the cause of rising wages, there remains the issue of how far higher productivity is simply the result of capital deepening induced by higher wages.

All of the above suggests that tests of the hypothesis that increasing wages above the market clearing level minimizes labor costs will have to be conducted with highly disaggregated data, probably at the level of individual firms. Even then it is not sufficient just to demonstrate that higher wages result in higher productivity among workers who are homogeneous in other respects.[4] Rather, the wage elasticity of supply of efficiency units per worker must exceed unity. Otherwise the wage-related benefits to employers from increased productivity (or decreased nonwage costs of labor) will not exceed the costs of increased wages, implying that conventional labor market clearing adjustments take place through numbers hired and wage rates. To measure this elasticity of supply with precision, detailed measures of productivity, which are difficult to obtain, will be necessary.

A second focus of attention was on the measurement of wage gaps between geographic areas for the behaviorial analysis of migration, which is agreed to be essential both for the estimation of the labor supply function in all but the most aggregate labor market models and for regional projections of population growth that are more than extrapolations of past trends. Schultz emphasizes the need for multivariate analysis of wages as a complement to econometric analyses of the determinants of migration, to guard against the possibility that differences in the demographic composition, or in the employment experience of the labor forces whose wages are compared, create the illusion of a wage gap. However, it was noted in discussion that regional wage functions that only include proxies for human capital as independent variables may provide a misleading view of economic returns to the average migrant. This is because where the labor market in the receiving region is segmented, those migrants successful in obtaining a high wage job may earn markedly more than the average worker with the same characteristics, while unsuccessful migrants, who remain unemployed or obtain employment in sectors where earnings are flexible, may earn markedly less. Thus, in addition to those variables Schultz suggests, the earnings function should also include a variable capturing this distinction. Its significance would be a preliminary test of the relevance of the segmentation model. In some markets the distinction between casual and regular employees parallels this sectoral distinction; in these an employment status variable may be adequate. The division of the labor market into unionized and nonunionized, or protected (by minimum wages) and unprotected, areas may be alternatives. In other markets, finding an effective proxy for sector of employment may be more difficult. While much in the recent theory of labor markets in developing countries depends on the rate of adjustment of wages to imbalances in supply and demand, there is little work on distinguishing rapidly adjusting (flexible) real wages from slowly adjusting (rigid) real wages through observation of the labor market.

In segmented labor markets migrants respond to differences in the price of labor discounted by the probability of finding a job. To incorporate this notion of the expected price of labor into migration functions, Schultz recommends that regional functions for hours (weeks) of work should be estimated parallel to wage functions. Several drawbacks to using such functions to generate proxies of the probability of employment were noted, however, in discussion. The ratio of job-seekers to job openings in the high wage sector may be high, implying a low average probability. Nevertheless, if hours employed in the flexible wage sector are high, as both theory and empirical evidence suggest they are, average hours worked in the receiving area, standardized for a variety of demographic and other factors, may still exceed average hours in the source area. This may be true even under the extreme assumption that all workers unable to obtain employment in the high wage sector remain in open unemployment. Long hours worked in regular employment in the high wage region where employment opportunities are scarce may disguise the presence of substantial workers with zero hours. However, confirming that differences between regions in hours worked per year are due to differences in the employment rate rather than in the length of the work day in the high wage sector does not resolve the fundamental problem with this approach. The probability of employment for workers with the same demographic characteristics and employment experience may be greater in a region with a low employment rate because of regional differences in the rate of employment growth.[5] Conceptually these objections to this approach to estimating the expected price of labor can be overcome by simply replacing hours worked with a dependent variable measuring the probability of employment. But the definition of this variable raises such issues as how to take account of job-seekers employed in the flexible wage sector and how to treat differences between employed and unemployed workers in the efficiency of job search; the resolution of these issues is likely to complicate measurement considerably.

Also emphasized in discussion was that in developing countries, given labor's high functional share of income and the high proportion of workers who receive most or all of their income as returns to their labor, variations in labor income account for more of the total income inequality than all other sources combined. Thus determining the causes of variance in the price of labor (wages or income from self-employment) can make an important contribution to the understanding of inequality and poverty. By providing a means of investigating the role of human capital, labor market segmentation, and discrimination in the determination of wages the estimation of wage functions can also contribute to the more complex issue of the extent of income redistribution developing countries can efficiently tolerate.

Variation among regions in the proportion of intermediate goods that are in consumption is another reason why regional differences in real wages for workers with the same skills may be a poor indicator of the incentive to migrate. The definition of income appropriate for migration and labor market analysis is a third focus of discussion. It was noted that the prominent reasons for adopting the conventions in national income accounting—treating all government expenditure and all household expenditure as expenditure on final goods and services—do not apply with the same force in developing countries today. It is undoubtedly easier to separate out intermediate from final goods in the enterprise sector (where it is possible to adopt the convenient rule that all output sold by one business to another for resale is to be classified as intermediate) than in the household sector. This is mainly because it is legitimate to assume that enterprises are heavily specialized in production, whereas quite clearly households divide their time between production and consumption activities. The second and probably more important reason for the conventions is that, for the purposes to which national income accounts were to be put—to monitor aggregate economic performance and to test the predictions of the then new macroeconomic analysis—the errors in measurement resulting from the logical inconsistency were unlikely to be big enough to matter.

The hedonic theory of consumer demand and the theory of the allocation of time, taken together with the dramatic increase in our technical ability to analyze large, complex microdata sets generated by multipurpose household surveys, suggest that distinguishing intermediate from final consumption in the household sector is likely to be easier than it used to be. Likewise, the emphasis in developing countries on micro or behavioral analysis and on the analysis of the distribution of income suggests that the errors arising from the logical inconsistency in the treatment of intermediate goods are likely to be considerably greater. For one thing, the household sector is frequently the sole focus of distributional and behavioral analysis. Errors, as a percentage of income, will thus not be diminished by aggregating household acquisitions with those of other sectors free from such errors. Also the potential for error is greater when the difference between incomes rather than a single total is estimated. The composition of consumption is likely to differ significantly between rural and urban areas. If the gap between the actual and estimated level of income is consequently minimal in the large rural sector and large in the small urban sector, the ratio of the actual differences will be in excess of the ratio of the actual to measured aggregate income.

The hedonic theory, which assumes that utility does not depend on the consumption of commodities per se, as is conventionally assumed, but on the satisfaction of wants by qualities or characteristics inherent in physical goods and services, provides a useful framework for the allocation of acquisitions between the intermediate good and final good categories. It is clear, for example, that most expenditures on transport are intermediate. This should not be taken to imply, however, that the process of categorization of acquisitions can be mechanical and noncontroversial. It was noted that the change in the definition of income proposed by Collier and Sabot is open to the criticism that the lack of rigorous criteria for determining whether an expenditure is intermediate or final would undermine the objectivity of income. It could even be argued that by making the categorization of acquisitions a matter of consensus, estimates of the level of income or differences in income become what is desired. The rejoinder, of course, is that current conventions are no less arbitrary; only their widespread acceptance makes their inadequacies less discussed. Certainly, the charge of social critics that the increased costs of running society have been underestimated and increases in social welfare overestimated, must be based on the assumption that much of what is treated as final consumption should be intermediate.

Nor does this imply that every time economists estimate a migration function or analyze other aspects of the labor market requiring income comparisons, they must first complete a detailed analysis of consumption and prices; it was stressed that there may be shortcut methods of determining the magnitude of the errors incurred by ignoring this problem. But a search for shortcuts would be premature. First it is necessary to carry out detailed studies to determine the sensitivity of measures of income to changes in its definition, and to shift toward a more appropriate treatment of differences in relative prices of the sort suggested.[6] Contrary to a priori expectations, the conventional definition may prove robust; a shift of some acquisitions from quantities to prices may have little impact on total income or on the income differences between geographic areas. Until there are results of such studies, however, the logical inconsistency between the treatment of intermediate goods in production and in consumption casts a shadow over much applied research on migration and the labor market.

## OTHER AREAS FOR RESEARCH

Labor markets should not be viewed in isolation from the larger economic environment. The level of income per capita, the structure of the economy, and the performance of other factor and product markets will influence the degree of complexity of the task of efficiently allocating labor and the outcomes of particular labor market adjustment processes. For example, the greater differentiation on the supply and demand sides of the labor market found in countries with higher incomes makes the task of matching skills and job requirements more complex. A recurrent theme in the chapters of this book is the sensitivity of labor market outcomes to the nature and performance of capital markets. Lipton's emphasis on the difficulty poor rural residents have in obtaining finance for investments in education and migration is an indictment of capital markets. Their inefficiency and inequity share the responsibility for the tendency he sees of migration to widen the gap between high- and low-income rural dwellers. Likewise Schuh stresses the negative impact of the urban capital flows associated with migration, induced in part by capital market imperfections, on source area incomes. Stiglitz, Harris and Sabot, and Schultz all emphasize the potential influence of capital market performance on the consequences of migration for urban labor market balance. The inability to obtain the funds to finance the direct costs of migration and job search, which in a segmented labor market are likely to be considerable, may reduce the rate of migration, hence the rate of urban unemployment, to a level significantly lower than it otherwise would be. Also, the size, composition, and level of incomes in flexible wage sectors may be affected if employment in those sectors is an alternative means of financing search.

To assess these hypotheses will require, as a first step, detailed research on the costs of migration and job search, the means by which it is financed, and differences between rural subgroups in the ability to obtain finance or in the costs of finance. A second step would be the addition to migration functions of a variable measuring the ability to finance migration. Differences in this ability may help explain several important dimensions of migration selectivity, among them education. There is generally a positive correlation between education attainment and family income, suggesting that it is easier for the educated to finance human capital investments. They may also explain the asymmetry observed in a number of countries in the effects of source and receiving area wage changes on the rate of migration. An increase in source area incomes would have two countervailing effects: increasing the opportunity cost of migration, which would tend to slow the flow of migration; and decreasing the constraint poverty places on the ability to finance migration, which would tend to accelerate the flow of migrants. A decline in receiving area incomes would not have this second effect. The notable absence of this variable from quantitative analyses of migration decisions is almost certainly due to the difficulty of finding an appropriate definition and then, for any sensible definition, finding the appropriate data. There is little doubt that a more intensive study of interactions between factor markets would bear valuable fruit for understanding both the determinants and the consequences of migration.

Interactions between, on the one hand, product markets and characteristics of technology and, on the other hand, labor market outcomes were stressed in a comment on the taxonomy of models of unemployment in the chapter by Harris and Sabot. A labor market at full employment equilibrium may nevertheless have sectors in which wages are downwardly inflexible. Only in sectors where they are flexible will wages decline in response to a decline in aggregate demand. The resulting segmentation of the labor market and open unemployment may thus be cyclical. In previously segmented markets, the movement of aggregate demand would add a cyclical component to a chronic phenomenon. In either case, the question of the remedial impact on unemployment of fiscal or monetary policies is reopened. Similarly, if technical lack of substitution is the cause of high capital intensity in some sectors, it may increase the likelihood of wages in excess of the market clearing level, and the possibly beneficial impact on labor market imbalance of policies aimed at increasing the elasticity of substitution between capital and labor should be considered.

The discussion of search models also emphasized that it would be a mistake to seek a single explanation for unemployment. For example, the general search model and its special case, the segmentation model, are not mutually exclusive; wage rigidities and information gaps may both be contributing factors. This complicates the task of rigorously testing search models of unemployment. Some skepticism was expressed, however, as to how much inadequate labor market information contributes to the explanation of rates of unemployment, which frequently exceed 10 percent of the urban labor force. In the industrial countries, even among the strongest proponents of the concept of a "normal" rate of unemployment, estimates do not exceed 5 percent. Nevertheless, a need for detailed empirical studies of search and hiring behavior and how it varies between sectors and workers with different skills was recognized. Topics recommended for research included the effect on search behavior of different types of employment contracts, and of differences between socioeconomic subgroups of workers in the quantity and quality of labor market information to which they have access, hence in the accuracy of their perceptions as to employment opportunities. The operation of internal labor markets and their influence on search behavior are others.

The chapters in this volume identify subjects about which we still know little. However, these brief comments on unresolved issues should not be interpreted as an agenda for research. Rather they are an attempt to explore particular areas in depth. Similar examination of other areas such as the links between the market for education and the labor market, or the determinants of the demand for wage labor in different sectors, are bound to reveal other important topics about which we also know little.

More fundamentally, an agenda cannot be drawn up without first specifying the criteria for establishing priorities. Research cost and the strength of demand for results by policymakers are two criteria suggested by the discussion of the distribution between rural and urban areas of resources for research on migration. Because the rural sector is much larger than the urban in both area and population, the costs of research there are higher. The difference in size also means that the impact of migration on productivity and income distribution is likely to be much greater in urban than in rural areas, suggesting that the "returns" to research on migration are lower in rural than in urban areas. However, aggregate averages are often misleading. In this case, it was noted, they indicate the inadvisability of designing empirical studies of out-migration comprehensive in their geographic coverage. However, the magnitude of outflows is likely to vary considerably between rural regions; in those regions where it is high, the impact of out-migration on productivity and the distribution of income may be considerable. Studies of the consequences of out-migration in such regions may prove to be of great value to regional planners. Moreover, the impact of out-migration on aggregate measures of economic performance in rural areas is likely to increase as urbanization proceeds.

In conclusion, the emphasis by the authors of the chapters on the sensitivity of a variety of development policy issues to assumptions about labor markets implies a need for an enlarged program of labor market research in developing countries and for an agenda of topics. To judge from the chapters herein it is likely such an agenda will emphasize applied research and that high priority will be given to the analysis of wages and of interactions between the labor market and other markets.

## NOTES

1. A. Cairncross, "The Limitations of Shadow Prices," in A. Cairncross and M. Puri (eds.), *Employment Income Distribution and Development Strategy* (New York: Holmes and Meier, Inc., 1976).

2. Such a program aimed at refining accounting prices may require a sacrifice of improvements in tax, subsidy, or price-control programs that could increase the efficiency with which resources are allocated. Thus to determine whether detailed labor market research is justified would require a comparison of the net benefits of such a program with the net benefits of improvements in other programs.

3. See R. Sabot, *The Social Costs of Urban Surplus Labor* (Paris: OECD, Development Center, 1978) and A. Berry and R. Sabot, "Labour Market Performance in Developing Countries: A Survey," *World Development* 6 (November/December 1978), 1119–1242.

4. It was noted in discussion that it is not strictly correct to view the participation in the wage labor market of more productive workers (with higher

supply prices) at higher wages and the "creaming" of the labor supply by high-wage employers as a basis for the hypothesis, as at one point Stiglitz suggests. In this case, the wage level and the level of productive potential of workers is not causally related. Rather, labor is heterogeneous with respect to preexisting productive capacity, and the relationship here between wages and productivity no more causes labor market segmentation than educated workers earning more than uneducated workers causes it.

5. A recent survey of migration research in the United States concluded, "One of the most perplexing problems confronting migration scholars is the lack of significance of local unemployment rates in explaining migration." See M. Greenwood, "Research on Internal Migration in the United States: A Survey," *Journal of Economic Literature*, June 1975. The key to this puzzle may be that, as suggested above, if not standardized by the rate of growth of employment opportunities, the rate of unemployment is a poor proxy for the probability of employment with which potential migrants are likely to be concerned.

6. It is unlikely any existing sources will fulfill the requirements of such a study for data on earnings, expenditure, prices, and the allocation of time; sample surveys will have to be specially designed and administered. The procedure would be first to measure income and its distribution in the conventional way, and then, progressing from less to more controversial changes, to shift various categories of acquisitions from quantities to prices, assessing at each step the sensitivity of the standard two parallel analyses, one in which the allocation of time is taken into account and the other in which it is not.

# Index

# The Contributors

**Paul Collier** is a fellow of Keble College and on the staff of the Institute of Economics and Statistics, Oxford. His research on LDC labor markets is published in articles in *Oxford Economic Papers* and the *Oxford Bulletin of Economics and Statistics* and in a monograph (with D. Lal) "Poverty and Growth in Kenya" (forthcoming). He has also published on international economics.

**John R. Harris** is professor of economics and director of the African Studies Center at Boston University. Before coming to Boston University he was associate professor of economics and planning and codirector of the Migration and Development Study Group at the Massachusetts Institute of Technology. He has been a research associate of the Nigerian Institute of Social and Economic Research and of the Institute of Development Studies of the University of Nairobi. He has written extensively on migration in East Africa and in Indonesia and is currently involved in a national migration study in Botswana.

**Michael Lipton** is a fellow of the Institute of Development Studies and a professor of economics at the University of Sussex. His books include *Why Poor People Stay Poor, Urban Bias and World Development, Assessing Economic Performance*, and several books and papers on the economics of agricultural and rural development, on the Indian economy, and on international economic relations.

**Richard H. Sabot** is a member of the Development Economics Department of the World Bank, where he has been since leaving the staff of the Institute of Economics and Statistics, University of Oxford. His theoretical and applied research has focused on labor markets in low-income countries and on the design and use of appropriate large-scale micro-data bases for the analysis of the behavior of buyers and sellers of labor services and of the consequent employment and income outcomes. His most recent books are *The Social Costs of Urban Surplus Labor, Economic Development and Urban Migration,* and (with J. Knight) *Why Wages Differ* (forthcoming). Currently he is directing the World Bank's comparative study of the labor market consequences of educational expansion.

**G. Edward Schuh** is professor and head, Department of Agricultural and Applied Economics, University of Minnesota. He has been senior staff economist, President's Council of Economic Advisors (1974-75) and deputy undersecretary of agriculture (1978-79). He has published three books on the agricultural development of Brazil and many technical papers for professional journals. Dr. Schuh has a Ph.D. from the University of Chicago, is a fellow of the American Academy of Arts and Sciences, and is president-elect of the American Agricultural Economics Association.

**T. Paul Schultz** is Malcolm K. Brachman Professor of Economics, Yale University. He is coauthor of *Structural Change in a Developing Country* and author of *Economics of Population* and various journal articles and contributions to books on microeconomic and demographic behavior in high- and low-income countries. His work has sought to develop a conceptual framework from household demand theory and suitable econometric tools to understand fertility, labor force, migration, and health behavior of individuals and thereby construct a microeconomic foundation for the study of the personal distribution of income. Dr. Schultz received his Ph.D. from MIT in 1966 and started the Population and Labor Economics Program at the Rand Corporation in 1970.

**Joseph E. Stiglitz** is currently professor of economics at Princeton University. Recently Drummond Professor of Political Economy at Oxford University, he has also taught at MIT, Yale, and Stanford. He is the author (with A. B. Atkinson) of *Lectures in Public Economics* and a forthcoming book, *The Economic Impact of Commodity Price Stabilization* (with D. Newbery). He is currently coeditor of the *Journal of Public Economics,* has served on the editorial board of the *American Economic Review,* and has served as an associate editor of the *Journal of Economic Theory* and the *Review of Economic Studies.* He is a fellow of the Econometric Society. In 1979, he received the John Bates Clark Award of the American Economic Association.